Meeti

Their Law an

THE M & E HANDBOOK SERIES

Meetings
Their Law and Practice

L. Hall ACIS, AMBIM
*Formerly Senior Lecturer in Secretarial Practice
at the City of London Polytechnic*

revised by
Philip Lawton LLB
*Barrister, Senior Lecturer in Law,
Lancashire Polytechnic*
and
Eric R. Rigby BEd
*Senior Lecturer in Law, Department
of Professional Administration, Wigan
College of Technology*

THIRD EDITION

MACDONALD AND EVANS

Macdonald & Evans Ltd.
Estover, Plymouth PL6 7PZ

First published 1966
Reprinted 1969
Reprinted 1970
Reprinted 1971
Reprinted (with additions) 1973
Reprinted (with additions) 1974
Reprinted 1975
Reprinted 1976
Second Edition 1977
Reprinted 1979
Reprinted 1981
Third Edition 1985

© Macdonald & Evans Ltd. 1984

British Library Cataloguing in Publication Data

Hall, L.
    Meetings: their law and practice.—3rd ed.
    1. Meetings
    I. Title II. Lawton, Philip III. Rigby, Eric R.
    060.4'2 AS6

ISBN 0-7121-0449-6

This book is copyright
and may not be reproduced in whole
or in part (except for purposes of review)
without the express permission
of the publishers in writing.

Filmset by J & L Composition Ltd, Filey, N. Yorkshire
Printed and bound in Great Britain by
Hollen Street Press Ltd, Slough

Preface to the First Edition

In preparing these study notes it has been the author's intention to reduce the subject of meetings to its essentials and, it is hoped, meet the requirements of students preparing for the final examinations of the *Institute of Chartered Secretaries and Administrators*.

It is not suggested that these notes should replace the textbooks recommended for the use of students taking college or correspondence courses; indeed, textbooks are an essential part of their course. Nevertheless, for many years it has been the author's experience as lecturer that students are always appreciative of "hand-outs," and this handbook will supply that need, particularly for the purpose of revision.

In order to derive maximum benefit from this HANDBOOK the text ought to be used in conjunction with the examination questions appearing at the end of each chapter. Most of the questions are taken from past examination papers of the *Institute of Chartered Secretaries and Administrators* and the *Building Societies Institute* to whom the author tenders grateful acknowledgment. It will be noted that the majority of the questions are cross-referenced to the relevant chapters and paragraph(s) of the text. Those which give no reference might be classified as questions (a) requiring the application of knowledge already derived from the reading of the text plus a certain amount of imagination and originality, *e.g.* in report-writing or the drafting and/or re-writing or correction of rules, agenda, notices, motions, amendments, resolutions and minutes; (*b*) outlining procedures and secretarial duties before, during and after meetings; (*c*) demanding knowledge of both company law and law of meetings; (*d*) calling for discussion concerning, or interpretation of, legal decisions. Practice in answering questions of this type is an essential part of a student's training for the professional secretarial examinations.

1966   LH

Preface to the Third Edition

We feel sure that Mr. Hall's undoubted ability to extract and express the key points of the subject matter will be greatly missed and have endeavoured to maintain his standard of clarity in this new edition.

In view of the development for BTEC courses in Public Administration and Business Studies of an optional meetings module, we feel that it is appropriate to include a brief section on local authority meetings which may also prove useful reference for people studying on the ICSA public service stream. A new chapter on the nature of companies and the context of company meetings has also been added. We also felt it necessary to restructure the book by reorganising and extending its various parts which a glance at the contents pages will show. Some parts and chapters have been merged and/or repositioned. This was done in order to more closely mirror the modern style of professional examinations and allow a clearer exposition of subject matter. We have of course taken account of statute and case law developments since the last edition in particular the Companies Acts 1980 and 1981. Specimen examination questions have been thoroughly revised and updated and are contained in a new appendix. We wish to thank the Institute of Chartered Secretaries and Administrators for granting permission to use past examination questions.

1984   PL
                                                                                                              ER

Contents

Preface to the First Edition   v
Preface to the Third Edition   vi
Table of Cases   xi

PART ONE: MEETINGS IN GENERAL

I   *Holding a Meeting*   1
     Legality of meeting; legislative provisions; police powers; public meetings on private premises; attendance of outsiders

II   *Convention, Constitution and Conduct of Meetings*   15
     Number of persons attending; validity of meeting

III   *Regulations governing Meetings*   19

IV   *The Chairman*   23
     Appointment and qualifications; duties and privileges; removal

V   *The Agenda*   28
     General; preparation; use in preparation of minutes

VI   *Notices*   34
     Purpose, content and entitlement; method of service; notice and convention of meetings

VII   *Quorum*   39

VIII   *Motions*   41
     Form and presentation; amendments; other types of motion

CONTENTS

IX *Formal (Procedural) Motions* — 48
Use of formal motions; types of formal motion

X *Summary of Procedure at a Meeting* — 54

XI *Adjournments* — 56

XII *Minutes* — 59
The taking of minutes; reading and alteration

Part Two: DEFAMATION

XIII *Defamation* — 65
The action; defences; special rules as to qualified privilege; inference of defamation

Part Three: COMPANY MEETINGS

XIV *Companies and Company Meetings* — 75
Introduction to company law; types of company; legal status; company meetings; the future

XV *The Agenda* — 85
Convening of Meetings; notice

XVI *Quorum* — 95

XVII *Motions and Resolutions* — 102
General; notice; types of resolution; registration and circulation; resolution without meeting

XVIII *Voting* — 112

XIX *Polls* — 114

XX *Proxies* — 118
Appointment of person as proxy; the proxy document, revocation and rejection; validity of proxy

XXI	*Minutes*	124
XXII	*The Annual General Meeting*	126
XXIII	*Extraordinary General Meetings*	129
XXIV	*Class Meetings* Purpose of meetings; methods of variation; conduct of meeting	132
XXV	*Board Meetings* Business at board meetings; conduct of board meetings	138
XXVI	*Committee Meetings* Appointment and purpose; types of committee	145
XXVII	*Meetings in a Winding Up by the Court* How a winding up is effected; procedure	149
XXVIII	*Meetings in a Voluntary Winding Up* How a winding up is effected; procedure; form and proceedings	157
XXIX	*Directors' Report* Statutory requirements; Stock Exchange requirements	165

Part Four: LOCAL GOVERNMENT

XXX	*The Structure of Local Government*	171
XXXI	*Principal Council Meetings* Types of meeting; conduct of meeting	173
XXXII	*Parish and Community Council Meetings* Types of meeting; conduct of meeting	178

XXXIII	*The Committee System*	178
	Membership and types of committee; conduct of committee meetings	

XXXIV	*Disqualification from Voting*	180

PART FIVE: PREPARATION FOR MEETINGS

XXXV	*Practical Work of the Secretary*	181

Appendices
I	Glossary of Terms in Relation to Meetings	193
II	Examination Techniques	200
III	Specimen Examination Questions	204
Index		213

Table of Cases

Aberdeen Rail Co. *v.* Blaikie Bros (1854) 1 M.A.C.Q. 461   97
Aldred *v.* Miller [1924] S.C. 117   2
Allen *v.* Gold Reefs of West Africa [1900] 1 Ch. 656   86
Ashbury Carriage Co. *v.* Riche (1865) L.R. 7 H.L. 453   79

Bamford *v.* Bamford [1970] Ch. 212   79
Barron *v.* Potter [1914] 1 Ch. 895   39, 142
Beatty *v.* Gillbanks [1882] 9 Q.B.D. 308   3
Betts *v.* MacNaughton (1910) 1 Ch. 430   103
Blackshaw *v.* Lord [1983] 2 All E.R. 311   69
Boston Deep Sea Fishing and Ice Co. *v.* Ansell (1888) 39 Ch. 339   97
Bruner *v.* Moore [1904] 1 Ch. 305   195
Burden *v.* Rigler [1911] 1 K.B. 340   2
Burton *v.* Bevan [1908] 2 Ch. 240   143
Bushel *v.* Faith [1970] 1 All E.R. 53   113

Cane *v.* Jones [1981] 1 All E.R. 533   83, 110, 127
Caratal New Mines, *Re* [1902] 2 Ch. 498   109
Catesby *v.* Burnett [1916] 2 Ch. 325   26, 57
Cawley *v.* Jones [1967] 3 All E.R. 743   8
Citizens' Theatre Ltd, *Re* [1946] S.C. 14   109
Collins *v.* Revison [1754] 1 Sayer 138   2, 11
Compagnie de Mayville *v.* Whitley [1896] 1 Ch. 788   142
Cook *v.* Deeks [1916] 1 A.C. 554   98
Cooper *v.* Lawson [1838] 8 A & E. 746   67
Cousins *v.* International Brick Co. [1931] 2 Ch. 90   121

De Morgan *v.* Metropolitan Board of Works (1880) 5 Q.B.D. 155   2
Duncan *v.* Jones [1936] 1 K.B. 218   3
Duomatic Ltd, *Re* [1969] 2 Ch. 365   81, 111

East *v.* Bennett Bros. [1911] 1 Ch. 163   15, 96
Edinburgh Workmen's Houses Improvements Co. Ltd 1934,
    Re (1934)   91
Edwards *v.* Bell (1824) 1 Bing 403   67

TABLE OF CASES

E.E.T.P.U. *v.* Times Newspapers Ltd [1980] 1 All E.R. 1097   65
Emmadart Ltd, *Re* [1979] Ch. 540   81
Ernest *v.* Loma Gold Mines [1897] 1 Ch. 1   117, 122
Express Engineering Works, *Re* [1920] 1 Ch. 466   16, 35, 100

Field *v.* Receiver for the Metropolitan Police District [1907] 2 K.B. 853   3, 4
Fireproof Doors, *Re* [1916] 2 Ch. 142   63, 64, 96, 125
Foss *v.* Harbottle (1843) 2 Hare, 461   82, 103
Foster *v.* Foster [1916] 1 Ch. 532   142
Freeman and Lockyer *v.* Buckhurst Park Properties [1964] 2 Q.B. 480   79

Garden Gully Quartz Mining Co. *v.* McLister [1875] 1 A.C. 39   142
Grant *v.* U.K. Switchback Railway Co. (1889) 40 Ch. D. 135   81
Greenhalgh *v.* Arderne Cinemas [1946] 1 All E.R. 512   136

Harben *v.* Phillips (1883) 23 Ch.D. 14   118
Hartley Baird Ltd, *Re* [1954] 1 Ch. 143   39, 100
Haycraft Gold Reduction Co., *Re* [1900] 2 Ch. 230   17, 37, 89
Henderson *v.* Bank of Australasia (1890) 45 Ch.D. 330   16, 17, 37, 43
Henderson *v.* Louttit (1894) 21 R. 674   39, 100
Holders Investment Trust Ltd, *Re* [1971] 1 W.L.R. 583   136
Hooper *v.* Kerr [1900] 83 L.T. 729   17, 37, 89
Horbury Bridge Coal Co., *Re* (1879) 11 Ch.D. 109   20, 41, 112
Hurst *v.* Picture Palaces [1915] 1 K.B. 1   2, 12

Irvine *v.* Union Bank of Australia (1877) 2 App. Cas. 366   79

Jackson *v.* Hamlyn & Others (Gordon Hotels Case) [1953] 1 Ch. 577   57, 122
John Shaw (Salford) Ltd *v.* Shaw [1935] 2 K.B. 113   80, 82

Kamara and others *v.* D.P.P. [1973] 2 All E.R. 1242   4
Kaye *v.* Croyden Tramways Co. (1898) 1 Ch. 358   16, 37, 79
Kerr *v.* Mottram [1940] Ch. 657   63, 64

Lawrenson *v.* Oxford 1981   8
Liverpool Household Stores Ltd, *Re* (1890) 59 L.J. Ch. 616   96, 146
London Flats, *Re* [1969] 1 W.L.R. 79   15
Lucas *v.* Mason (1875) L.R. 10 Ex. 251   11

Machell *v.* Nevinson (1890) cit. 11 East. 84   16

TABLE OF CASES

Marshal Valve Gear Co. *v*. Manning & Co. (1909) 1 Ch. 267 81
Menier *v*. Hoopers Telegraph Works Ltd (1874) L.R. 9
  Ch. App. 350 98
Moorgate Mercantile Holdings, *Re* [1981] 1 All E.R. 40
  88, 102, 104, 107
Morris *v*. Kanssen [1946] A.C. 459 141, 142
Musselwhite *v*. Musselwhite and Son Ltd [1961] 1 Ch. 964 87

National Dwellings Society *v*. Sykes [1894] 3 Ch. 159 17, 25, 26, 57
Nationwide Building Society *v*. Punt (1983) *Financial Times*,
  30th November 108
Nell *v*. Longbottom [1894] 1 Q.B. 767 19, 26, 142
Newman Industries *v*. Prudential Assurance Co. 1983 91
North Eastern Insurance Co., *Re* [1919] 1 Ch. 198 97
Northern Counties Securities Ltd *v*. Jackson and Staple [1974] 1
  W.L.R. 1133 88
North-West Transportation Co. Ltd *v*. Beatty (1887) 98

Oxted Motor Co., *Re* [1921] 3 K.B. 32 16, 36

Parker and Cooper *v*. Reading [1926] Ch. 975 110
Pearce, Duff & Co., *Re* [1960] 3 All E.R. 222 93
Pender *v*. Lushington (1877) 6 Ch. D. 70 00
Portuguese Consolidated Copper Mines, *Re* (1889) 42 Ch. D. 160
  16, 35, 143
Prudential Assurance Co. Ltd *v*. Newman Industries (No. 2)
  (1980) 3 W.L.R. 543; (1982) 1 W.L.R. 31, C.A. 82

R. *v*. Burns (1886) 16 Cox. C.C. 355 4
R. *v*. Caird (1970) 54 Cr. App. Rep. 499 4
R. *v*. D'Oyly (1840) 12 A. & E. 139 26, 56
R. *v*. Edwards and Roberts (1978) 67 Cr. App. Rep. 228 8
R. *v*. Langhorne (1936) 6 N. & M. 203 16, 35, 143
R. *v*. Liverpool City Council 13
R. *v*. Shrewsbury (1735) cases Lee, temp. Hardwicke 147 35
R. *v*. Wimbledon Local Board (1882) 8 Q.B.D. 459 114, 196
Railway Sleepers Supply Co., *Re* (1885) 29 Ch.D. 204 36, 193
Rands *v*. Olroyd [1958] 3 All E.R. 344 180
Regents Canal Iron Co., *Re* (1867) W.N. 79 96
Rights and Issues Investment Trusts *v*. Style Shoes [1965]
  Ch. 250 113
Rolled Steel Products Ltd *v*. British Steel Corp. [1982]
  3 All E.R. 105 79

TABLE OF CASES

Royal British Bank Ltd v. Turquand (1856) 6 E.R.B. 327 — 79

Salisbury Gold Mining Co. v. Hathorn & Others [1897] A.C. 268 — 49, 57
Salmon v. Quinn and Axtens [1909] A.C. 442 — 82
Saloman v. Saloman & Co. [1897] A.C. 22 — 78
Sanitary Carbon Co., *Re* [1877] W.N. 223 — 15, 96
Saxtons Ltd v. Miles Ltd 1983 B.C.L.C. 70 — 163
Scadding v. Lorant (1851) 3 H.L.C. 418 — 56
Shankey Contracting Ltd *Re* — 110
Sharp v. Dawes (1876) 2 Q.B.D. 29 — 1, 15, 96
Silkin v. Beaverbrook Ltd [1958] 1 W.L.R. 743 — 67
Slee v. Meadows (1911) 75 J.P. 244 — 2
Smith v. Paring-Mines [1906] 2 Ch. 193 — 57, 196
Smyth v. Darley (1849) 2 H.L. Cas. 789 — 16, 35

Tenby Corporation v. Mason [1908] 1 Ch. 457 — 12
Thomas v. Bradbury, Agnew & Co. [1906] 2 K.B. 62 — 68
Thomas v. Sawkins [1935] 2 K.B. 249 — 10
Tolley v. Fry & Sons Ltd [1931] A.C. 333 — 73

West Canadian Collieries, *Re* [1962] 1 All E.R. 26 — 87
White v. Bristol Aeroplane Co. [1953] Ch. 65 — 136
Williams v. Manchester Corp. 1897 — 179
Wills v. Murray (1850) 4 Ex. 843 — 56, 198
Windward Islands Enterprises (U.K.) Ltd, *Re* 1983 B.C.L.C. — 130
Wise v. Dunning [1902] 1 K.B. 167 — 3
Wood v. Leadbetter (1845) 13 M. & W. 838 — 12

York Tramways v. Willows (1882) 8 Q.B.D. 685 — 95, 96, 142
Young v. Ladies' Imperial Club [1920] 2 K.B. 523 — 16, 35
Yuill v. Greymouth Point Elizabeth Railway Co. [1904] 1 Ch. 32 — 40, 142

PART ONE

MEETINGS IN GENERAL

CHAPTER I

Holding a Meeting

1. Definitions. In *Sharp* v. *Dawes* (1876) a meeting was defined as "an assembly of people for a lawful purpose" or "the coming together of at least two persons for any lawful purpose". It follows, therefore, that the word "meeting" covers a wide range of assemblies, from the formal meeting of a board of directors of a registered company to the social meeting of friends.

The behaviour of people at any kind of meeting is governed by the law of the land as it affects each individual. For many types of assembly this is quite sufficient and there is no need for special rules and regulations for such assemblies as theatre and cinema audiences or friends who go out for a meal together. The law relating to meetings is therefore confined to the regulation of assemblies which consider matters of general public concern or the consideration of affairs which are of common concern to members of the assembly.

Furthermore, these meetings are divided into two types:

(*a*) *public meetings* which consider matters of public concern and to which all members of the public have access, subject to the physical limitations of the place where the meeting is held, but irrespective of whether persons attending the meeting are required to pay; and

(*b*) *private meetings* which are attended by people who have a specific right or special capacity to attend, such as the committee of a brass band or golf club or the members of a registered company.

LEGALITY OF MEETING

2. Place of meeting.

(*a*) *Meetings in public places:*

(*i*) There is no common law right to hold meetings in public places, such as highways, parks, etc.

(*ii*) Nevertheless, an individual having a right to be there is presumed to have a right to join with others who happen to be there, i.e. his is not so much a positive right to meet there as a negative right not to be removed, so long as there is no infringement of statutory or local regulations.

(*iii*) The following cases are important in this connection:

Aldred v. *Miller* (1924): A meeting held in a *highway* is not necessarily unlawful, unless there is interference with the primary function of the highway to afford passage.

Burden v. *Rigler* (1911): Although there is no right to hold such a meeting, the fact that a public meeting is held upon a highway does not necessarily render the meeting unlawful, unless other circumstances exist to do so, e.g. the causing of an obstruction.

De Morgan v. *Metropolitan Board of Works* (1880): In this case, it was held that no right on the part of the public to hold meetings on a *common* is known to the law.

Slee v. *Meadows* (1911): Local authorities can regulate the holding of public meetings in areas within their jurisdiction.

(*b*) *Meetings in private places:*

(*i*) People who meet on private property without the permission of the owner or other lawful occupier are trespassers, and can, of course, be requested to withdraw—but payment of an admission charge implies permission granted.

(*ii*) If, after being requested to withdraw, the trespasser persists in his offence, the lawful occupier (or his agent) can remove him.

(*iii*) Only such force as is reasonably necessary to effect the removal may be used; if unreasonable violence is used, the trespasser will have a right of action for assault: *Collins* v. *Revison* (1754).

(*iv*) If payment is made for admission, that apparently constitutes a form of licence to attend; therefore a person who has paid for admission cannot be removed from the private premises so long as he behaves himself in an orderly manner and does not infringe any of the rules by which he is bound: *see Hurst* v. *Picture Palaces* (1915) and other cases on this subject.

3. Illegal assemblies. A meeting may be illegal either at common law or by statute.

As stated in **2** above, the place in which a meeting is held does not of itself necessarily affect its legality. Other factors or circumstances connected with a meeting may render it illegal, as will be shown in the following cases:

(*a*) *An unlawful assembly* is created at common law, where there is a breach of the peace, or where a breach of the peace is imminent; thus:

I. HOLDING A MEETING

(*i*) In *Field* v. *The Receiver for the Metropolitan Police District* (1907), it was held that "whenever as many as *three* persons meet together to support each other, even against opposition, in carrying out a purpose which is *likely* to involve violence, or to produce in the minds of their neighbours any reasonable apprehension of violence, they then constitute an *unlawful assembly*."

(*ii*) *Beatty* v. *Gillbanks* (1882). In this case, it was held that a lawful assembly does not become unlawful simply because the participants must know, in view of their previous experiences, that a breach of the peace would result from their meeting.

NOTE: The original decision of the magistrates was to bind over Beatty (of the Salvation Army) on a charge of unlawful assembly. But this decision was later reversed, as it was pointed out that an unlawful organisation had deliberately set out to prevent the lawful assembly of the Salvationists.

(*iii*) *Wise* v. *Dunning* (1902). It was held, in this case, that the defendant, who held public meetings in a public place in Liverpool, had, by speech and action, been highly provocative. Breaches of the peace resulted, and the defendant was bound over by the magistrates.

NOTE: Apart from the fact that there had been greater and, perhaps, more direct provocation in the *Wise* v. *Dunning* case, it might also be mentioned that there had been a breach of a local bye-law, whereas in the *Beatty* v. *Gillbanks* case there had been no illegal act on the part of the Salvationists.

(*iv*) *Duncan* v. *Jones* (1936). In this case, a police officer, anticipating a breach of the peace, forbade the defendant to address a public meeting. The defendant persisted and tried to hold the meeting, and was found guilty of wilfully obstructing the police in the execution of its duty, namely in preventing a breach of the peace.

NOTE: This appears to be based upon the principle that if it is found impossible to preserve order by any other means, the police may order the dispersal of even a lawful assembly, if a breach of the peace is anticipated to result from it. Refusal to disperse would then amount to an obstruction of the police in the execution of its duty.

It must be apparent, from consideration of the above decisions, that a breach of the peace may be created among those actually participating in or forming part of a meeting, or it may arise because of the effect of the meeting on members of the public in the vicinity.

It must, however, be admitted that the legal position relating to unlawful assemblies is still rather doubtful.

(*b*) *Rout.* This is a disturbance of the peace by three or more persons who have assembled with the intention of doing something amounting to a riot and, although they have gone some way towards carrying out that intention, have not yet executed it. It is, in effect, an *incomplete* riot.

(*c*) *Riot.* An unlawful assembly may become a riot at common law. At *common law*, five elements are necessary to constitute a riot:

(*i*) three or more persons;

(*ii*) a common purpose;

(*iii*) execution or inception of that common purpose;

(*iv*) an intention to help one another, by force if necessary, against any who may oppose them in the execution of their common purpose; and

(*v*) force or violence displayed in manner calculated to alarm at least one person of reasonable firmness and courage. (*Field* v. *The Receiver for the Metropolitan Police District* (1907), *R* v. *Caird* (1970).)

(*d*) *Sedition and seditious assembly.* An attempt to incite disaffection against the person of Her Majesty or to bring the Government or the constitution into contempt by inciting public violence is said to be sedition: *R.* v. *Burns* (1886). A meeting will become a seditious assembly, as provided in the Seditious Meetings Act 1817 (s.23), if:

(*i*) it consists of more than 50 persons;

(*ii*) it is held within a mile of Westminster Hall during sittings of Parliament or the Superior Courts; and

(*iii*) its purpose is to prefer a petition, complaint or address to the Queen or either House of Parliament, or to alter matters of Church or State.

(*e*) *Affray.* This is fighting, violence or a display of force which would intimidate reasonable people. An affray can occur in a private building as well as in a public place. (*Kamara and others* v. *DPP* (1973).)

4. Preservation of order.

(*a*) In most meetings, disorder can be traced to the following principal causes:

(*i*) *Organised opposition.* This consists of people whose main object is to disturb or even break up a meeting. Usually they prefer to congregate at the back of the meeting. If this is apparent before the meeting starts, the stewards must ensure that such people are kept to the front of the meeting and kept apart as much as possible. This weakens their organisation and, if they do attempt a disturbance, it simplifies the work of the "chuckers-out".

(*ii*) *Irrelevant interruption of speeches.* Some of these may be of a violent character, but in most cases they are caused by audible running commentaries or by small groups of members who form themselves into "whispering sub-committees". Both of these distract and annoy, but a tactful chairman ought to be able to quell these disturbances without calling upon the stewards.

(*iii*) *Intolerant speakers* may make insulting remarks concerning those who are opposed to them. In such cases, it is the chairman's task to deal tactfully with the situation, otherwise, if the speaker is allowed to continue on the same lines, the subsequent speeches will almost certainly develop into a "slanging match", and the meeting will end in disorder.

(*b*) If the chairman is unable to preserve order under his own powers, he may, in certain circumstances, seek the statutory remedies provided by the following Acts:
   (*i*) the Public Meeting Act 1908; or
   (*ii*) the Public Order Act 1936.

LEGISLATIVE PROVISIONS

5. Public Meeting Act 1908.

(*a*) *The main provisions* of this Act are as follows:
   (*i*) Any person who at a lawful public meeting acts in a disorderly manner for the purpose of preventing the transaction of the business for which the meeting was called together shall be guilty of an offence.
   (*ii*) If the offence is committed at a *political* meeting held in any parliamentary constituency between the date of the issue of a writ for the return of a Member of Parliament for such constituency and the date at which a return to such a writ is made, he shall be guilty of an illegal practice within the meaning of the Corrupt and Illegal Practices Prevention Act 1883.
   (*iii*) Any person who *incites* others to commit an offence under this section shall be guilty of a like offence.

(*b*) Thus, the Act made *deliberate interruption* of a public meeting an offence, and imposed appropriate penalties. It did not, however, give any additional powers to the police for the purpose of enforcing the Act.

(*c*) This defect was remedied to some extent by the Public Order Act 1936 (s.6), which provided, *inter alia*, that:

(*i*) If a police officer reasonably suspects a person of committing an offence under the Public Meeting Act 1908, he may, *at the request of the chairman*, demand immediately the person's name and address.

(*ii*) If the person concerned *refuses* such request or gives a false name and address, he commits an offence.

(*iii*) In the event of such refusal, or if the constable reasonably suspects the person concerned of giving a false name and address, he may *arrest him immediately without warrant*.

6. The Public Order Act 1936.

(*a*) *The purposes of this Act* are clearly stated in its title as "An Act *to prohibit the wearing of uniforms* in connection with political objects and the maintenance by private persons of associations of military or similar character; and to make further provision for the preservation of public order on the occasion of *public processions* and in public places" (authors' italics).

NOTE: This Act was passed during a period when certain parties in this country favoured the wearing of uniforms, the carrying of weapons and the organising of processions. As the result of such displays, disorder and violence at public meetings and in public places had been causing considerable alarm.

(*b*) Apart from the provisions of s.6 of the Act, already referred to in 5 above, *its main effect is to forbid:*

(*i*) The wearing of uniforms in connection with political objects.

(*ii*) Quasi-military organisations.

(*iii*) The carrying of offensive weapons at public meetings or processions.

(*iv*) Offensive conduct conducive to a breach of the peace.

7. Main provisions of the Public Order Act 1936.

The following are the main provisions of the Act in greater detail:

(*a*) *Political uniforms* (s.1)*:* A person is guilty of an offence who, in any public place or at any public meeting, wears a uniform which signifies his association with any political organisation or with the promotion of any political object.

But the chief of police may, with the consent of the Secretary of

State, permit the wearing of a uniform at ceremonial, anniversary or other occasions, if he is satisfied that there is no risk of public disorder.

> NOTE: Organisations such as the Boy Scouts' Association and the Salvation Army are obviously non-political and are not concerned with the promotion of political objects.

(*b*) *Quasi-military organisations* (s.2)*:* If members or followers of an association (whether incorporated or not) are organised, trained or equipped for employment in usurping the functions of the police, or of the armed forces of the Crown; or are organised and trained or organised and equipped for employment in the use or display of force to promote a political object, or in such manner as to cause a reasonable apprehension of such purpose, then any person who takes part in the control or management of the association or in the organising or training, is guilty of an offence.

> NOTE: This does not prevent the convenors of a public meeting on private premises from employing a reasonable number of stewards to preserve order; nor does it prevent the giving of instructions to them as to their duties, nor the provision of badges or other distinguishing signs.

(*c*) *Processions* (s.3)*:* Chief officers of police are given power:
 (*i*) to make regulations for the conduct of processions where there is reasonable grounds to fear serious disorder, e.g. to re-route a procession so as to avoid a certain neighbourhood;
 (*ii*) to request the public authority to prohibit public processions in a particular district for a period not exceeding three months, if he considers that the regulations which he has power to make are unlikely to be effective.

> NOTE: Such a prohibition against public processions also requires the consent of the Secretary of State; thus, although the Commissioner of the City of London Police or the Commissioner of the Metropolitan Police may himself make an order prohibiting a public procession, it is still subject to the consent of the Secretary of State.

(*d*) *Offensive weapons* (s.4)*:* It is an offence for any person while present at a public meeting or on the occasion of a public procession, to have with him an offensive weapon, otherwise than in pursuance of lawful authority.

(*e*) *Breach of the peace* (s.5)*:* It is an offence for any person, in any public place or at any public meeting, to use threatening, abusive, or insulting words or behaviour, or to distribute or display any writing, sign or visible representation which is threatening, abusive or insulting, with intent to provoke a breach of the peace or whereby a breach of the peace is likely to be occasioned.

(*f*) *Racial hatred* (s.5A): It is an offence for any person to publish or distribute any written matter which is threatening, abusive or insulting, or to use in any public place or at any public meeting words which are threatening, abusive or insulting in a case where, having regard to all the circumstances, hatred is likely to be stirred up against any racial group by the matter or words in question.

(*g*) *Extension of police powers* under Public Meeting Act 1908 (s.6): In the words of sub-section (3), the following is to be added to section 1 of the Public Meeting Act 1908:

"If any constable reasonably suspects any person of committing an offence under the foregoing provisions of this section, he may *if requested to do so by the chairman of the meeting* require that person to declare to him immediately his name and address, and if that person refuses or fails so to declare his name and address or gives a false name and address he shall be guilty of an offence under this sub-section and liable on summary conviction thereof to a fine not exceeding £2, and if he refuses or fails so to declare his name and address or if the constable reasonably suspects him of giving a false name and address, the constable may without warrant arrest him."

8. Definitions in the Public Order Act 1936. The following are defined in the Act:

(*a*) *Meetings:* "A meeting held for the purpose of the discussion of matters of public interest, or for the purpose of the expression of views on such matters."

(*b*) *Public meeting:* "Any meeting in a public place and any meeting which the public or a section thereof are permitted to attend, whether on payment or otherwise."

(*c*) *Public place:* "Any highway, public park or garden, any sea beach, and any public bridge, road, lane, footpath, square, court, alley or passage, whether a thoroughfare or not; and including any open space to which, for the time being, the public have or are permitted to have access, whether on payment or otherwise." In *Cawley* v. *Frost* (1976) it was decided that a football ground could be a "public place", whilst in *R* v. *Edwards and Roberts* (1978) it was decided that although the public may be able to obtain access to private premises through the private front garden of a house if they have some lawful purpose for so doing, this will not make such gardens public places within s.9(1) of the Public Order Act 1936. Finally, in *Lawrenson* v. *Oxford* (1981) it was held that a public house was a "public place" within the meaning of the Act:

"The references to 'permission' and 'payment or otherwise' do, in my view, indicate that it is not necessary to go so far as to say that once a person becomes an invitee, the place cannot be regarded as a 'public place'. There will be places where the public can be excluded, but when they are not excluded, they are a public 'place' for the purpose of the definition contained in the Act" (Woolf J.).

(*d*) *Private premises:* "Premises to which the public have access, whether on payment or otherwise, only by permission of the owner, occupier or lessee of the premises."

(*e*) *Public procession:* "A procession in a public place."

POLICE POWERS

9. Police powers and duties. Reference has already been made to the statutory powers of the police under s.6 of the Public Order Act 1936. It was, however, stressed that the right to exercise such powers arises out of the prior request of the chairman of the meeting concerned.

The powers and duties of the police relating to entry of meeting places, and the arrest or removal of disorderly persons, are not by any means clearly defined, and must obviously depend upon where the meeting is held. The position at common law is summarised in the following paragraphs.

10. Meetings held in public places. The police may:

(*a*) *Remove or arrest* individuals or disperse the meeting, where a breach of the peace occurs, or is reasonably anticipated.

(*b*) *Exercise the necessary authority* to prevent obstruction, or to control unlawful assemblies.

11. Meetings held on private property.

(*a*) The powers and duties of the police in relation to meetings held on private property (whether held for public purposes or not) were stated in a Home Office report of 1909, namely:

(*i*) The police have no power to enter, except by leave of the occupiers of the premises or promoters of the meeting—or where they have reason to believe that a breach of the peace is being committed.

(*ii*) Although it is no part of the police duties to eject trespassers from private premises, they *may* (in their capacity as private citizens) assist in ejecting them, if requested to do so by the occupiers of the premises or promoters of the meeting—but they are not under legal obligation to do so.

(*iii*) Where there is an actual breach of the peace, they may, and indeed have a duty to, intervene. In that event, even if they have not seen any such breach committed, they may arrest without warrant a person charged by another for such a breach, where there are reasonable grounds to anticipate that the breach is likely to be continued or immediately renewed.

NOTE: Private property would include a *public* building which had been hired by the convenors of the meeting for the occasion.

(*b*) *The decision in Thomas* v. *Sawkins* (1935) modified the somewhat narrow interpretation of police powers stated above; in this case:

(*i*) The police forced their way into a public meeting held in a hall hired by the promoter for the occasion, having been refused permission by the promoter.

(*ii*) The promoter brought an action for technical assault.

(*iii*) *It was held* that the police are empowered to enter a meeting held on private premises, not only where a breach of the peace has been or is being committed, but also when they have reasonable grounds for believing that a breach of the peace is *likely to be* committed.

(*c*) Although the position may vary considerably between local authorities, the assistance of the police in controlling meetings on private property can usually be procured, so long as the promoters are prepared to meet the cost of such special service.

(*d*) Several years ago, however, the Home Office, showing some concern over frequent cases of organised interference at political meetings, suggested that the police should (at the invitation of the promoters), be present at such meetings without charge, when it is anticipated that there will be interference which would be likely to lead to a breach of the peace.

(*e*) *Entry and search without search warrant.* The Police and Criminal Evidence Bill 1984 provides that a constable who has reasonable grounds for believing that the person whom he is seeking is on the premises may enter and search the premises, using such reasonable force as is necessary for the purpose:

(*i*) of executing

(1) a warrant of arrest issued in connection with or arising out of criminal proceedings; or

(2) a warrant of commitment issued under s.76 of the Magistrates' Courts Act 1980;

(*ii*) of arresting a person for an arrestable offence;

(*iii*) of arresting a person for an offence under

(1) s.1 (prohibition of uniforms in connection with political objects), s.4 (prohibition of offensive weapons at public meetings and processions) or s.5 (prohibition of offensive conduct conducive to breaches of the peace) of the Public Order Act 1936;

(2) any enactment contained in ss. 6 to 8 or 10 of the Criminal Law Act 1977 (offences relating to entering and remaining on property). Only a constable in uniform may exercise powers of entry and search for this purpose;

(*iv*) of recapturing a person who is unlawfully at large and whom he is pursuing; or

(*v*) of saving life or limb or preventing serious damage to property (the reasonable belief requirement does not apply to (*v*)).

The power of search is only a power to search to the extent that is reasonably required for the purpose for which the power of entry is exercised.

NOTE: When this section became law all the rules of common law under which a constable has power to enter premises without a warrant were abolished *except* for any power of entry to deal with or prevent a breach of the peace.

PUBLIC MEETINGS ON PRIVATE PREMISES

12. Promoter's rights. Where a public meeting is held on *private* premises (including public premises hired by the promoter for the occasion), the promoter's right of expulsion may be summarised as follows:

(*a*) *Where no admission charge is made*, any person who attends does so only by leave of the promoter; consequently:

(*i*) *He can be requested to leave the meeting* at any time, whether he has behaved in an orderly manner or not.

(*ii*) *If he refuses to leave*, or fails to do so within a reasonable time, he becomes a *trespasser*, and may be forcibly removed.

NOTE: Only reasonable force may be used, otherwise the person forcibly removed may bring an action for assault, as in *Collins* v. *Revison* (1754); *see also Lucas* v. *Mason* (1875).

(*b*) *Where a charge for admission has been made* to enter private premises, the person paying the admission charge is obviously in a much stronger position:

(*i*) If he is improperly requested to withdraw, or improperly ejected, he is entitled to sue the promoters for breach of contract, i.e. for the cost of admission: *Wood* v. *Leadbetter* (1845).

(*ii*) If he has conducted himself properly and observed the conditions contained in his contract with the promoters, his licence conferring admission to the premises cannot be revoked before its purpose has been achieved and, if, as in *Hurst* v. *Picture Palaces* (1913), after refusing to withdraw, he is ejected, he may bring an action for assault.

(*c*) *To summarise* the position:

(*i*) The promoter has a right to request a person to leave a meeting held on private premises; if, however, he has paid for admission, his expulsion from a meeting can be legally justified only on the grounds of his failure to conduct himself in a proper manner.

(*ii*) In either case, i.e. whether he paid an admission charge or not, and whatever the grounds for his expulsion, only reasonable force may be used.

ATTENDANCE OF OUTSIDERS

13. Admission of the Press.

(*a*) *At public meetings*, representatives of the Press have the same right to attend as any other member of the public.

(*b*) *At a public meeting held on private premises* (including public premises hired for the occasion), Press representatives have no better right to be admitted than any member of the public; consequently, if they attend uninvited, they may be requested to withdraw.

(*c*) *At meetings of local authorities*, the Press has had the right of admission since 1908, and the public since June 1961. The legal position may be summarised as follows:

(*i*) Originally, it was held that neither the Press nor the public had any legal right to be present at meetings of a local authority: *Tenby Corporation* v. *Mason* (1908).

(*ii*) *The Local Authorities (Admission of the Press to Meetings) Act* 1908 changed the position in law by providing that:

(1) Representatives of the Press *shall* be admitted to the meetings of every local authority.

(2) A local authority may *temporarily exclude* such representatives as often as may be desirable at any meeting when, in the opinion of the members present, expressed by resolution, such exclusion is advisable *in the public interest*, by reason of the special nature of the business then being, or about to be, dealt with.

I. HOLDING A MEETING

14. The Public Bodies (Admissions to Meetings) Act 1960. This has remedied some of the inadequacies of the 1908 Act and will, it is hoped, prevent cases of deliberate evasion of that Act, although such cases were comparatively rare. The main provision of the 1960 Act, which came into force on 1st June, 1961, are as follows:

(*a*) *The public has the same right as the press* to attend the meetings of local authorities (s.1 and Sched, para 1).

(*b*) *The right of admission* of both press and public applies also to *committee meetings*, although this right applies only to education committees, certain joint committees and to committees composed of the whole of the members of the parent body (s.2(1)). The Local Government Act 1972, s.100, requires any meeting of a committee, appointed by a local authority or authorities to discharge functions under arrangements made by the authority or authorities, to be open to the public.

NOTE: Presumably this section of the 1960 Act was intended to prevent a practice, adopted by certain local authorities, of "going into committee" when it wished to exclude the Press from a council meeting.

(*c*) The press is given the right, on payment of expenses, to call for a *supply of agenda papers* of meetings which the public are entitled to attend.

NOTE: In order to safeguard the position as regards defamatory statements, reports, agenda papers and other documents issued to the press are subject to qualified privilege.

(*d*) A local authority reserves the right to pass a *resolution excluding both press and public* "wherever publicity would be prejudicial to the public interest by reason of the confidential nature of the business or for other special reasons stated in the resolution and arising from the nature of the business of the proceedings" (s.1(2)). In *R* v. *Liverpool City Council* (1975) the business of a meeting was to consider applications for hackney carriage licences and it was decided to hear each application without competitors being present. This was held to be a valid course of action within "special reasons" as stated in the Act, but as the minutes did not refer to this special reason the Act had not been complied with.

NOTE: The Act imposes no penalty for improper or unnecessary exclusion of press or public from a meeting. This criticism has, in fact, been made of the Act throughout, as it does not anywhere refer to the penalty for any breach of the various sections.

PROGRESS TEST 1

1. What is a public meeting? Is there a right at common law to hold meetings in public places? (**1, 2**)

2. Explain briefly some of the more important provisions of the Public Order Act 1936. (**6**)

3. What do you understand by the term "public meeting"? Would a meeting of a company or of a registered body be so regarded? Name any circumstances where common law rights (if any) in this connection are affected by statute. (**1, 2, 6**)

4. Is there any general right to assemble in a public place, or a right to meet on the public highway? Does this prevent a meeting being held in either of the two places? Give the reasons supporting your contention. (**2, 8**)

CHAPTER II

Convention, Constitution and Conduct of Meetings

NUMBER OF PERSONS ATTENDING

1. Sharp v. Dawes (1876). In this case a meeting was defined as "the coming together of at least two persons for any lawful purpose." Thus, it may be stated that a meeting usually consists of two or more persons.

2. In Re Sanitary Carbon Co. (1877). This case appeared to lend support to the above decision, as it was held that a meeting of a company attended by one shareholder only was not validly constituted—even though that shareholder held the proxies of all the other members.

3. Re London Flats (1969). The articles of a company required a quorum of two. It was held that a decision made by one shareholder after the other had left the room was a nullity.

4. One person can, however, constitute a valid meeting. Despite the above decisions, one person can constitute a valid meeting; e.g.

(*a*) Where one person held all the shares of a particular class, that person alone was held to constitute a valid meeting of that class of shareholder: *East* v. *Bennett Bros.* (1911).

(*b*) Where the rules permit, it is possible to appoint a committee of one, and thus hold a committee "meeting" of one member.

NOTE: several other cases occur in connection with company meetings, where a "meeting" of one person might be valid.

(*c*) Section 131 of the Companies Act 1948 states that the Department of Trade may direct a valid meeting to be held even if only one creditor has lodged proof.

(*d*) Section 135 states that the courts may direct a valid meeting to be held even if there is only one person entitled to attend.

(*e*) Where the director has fixed a quorum of one.

VALIDITY OF A MEETING

5. The requisites of a valid meeting. The validity of a meeting may be questioned for a number of reasons; therefore, in order to ensure that decisions taken at a meeting are not subsequently nullified, the convenors must conform to certain basic requisites, namely:

(a) A meeting must be properly *convened*.
(b) It must be properly *constituted*.
(c) It must be properly *held* in accordance with the rules governing the meeting.

6. Failure properly to convene. This might arise out of:

(a) *Omission to send notice* to every person entitled to attend, but the omission may be excused, e.g.

(i) Where the rules governing the meeting provide that *accidental omission* to send notice to, or the non-receipt of notice by, any person entitled to receive notice shall not invalidate the proceedings of the meeting concerned.

(ii) Where *all* persons entitled to attend are present without notice and all "expressly assent to that which is being done": *Express Engineering Works* (1920).

(iii) Where those not summoned were *beyond summoning distance*, e.g. where a member was abroad: *Smyth* v. *Darley* (1849); or where a member was *too ill to attend* in any case: *Young* v. *Ladies' Imperial Club* (1920).

NOTE: It is, however, always advisable to send proper notice to all persons entitled to attend a meeting, and not to rely upon the apparent disability of a member at the time as an excuse for failing to summon him. Even if the member informs the convenors that he will not be able to attend the meeting, that should not be relied upon as a waiver of notice: *Re Portuguese Consolidated Copper Mines* (1889), *Rex* v. *Langhorne* (1836).

(b) *Inadequate (short) notice*; if, for example, only 7 days' notice is given instead of the 21 days' notice required by the regulations.

NOTE: In this case, too, inadequacy of notice might be excused if all, or a specified proportion of, the members so agree: *Machell* v. *Nevinson* (1809), *In Re Oxted Motor Co.* (1921).

(c) *Ambiguity of the notice*; that is, it must be free from anything calculated to confuse or mislead: *Kaye* v. *Croydon Tramways* (1898), *Henderson* v. *Bank of Australasia* (1890).

(d) *Omission of important contents*; in particular failure to mention that special business is to be transacted. It is, of course, also essential to state place, date, day and time of the meeting; although it would usually be permissible to dispense with an indication of the actual time, where one meeting is to be held immediately after

II. CONVENTION, CONSTITUTION AND CONDUCT OF MEETINGS 17

another; in that case, the notice may indicate that the second meeting will commence "at the conclusion" of the first meeting.

(*e*) *Unauthorised issue of notice*; thus, the issue of notice by the secretary without the authority of the convening body is inadequate and the meeting rendered invalid: *Re Haycraft Gold Reduction Co.* (1900). Nevertheless, if the notice is adopted and ratified by the proper summoning authority *before* the meeting is held, it may become a good notice; in which case the meeting is not invalid: *Hooper* v. *Kerr* (1900).

7. Failure to ensure that a meeting is properly constituted. The constitution of a meeting might be questioned and decisions taken might be invalidated on the following grounds:

(*a*) *Irregularity of chairman's appointment.* It is the first duty of the chairman to ensure that his own appointment is valid. If he has not been validly appointed in accordance with the rules, the meeting is not properly constituted.

(*b*) *Absence of quorum.* The quorum prescribed by the rules must be present. Absence or inadequacy of the quorum may arise in the following cases:

(*i*) *Failure to muster a quorum.* If the prescribed quorum is not present when the meeting is due to start, the meeting should be formally adjourned because, legally, there is no meeting.

(*ii*) *Failure to maintain a quorum.* If a quorum is not maintained it would be open to anyone to draw the chairman's attention to the matter. It is then the chairman's duty to declare a "count out" and to adjourn the meeting.

8. Failure to hold the meeting in accordance with the regulations governing the meeting; e.g.

(*a*) Chairman's failure to ensure that the sense of the meeting is properly ascertained with regard to any question which is properly placed before it: *National Dwellings Society* v. *Sykes* (1894).

(*b*) Chairman's refusal to allow the proposal of a legitimate and relevant amendment: *Henderson* v. *Bank of Australasia* (1890).

NOTE: In this case the court set aside the resolution on the grounds of the chairman's failure to admit a relevant amendment to it.

PROGRESS TEST 2

1. Define a meeting, and cite any cases to support or qualify your definition. **(1–3)**

2. Discuss the rule that one person cannot constitute a meeting. **(3, 4)**

3. Contrast the effects of the following cases as they affect the constitution of a meeting: (*a*) *Sharp* v. *Dawes* (1876); (*b*) *East* v. *Bennett Bros.* (1911). (**1, 4**)

4. What are the requisites of a valid meeting? Mention three leading cases on the law of meetings and the points decided. (**1–5**)

5. In what respects might the validity of a meeting be questioned? (**5–8**)

CHAPTER III

Regulations Governing Meetings

The following are matters which ought to be included in the regulations governing meetings:

1. **Appointment of officials.**

   (*a*) Appointment of chairman, deputy chairman, secretary etc.
   (*b*) Duration of appointment.
   (*c*) Filling casual vacancies.

2. **Chairman's powers.**

   (*a*) Power to use a casting vote—which he has no power to use at common law: *Nell* v. *Longbottom* (1894).
   (*b*) Powers of adjournment.
   (*c*) Power to decide points of order etc.

3. **Convening meetings.** In particular:

   (*a*) Form of notice.
   (*b*) Period of notice, e.g. for "special" business.

4. **Constitution of the quorum;** i.e.

   (*a*) Minimum number of members necessary to transact business; also, whether proxies may be included in the quorum.
   (*b*) Provision for adjournment if quorum is not present.

5. **Order of business.**

   (*a*) Listing various routine items which are to constitute "ordinary" business; all other items to be regarded as "special" business.
   (*b*) Indicating the order in which "ordinary" business items will be dealt with.

   NOTE: This would not, however, prevent the meeting from amending the recognised order.

6. **Voting.** The method or methods to be adopted, and the rules to be applied in each case; e.g.

(a) *Show of hands:* the common law method of voting.

(b) *Poll*, where, for example, the number of votes a person is entitled to use may be dependent upon the number of shares he holds.

NOTE: There is a common law right to demand a poll vote, but the rules may exclude or restrict that right.

(c) *Voice*, which includes:

(i) *acclamation*, when the voting is unanimous, or nearly so; and

(ii) *oral consent or negation*, i.e. voting "aye" or "nay" or "yes" or "no".

(d) *Ballot:* a method which is used when secrecy of the voting is desired, for example, in electing officials, etc.

(e) *Division.* The parliamentary method, the members being counted by tellers as they divide and proceed to their respective lobbies.

7. Debate. The rules governing the conduct of debate. These ought to include various rules supporting the chairman's authority, as these would enable him to ensure that debate is conducted in an orderly and efficient manner, e.g.

(a) *The order of speaking* to be decided by the chairman.

(b) *Seconding of motions:* whether a seconder is required. At common law a seconder is *not* required: *Re Horbury Bridge Coal Co.* (1879).

(c) *Withdrawal of a motion.* When a motion is before the meeting, it cannot be withdrawn except with the consent of the meeting.

(d) *Time limit* (if any) fixed for speeches, and provision for extension of the time limit in exceptional circumstances.

(e) *Second speech.* Only the mover of the original motion may speak twice on that motion.

(f) *Remedies available* for dealing with disorder and points of order.

(g) *Equality of opportunity.* Although it may not be written into the rules, it is the duty of the chairman to ensure that, so far as it is possible, each member shall have an equal opportunity of speaking.

NOTE: Other "rules" are a matter of custom or common courtesy towards the chair, and are rarely set out in written form; for example, a speaker is usually expected to stand while addressing the chairman; when the chairman rises the speaker should resume his seat.

8. Motions.

(*a*) *Form of motion*, e.g. whether it is required to be in writing.
(*b*) *Disposal:* that is, how a motion may be disposed of, e.g. it may be "dropped" or "shelved".

9. Amendments.

(*a*) *Form of amendment*, e.g. whether it is required to be in writing.
(*b*) *Order* in which amendments are to be put to the meeting.
(*c*) *Amendments to amendments:* the method of dealing with amendments to amendments, if permitted by the rules.

10. Resolutions.

(*a*) *Form of resolution* for special purposes, requiring a specified majority, e.g. where a two-thirds or three-fourths majority may be required.
(*b*) *Resolutions in writing*, permitting the passing of a resolution in writing, e.g. where it is signed by all members of an executive committee such a resolution may be as valid as if it had been passed at a duly constituted meeting of that committee.

11. Proxies.

(*a*) *Power to appoint* a proxy (or proxies) bearing in mind that there is *no* power to do so at common law.
(*b*) *Form(s) of proxy*, if any, permitted, e.g. a two-way proxy may be permitted.
(*c*) *Rights* of a proxy at meetings.
(*d*) *Deposit* of proxy forms, e.g. it may be necessary to deposit them not less than (say) 48 hours before the meeting concerned is due to commence.

12. Adjournment. Rules governing adjournment of:

(*a*) debate; and
(*b*) meetings, in so far as they are not dealt with in defining the powers of the chairman.

13. Committees.

(*a*) *Appointment.* Power to appoint committees.
(*b*) *Constitution* and powers of committees.

14. Alteration of rules governing meetings, e.g.

(a) *Procedure*, kind of resolution, period of notice required.
(b) *Restrictions* if any, upon the power to alter rules.

15. Suspension of rules governing meetings, e.g.

(a) *Circumstances* in which suspension may be permitted.
(b) *Procedure*, kind of resolution, period of notice required.

16. Rescission of resolutions.

(a) *Time limit;* the period which must elapse before a resolution can be rescinded, e.g. a period of six months may be required.
(b) *Procedure*, kind of resolution, period of notice required.

17. Minutes.

(a) *The keeping of minutes*—where they are to be kept and by whom.
(b) *Precautions* to be taken to safeguard the minutes.

PROGRESS TEST 3

1. Enumerate some of the usual contents of the regulations, rules or standing orders governing meetings of any association, society or other body with which you are familiar. (**1–17**)

2. The rules governing the meetings of a society are silent on the following subjects:

(a) Chairman's power to use a casting vote;
(b) Members' right to demand a poll vote;
(c) Seconding of motions.

What is the position in each case at common law? (**2, 6, 7**)

3. Suggest at least six rules governing the conduct of debate that might usefully be included in the regulations governing meetings of a social club. (**1–17**)

CHAPTER IV

The Chairman

APPOINTMENT AND QUALIFICATIONS

1. Manner of a chairman's appointment. This depends upon the kind of meeting over which he is to preside; e.g.

(*a*) The chairman of a limited company is appointed in accordance with that company's Articles of Association.

(*b*) The chairman of county council meetings is appointed in accordance with regulations laid down by statute.

(*c*) The chairman of any meeting for which no specific rules are provided may be appointed for that meeting by the majority vote of those present, before dealing with any of the business for which the meeting is being held.

2. Duration. The duration of the chairman's appointment is also dependent upon the regulations (if any) which govern the meeting; thus, he may be appointed for one particular meeting only, for a fixed period of (say) one year, or even for life.

A deputy chairman will preside in the absence of the elected chairman. A regular deputy chairman is often appointed in manner prescribed in the rules, and for a fixed period; if, however, there is no regular deputy, the meeting must elect one if the elected chairman is absent or is, for any reason, unable or unwilling to act.

3. Qualifications. To enable a chairman to carry out his duties successfully, and to exercise his powers for the greatest benefit of the meeting he must obviously possess an adequate knowledge of meeting procedure.

But the successful chairman must also possess certain essential qualities; in particular:

(*a*) *Personality.* He must have the ability to command respect of the meeting, and this largely depends upon his personality and bearing.

(*b*) *Impartiality.* He must possess a sense of fairness, and make his decisions with strict impartiality. If he is not the head of the organisation he should leave the chair when he wishes to address the meeting himself in formal debate.

(*c*) *Strength of character.* He must be courteous and yet have the strength of character to be firm when ruling on points of order and in enforcing the rules of the meeting. Strength of character must not, however, be confused with the overbearing, dogmatic and obstinate attitude of the inadequate chairman who may, for a time, force his ideas upon the meeting but certainly loses its respect.

(*d*) *Resourcefulness.* To enable him to make quick decisions, deal with quarrelsome members and answer awkward questions, he must have an adequate supply of tact, patience and good humour; these are essential in the make-up of the resourceful chairman.

(*e*) *Ability to maintain discipline.* To possess and exercise this ability he must set a good example by his own punctual and regular attendance at meetings, and by his own sense of orderliness.

(*f*) *Clarity of speech.* The making of lengthy speeches is not one of the chairman's normal duties; if, therefore, he is able to announce clearly the decisions of the meeting, that is all that is normally required of him. The garrulous chairman is generally regarded as a poor one; in fact, a good chairman is often the one who says least.

4. The status of a president. There is often some confusion over the respective function and status of "chairman" and "president". It is, of course, normal practice in the USA to appoint a "President" of a corporation rather than a "Chairman".

In this country, however, the status of a president may be explained as follows:

(*a*) *Where he is appointed as alternative to a chairman*, he exercises the full powers of a chairman within the regulations governing the meetings over which he presides.

NOTE: Where a limited company follows this practice, care must be taken to ensure that the Articles of Association give the necessary authority.

(*b*) *Where his appointment is additional to that of chairman:*

(*i*) His nomination to the presidential chair is often by way of appreciation for long service with the company or other body.

(*ii*) His office may be merely nominal, in which case he will function in a consultative rather than authoritative capacity, and in no way detract from the authority of the chairman.

DUTIES AND PRIVILEGES

5. Duties. Some of the chairman's duties may be set out in the regulations governing meetings, but many more are implicit in his appointment or arise out of common law. Thus, his duties, whether express or implied, may be summarised as follows:

(*a*) *Notice:* Before the meeting commences he ought to satisfy himself that it has been properly convened.

(*b*) *Constitution:* He must also ensure that the meeting is properly constituted, i.e.

(*i*) that his own appointment is in order; and

(*ii*) that a quorum is present.

(*c*) *Conduct:* During the whole course of the meeting, he must ensure that the proceedings are conducted strictly in accordance with the rules which govern the meeting.

(*d*) *Preservation of order:* He has a duty to preserve order. For this purpose he may have power to order the withdrawal of offenders, but this is a power which depends upon the nature of the meeting and where it is held.

(*e*) *Order of business:* He must ensure that business is dealt with in the order set out in the agenda paper—unless the meeting consents to a variation of the order.

(*f*) *Discussion:* He has a duty to allow reasonable time for discussion; on the other hand:

(*i*) He must restrain irrelevant discussion.

(*ii*) He must allow no discussion unless there is a motion before the meeting.

(*iii*) He must give equal opportunity to those who wish to speak. Those in the minority must be allowed to express their views on the subject under discussion; nevertheless, a small, noisy minority must not be permitted to monopolise the proceedings.

(*g*) *"Sense of the meeting":* He must ensure that the sense of the meeting is properly ascertained with regard to any question which is properly before the meeting. *See National Dwellings Society* v. *Sykes* (1894); for example, by putting motions and amendments to the meeting in proper form.

6. Powers. The chairman derives his powers principally from the rules which govern the meeting over which he presides, but also, to some extent, from common law. His powers from either or both of these sources may be summarised as follows:

(*a*) *To maintain order:* To this end he must use his discretion in dealing with emergencies as they arise.

(*b*) *To decide points of order* as they arise, and to give and maintain his rulings on any points of procedure.

(*c*) *To use a casting vote* where there is an equality of votes, and if the rules confer this power.

NOTE: A chairman has *no* casting vote at common law: *Nell* v. *Longbottom* (1894).

(*d*) *To order the removal of disorderly persons.* Where necessary, reasonable force may be used to effect the removal, if the person concerned has failed to withdraw after being requested to do so by the chairman. At a private meeting the chairman has the power to order the removal of any person who has no right to be present. In both the above categories a trespass is committed.

(*e*) *To adjourn the meeting.* Unless the rules give him express power to adjourn in specified cases, the chairman derives his power of adjournment from the meeting. If he were to adjourn without the consent of the meeting, another chairman may be appointed by the meeting and business resumed. See *National Dwellings Society* v. *Sykes* (1894), *Catesby* v. *Burnett* (1916).

NOTE: The only case in which a chairman appears to have the power to adjourn at common law arises when a meeting is adjourned for the express purpose of taking a poll: *R* v. *D'Oyly* (1840).

7. Addressing the Chair. The following rules apply:

(*a*) *A male chairman* is usually addressed as "Mr. Chairman"; alternatively, he may be addressed as "Sir",—or, for example, where the chairman is a church dignitary, as "My Lord".

(*b*) *When a woman is in the chair*, there are several possibilities, e.g.

(*i*) "Mr. Chairman", and even "Sir", are used in some cases, on the ground that it is the chair which is being addressed.

(*ii*) "Madame Chairman" (or "Madame President");

(*iii*) "Madame"; or

(*iv*) By name, e.g. "Mrs. Carter, Ladies and Gentlemen——"

(*c*) *When addressing the chair and others collectively:*

(*i*) *Normally*, the chairman takes precedence; that is, he should be addressed first, as in "Mr. Chairman, Ladies and Gentlemen——"

(*ii*) *If a distinguished guest is present*, he [the guest] should be given precedence; for example, "My Lord, Mr. Chairman, Ladies and Gentlemen", etc.

REMOVAL

8. Removal of chairman. This will normally be controlled by the regulations of the body concerned. However, a chairman who has been elected by the meeting can be removed by the meeting. This is normally achieved by a member proposing a vote of no confidence in the chair, this being seconded and carried.

PROGRESS TEST 4

1. What are the qualities a chairman ought to possess to enable him to carry out his duties and exercise his powers for the greatest benefit of the meeting? (**3**)

2. State the main duties of a chairman and the possible effects of his failure to carry out these duties. (**5**)

3. Comment on the following statement: "The chairman's duty is to carry out the wish of the majority." (**5**)

4. What is the duty of the chairman as regards the maintenance of orderly behaviour and the adjournment of meetings, and the use of his casting vote? (**5, 6**)

CHAPTER V

The Agenda

GENERAL

1. Definition. Literally, the word "agenda" means "things to be done", but in practice it is more commonly applied to the *agenda paper*, which lists the items of business to be dealt with at a meeting.

2. Form of agenda. An agenda may take various forms, according to requirements and, in some cases, to the kind of meeting to which it refers, namely:

(*a*) *A "skeleton" form of agenda*, i.e. in bare outline or summary form, giving headings only of the items to be dealt with. As a rule, this form is used when it is to be included as part of the notice circulated to those entitled to attend the meeting.

(*b*) *A detailed form of agenda*, with a complete heading to identify the meeting, and setting out in draft form the resolutions to be submitted to the meeting.

(*c*) *The chairman's copy of the agenda paper* may be supplied with more detail than the copies issued to those attending the meeting, and a wide margin may also be left on his copy for the purpose of note-taking.

NOTE: The secretary may also provide himself with a more detailed copy of the agenda paper. After the meeting, he can then convert successful resolutions into draft minutes (*see* **7,** below).

PREPARATION

3. Contents of an agenda paper. The following points are important in this connection:

(*a*) *Heading:* The agenda paper should be suitably headed, to indicate the kind of meeting, also where and when it is to be held.

NOTE: Although it may not always be necessary in practice, for examination purposes it is recommended that the name of the organisation holding the meeting should be shown as a bold heading at the top of the agenda paper.

(*b*) *Arrangement:* Items must be arranged in the order (if any) indicated in the rules governing the meeting. Whether the rules indicate the order or not, the items ought to be arranged in a logical order. A typical order of business would be as follows:

(*i*) Apologies for absence
(*ii*) Minutes of the previous meeting
(*iii*) Correspondence
(*iv*) Reports of chairman, treasurer, etc.
(*v*) Non-routine business of an important nature
(*vi*) Date of next meeting.

NOTE: It is often considered advisable to deal first with the routine items of business, so as to leave more time for special or non-routine business, which may need more time for discussion.

(*c*) *Items of business included:* No business should be placed on the agenda paper unless it comes within the scope of the notice convening the meeting, and is within the power of the meeting to deal with it.

(*d*) *Any other business:* Although it is very common to find this item on agendas its use is not advisable. The main problems posed by its use are:

(*i*) members may be forced to consider and debate items for which they have not prepared;

(*ii*) the item is usually at the end of the agenda and members may be prepared to vote in favour of a motion merely because they are ready to go home.

Therefore if this item is used the chairman must confine its use to the consideration of informal or unimportant matters.

(*e*) *Ease of reference:* To ensure ease of reference:

(*i*) The contents ought to be sufficiently clear and explicit to enable members to understand what business is to be dealt with.

(*ii*) In a lengthy agenda, each item should be numbered, and in the more detailed form of agenda it is often advisable to use headings and even sub-headings to show the subjects to be dealt with.

4. Preparation. The rules of an organisation may state what is to be included in an agenda, if not, the head of the organisation will be responsible and he will normally delegate the preparation to the secretary. Obviously it is impossible to lay down a standard method of preparing an agenda paper, as so much depends upon the nature and importance of the meeting concerned; however, the following points ought to be borne in mind in most cases:

(*a*) *Ensure that no relevant item of business is omitted;* this can be achieved in various ways, namely:

(*i*) *Consult the chairman* and any other officials who may have business to include.

(*ii*) *Refer to the minutes* of the last meeting for any business or decisions which were then deferred, and for reminders of the routine annual, half-yearly or quarterly recurring items.

(*iii*) *Keep a special file or folder* of documents, such as reports, correspondence, etc., which are likely to be required at the next meeting. Prior to that meeting, sort and arrange these documents.

(*b*) *Refer to the rules* governing the meeting, particularly if they regulate the order in which items of business are to be dealt with. Care must be taken to arrange the items in a logical order for the following reasons:

(*i*) If it is properly drawn up and well-arranged, an agenda is self-explanatory; furthermore, it prevents confusion, reduces the number of questions put to the chairman, and shortens the meeting.

(*ii*) The chairman is less likely to have to request the meeting to agree to an alteration in the order of business.

(*c*) *Where motions are to be submitted in writing*, ensure that they are received within any time limit imposed by the rules. In a detailed form of agenda, it may be the practice to include them in the agenda, in the actual words of the motion, if the rules so provide.

NOTE: In the chairman's copy of the agenda, the names of proposers and seconders of the motions may be stated.

(*d*) *Obtain approval* of the agenda in its final form, prior to inclusion in the notice or separate circulation. Such approval may be obtained informally from the chairman or, e.g. in the case of a limited company, by formal resolution of the board of directors.

5. Specimen of a "skeleton" agenda.

The Paramount Company Limited.

AGENDA

for the Seventh Annual General Meeting
to be held at City Hall, Bishopgate, London E.C.
on Monday, 12th July, 19—.

1. Auditors' Report.
2. Directors' Report and Accounts.
3. Dividend.
4. Election of Directors.
5. Remuneration of Auditors.

V. THE AGENDA

6. Specimen of a more detailed agenda, based on the above "skeleton" agenda and suitable for the chairman.

The Paramount Company Limited

AGENDA

for the Seventh Annual General Meeting
to be held at City Hall, Bishopgate, London E.C.
on Monday, 12th July, 19—.

Item No.	Agenda	Chairman's notes
1	*Notice:* The Secretary to read the notice convening the meeting.	Read.
2	*Auditors' Report* to be read by the Secretary.	Read.
3	*Directors' Report and Accounts:* The Chairman will ask the meeting whether the directors' report and accounts shall be read, or taken as read.	Taken as read.
4	Chairman will address the meeting, and conclude by proposing: "That the Directors' Report and Accounts for the year ended 31st March, 19—, as audited and reported on by the company's auditors, be and they are hereby approved and adopted."	
	Chairman will ask Mr. F. Carr (probably a director) to second the motion.	Seconded by Mr. F. Carr.
	Chairman will invite questions, and after dealing with any questions, put the motion to the meeting, and declare the result.	Moved and carried unanimously.
5	*Dividend:* The Chairman will move: "That a dividend of 15 per cent less income tax, recommended in the directors' report for the year ended 31st March, 19—, be and it is hereby declared payable	

Item No.	Agenda	Chairman's notes
	on 19th July, 19—, to all shareholders whose names appeared on the Register of Members on 30th June, 19—.	
	The Chairman will ask Mr. B. Craig (another Director) to second the motion.	Seconded by Mr. Craig.
	Chairman to put the motion to the meeting, and declare the result.	Moved and carried.
6	*Election of Director(s):* The Chairman will propose: "That Mr. Frederick Cooper, the Director now due to retire by rotation, be and he is hereby re-elected a Director of the Company."	
	Chairman will ask Mr. A. Cookson (a shareholder) to second the motion.	Seconded by Mr. Cookson.
	Chairman will put the above motion to the meeting and declare result.	Moved and carried.
7	*Appointment of Auditors:* The Chairman will ask Mr. W. Scott (a shareholder) to move, and Mr. R. Jenkins (a shareholder) to second the following motion: "That Messrs. Price and Harris be and they are hereby re-appointed Auditors of the Company, to hold office from the conclusion of this meeting until the conclusion of the next annual general meeting, at a remuneration of 8,000 (eight thousand) pounds."	Moved by Mr. Scott, seconded by Mr. Jenkins, and carried.
	Chairman will put the motion to the meeting, and declare result.	
8	*Chairman will declare proceedings at an end*, and (where applicable) reply to vote of thanks.	

USE IN PREPARATION OF MINUTES

7. Retention of agenda papers.

(*a*) *Chairman's copy of the agenda paper:* Although the chairman's notes on his copy of the agenda paper may sometimes be of assistance to the secretary when writing up his minutes, it is considered that, the minutes having been approved and signed, the chairman's copy of the agenda paper ought to be destroyed.

(*b*) Failure to do so might cause confusion later, if it is found that the hastily-drafted notes of the chairman do not coincide with the secretary's minutes as finally drafted.

(*c*) Nevertheless, at least one copy of the agenda paper should be retained by the secretary from which to prepare his minutes —particularly if he uses a detailed form of agenda paper with a wide margin for notes, similar to that provided for the chairman.

NOTE: As a rule, the secretary prefers to prepare notes for the minute book in a small note book, rather than on the agenda paper. (*See also* XII.)

PROGRESS TEST 5

1. What are the requisites of an agenda? Draft a specimen agenda for a meeting of one of the following: (*a*) annual meeting of an association; (*b*) board meeting of a company or association; (*c*) committee of a company or association. (**3**)

2. Describe the measures you would adopt in the preparation of an agenda for the council meeting of an association or similar body with which you may be familiar. Do you favour the retention of agenda papers? Give your reasons for retention or otherwise. (**4, 7**)

3. What are the advantages of a carefully prepared agenda to the chairman of a meeting and to the secretary, respectively? Draft an agenda for a board or committee meeting in order to illustrate and emphasise your conclusions. (**4**)

CHAPTER VI

Notices

PURPOSE, CONTENT AND ENTITLEMENT

1. The convening of meetings. As indicated in the last chapter, the secretary's first duty in preparing for a meeting is to prepare an agenda. His next important duty is to convene the meeting, i.e.

(*a*) Preparing (or supervising the preparation of) the notice of the meeting.

(*b*) Despatching notices to all persons entitled to attend the meeting.

2. Definition.

(*a*) The notice of a meeting is any form or method of communication adopted by the convenor(s) to summon to the meeting all persons entitled to attend.

(*b*) Thus, notice must be served in the form, or by the method, laid down in the rules governing the meeting; or

(*c*) If the rules make no such provision, then any reasonable form or method may be used, namely:

    (*i*) verbal notice;
    (*ii*) press notice;
    (*iii*) bill posting;
    (*iv*) handbills distributed from door to door;
    (*v*) separate handwritten or typewritten notices;
    (*vi*) notice board;
    (*vii*) broadcasting.

3. Contents. For meetings generally the principal contents are as follows:

(*a*) Place of the meeting.
(*b*) Date, day and time of the meeting.
(*c*) Business to be transacted.
(*d*) Details of any special business to be transacted.
(*e*) Kind of meeting, where applicable, e.g. annual general meeting.
(*f*) Date of the notice.

(g) Signature of the person convening (or authorised to convene) the meeting, usually the secretary's.

NOTE: The special requirements as regards notices convening *company* meetings are dealt with separately.

4. Entitlement to notice. In general, notice must be given to *all* persons entitled to attend the meeting; failure to do so might affect the validity of the meeting: *R* v. *Shrewsbury* (1735). But the omission to send notice may be *excused*, e.g.

(a) The rules often provide for *waiver* of notice, where the omission is accidental.
(b) Where *all* persons entitled to attend are present without notice, and *all* "expressly assent to that which is being done": *Re Express Engineering Works* (1920).
(c) Where those not summoned were *beyond summoning distance*, e.g. where a member was abroad: *Smyth* v. *Darley* (1849); or, where a member was *too ill to attend* in any case: *Young* v. *Ladies' Imperial Club* (1920).

NOTE: It is, however, always advisable to send proper notice to *all* persons entitled to attend a meeting, and not rely upon the apparent disability of a member at the time as an excuse for failing to summon him.

Even if the member informs the convenors that he will not be able to attend the meeting, that should not be relied upon as a waiver of notice: *Re Portuguese Consolidated Copper Mines* (1889), *Rex* v. *Langhorn* (1836).

5. Authority to convene. Notices must be issued, or communicated by whatever method the rules demand, by the person or body authorised to do so by the regulations governing the meeting concerned, e.g. by the secretary, or by the secretary on the instructions of a governing body. A meeting summoned without authority is invalid.

6. Period of notice. The following general rules are applicable:

(a) *The length of notice* required is usually provided for in the rules; if not, "reasonable" notice must be given.
(b) *Longer notice* is usually required for a meeting at which "special" business is to be transacted, e.g. 21 days' notice may be required, whereas only 14 days' notice may be required for ordinary business.

(c) Unless otherwise provided in the rules, it is implied that the number of days stated are *"clear days"*, i.e. they are *exclusive* of the day of service of the notice and of the day of meeting: *Re Railway Sleepers Supply Co.* (1885).

(d) Failure to give adequate notice may result in the meeting being rendered invalid; if, for example, only 7 days' notice is given instead of the (say) 21 days' notice required by the regulations concerned.

(e) *Inadequacy of notice* may, however, be excused if all, or some specified proportion of the members entitled to attend the meeting so agree: *Re Oxted Motor Co.* (1921).

METHOD OF SERVICE

7. Service of notice.

(a) As already indicated above, the period of notice required is usually measured in "clear days", which exclude the day of service of the notice and the day on which the meeting is to be held. But the day of service of the notice may have different interpretations.

(b) In some cases, the rules may indicate when notice is *deemed* to have been served, e.g.

(i) 24 hours after posting; or

(ii) at the time of posting.

(c) If the rules are silent on the subject, reference must be made to the Interpretation Act 1978. This provides that a notice is deemed to be served on the day on which, if posted, it would be delivered in the ordinary course of post.

8. Specimen of a simple form of notice, embodying a "skeleton" agenda.

THE GUILDHALL ASSOCIATION
75, Main Street,
Leeds, 8.
20th January, 19—.

NOTICE IS HEREBY GIVEN that a meeting of the Management Committee of this Association will be held at the Headquarters of the Association on Wednesday, the 6th February at 2.30 p.m. for the transaction of the business itemised in the appended agenda.

(*Signed*)..........................
General Secretary.

Agenda

1. Minutes of last meeting.
2. Consider matters arising.
3. Receive applications for membership.
4. Financial Statement.
5. Correspondence.
6. Receive reports from (*a*) Welfare Sub-Committee. (*b*) Building Committee.

NOTICE AND CONVENTION OF MEETINGS

9. Failure properly to convene a meeting, as already indicated, is one of the defects in respect of which the validity of a meeting might be questioned. It might, however, arise in various ways; in particular:

(*a*) *Omission to send notice* to every person entitled to attend, i.e. where there are no grounds for excusing the omission.

(*b*) *Inadequate (short) notice*, i.e. where no provision is made for excusing the inadequacy.

(*c*) *Ambiguity of the notice.* A notice must be free from anything calculated to confuse or mislead: *Kaye* v. *Croydon Tramways* (1898), *Henderson* v. *Bank of Australasia* (1890).

(*d*) *Omission of important contents*, such as the failure to mention that special business is to be transacted.

NOTE: Although it is, of course, normally essential to state place, date, day and time of the meeting, it would, no doubt, be permissible to dispense with any mention of the actual time, where one meeting is to be held immediately after another; in that case, the notice may indicate that the second meeting will commence "at the conclusion" of the first meeting.

(*e*) *Unauthorised issue of notice.* The issue of notice by the secretary without the authority of the convening body is inadequate and the meeting rendered invalid: *Re Haycraft Gold Reduction Co.* (1900).

Nevertheless, if the notice *is* adopted and ratified by the proper convening body before the meeting is held, it may become a good notice, in which case the meeting is not invalid: *Hooper* v. *Kerr* (1900).

PROGRESS TEST 6

1. State what a notice of meeting is, give its essentials; and discuss the legal effect of an imperfect notice.(**2, 3, 9**)

2. Enumerate some of the commonly used methods of convening meetings. If there are no regulations affecting the convening of meetings, what is the position as regards (*a*) period of notice, (*b*) place of the meeting? (**3, 6**)

3. State in brief, numbered paragraphs the essentials of a valid notice of a meeting. (**2–7**)

CHAPTER VII

Quorum

1. Definition. A quorum may be defined as the minimum number of persons entitled to be present at a meeting (or their proxies, if permitted) which the regulations require to be present in order that the business of the meeting may be validly transacted.

2. The casual meeting of sufficient members to constitute a quorum does *not*, however, constitute a valid meeting. It fails because proper notice of the meeting must be given to all persons entitled to attend it (*see* VI). Thus, where there are only two persons on a board of directors, their casual meeting together does not constitute a valid meeting, if either of them objects: *Barron* v. *Potter* (1914).

3. Absence of quorum. Absence or inadequacy of the quorum may arise in the following cases:

(*a*) *Failure to muster a quorum.* If the prescribed quorum is not present when the meeting is due to start, the meeting should be formally adjourned because, legally, there is no meeting.

NOTE: To save a meeting, some leniency is frequently permitted by the rules, e.g. half-an-hour extensions may be permitted, and if a quorum is not present within half-an-hour from the time originally appointed for the meeting, it must be adjourned to (say) the same day in the following week at the same time and place.

(*b*) *Failure to maintain a quorum.* If a quorum is not maintained, it is open to anyone present at a meeting to draw the chairman's attention to that fact. It is then his duty to declare a "count out" and to adjourn the meeting.

NOTE: Whether the chairman's declaration of a "count out" can effectively invalidate business subsequently completed at the meeting may depend, to some extent, upon the wording of the rules. In this connection, compare the cases of *Henderson* v. *Louttit* (1894), *Re Hartley Baird Ltd.* (1954) under "Company Meetings."

(c) *Effect of absence of quorum.* The general principle is that business transacted is invalid. However, third parties entering into contracts as a result of such decisions could enforce the contracts as the organisation would have implied authority to contract in the eyes of the third party.

(d) *Incompetent quorum.* Only persons competent to take part in the business of a meeting constitute a quorum; thus, at common law, a quorum must be a "disinterested" one: *Yuill* v. *Greymouth Point Elizabeth Railway Co.* (1904). Therefore, unless the rules permit, a person may be denied the right to vote at, and unable to form part of a quorum of, a meeting transacting business in which that person has conflicting interests.

NOTE: The rule of the "disinterested quorum" is dealt with more fully in XVI, **7**.

PROGRESS TEST 7

1. Explain in relation to a quorum: (*i*) its disinterestedness; (*ii*) its maintenance. (**3**)

2. What is the nature and purpose of a quorum? (**1**)

3. In what respects might a quorum prove incompetent to act? What is a "count out", and what is the chairman's duty when his attention is drawn to it? (**3**)

4. Explain how the absence or inadequacy of quorum might arise. (**3**)

CHAPTER VIII

Motions

FORM AND PRESENTATION

1. Definition. A motion is a proposition or proposal put forward for discussion and decision at a meeting.

2. Acceptance of a motion. After a motion has been put to the vote and agreed it becomes a resolution; that is, the resolution is the "acceptance" of the motion.

3. Form of motion. The following rules govern the form of the motion:

(*a*) A motion must be in the form required by the rules governing the meeting, e.g. it may be required in writing, signed by the proposer, and handed to the chairman.

(*b*) It must be within the scope of the notice convening the meeting, and relevant to the business for which the meeting was called.

(*c*) It must be proposed at the meeting and, if required by the rules, seconded.

> NOTE: A seconder is *not* required unless demanded by the rules governing the meeting: *Re Horbury Bridge Coal Co.* (1879).

(*d*) It must be set out in definite terms, and free from any ambiguity.

(*e*) It should *not* be negative in form. In general a motion should be affirmative; there are, however, certain exceptions to this rule, e.g. the "previous question" (referred to later in this chapter) is a formal or procedural motion which is quite correctly put in the form, "That the question be *not* now put."

(*f*) A motion and, if it is carried, the resulting resolution, should begin with the word "That——".

4. Presentation. A motion must be presented:

(*a*) In form and manner prescribed by the rules.

(b) By any person at the meeting who is qualified to do so, i.e. by the member himself or, if the rules permit, by a proxy appointed by the member.

(c) In the order shown on the agenda paper—unless the order is altered by decision of the meeting.

5. Disposal. A motion may be disposed of in various ways:

(a) In most cases, after adequate time has been allowed for discussing it, it is *put to the vote*, and either carried or rejected by the meeting.

(b) If various amendments have been accepted, it may be put to the meeting as a *substantive motion*, and either carried or rejected.

(c) It may be *shelved* if the "previous question" is moved and accepted by the meeting, i.e. "That the question be not now put."

(d) It may be *dropped:*
  (i) by the proposer himself, with the consent of the meeting; or
  (ii) because of failure to find a seconder, i.e. where the rules require a seconder to a motion.

(e) A motion for *adjournment*, if carried, disposes of a motion, but this may be only a temporary disposal, i.e. until the adjourned meeting is held.

6. A "dropped motion", as indicated above, is one which has been disposed of in one of the less customary ways: thus—

(a) The term "dropped motion" is more commonly associated with the case where a person who gave notice of a motion decides to withdraw it.

Strictly, such a motion "belongs" to the meeting, and it cannot be withdrawn without the meeting's consent; moreover, it cannot be revived without giving fresh notice.

(b) The term is also sometimes applied to a motion which has failed to find a seconder, where required by the rules.

AMENDMENTS

7. Definition. An amendment may be defined as a proposal to alter a motion submitted to a meeting; e.g.

(a) by adding, inserting or deleting words of the original motion;

(b) by substituting words, phrases or complete sentences for others in the original motion; or

(c) by any combination of the above forms of alteration.

VIII. MOTIONS

NOTE: An amendment must not be confused with a "rider", which adds to a motion, but does not amend it; see later reference in glossary.

8. Rules governing amendments. It may be found that rules do not deal as fully with amendments as they ought to do; consequently, the chairman is often given little assistance from that source, and a great deal is left to his discretion in deciding whether to accept or reject amendments.

He must, however, bear in mind that his failure to admit a relevant amendment might invalidate a resolution, as in *Henderson v. Bank of Australasia* (1890).

The following are the principal rules governing amendments which may be expressly stated or merely implied:

(*a*) *When moved:* An amendment may be moved after a motion has been proposed, but *before* the question is put to the vote.

(*b*) *Notice:* It can be moved *without* previous notice—unless required by the rules.

(*c*) *Form:*

(*i*) If previous notice *is* required, preferably it should be in writing, signed by the mover, and given or sent to the chairman (or secretary) before the meeting.

(*ii*) If previous notice is *not* required, it should be formally moved and, if the rules so provide, seconded.

(*iii*) It must not be a mere negative of the original motion; the same result can be achieved by voting against it.

NOTE: A direct negative *is* permissible in Scotland, where it is commonly used to reach a quick decision.

(*d*) *Proposer;* It may be moved or seconded (if required by the rules) by any member who has not already spoken on the motion; after that all members have a right to speak, i.e. even if they have already spoken on the original motion, unless the rules provide to the contrary.

NOTE: Where proxies are permitted by the rules, the mover (or seconder) of the amendment may not necessarily be a member.

(*e*) *Relevance:*

(*i*) It must be relevant to the original motion which it purports to amend.

(*ii*) It must not conflict with anything which the meeting has already agreed upon.

(*iii*) It must not go beyond the scope of the notice convening the meeting, nor beyond the power of the meeting, e.g. it must not introduce anything which, if accepted, might commit the meeting to something more onerous than was intended in the original motion or even beyond its power to decide.

(*f*) *Withdrawal:* It cannot be withdrawn without the consent of the meeting—as is the case with a motion.

(*g*) *Second speech:* As a rule, the mover of an amendment has no right of reply; this, of course, differs from the case of the mover of the original motion, who automatically has the right of second speech in discussion.

(*h*) *Only one amendment* should be permitted before the meeting at any one time; that is, the chairman ought to refuse to accept an amendment while another is already being discussed.

(*i*) *Persons debarred:* The chairman will not usually accept an amendment proposed by:

(*i*) the mover of the original motion; or

(*ii*) one who has already moved an amendment to the original motion.

NOTE: Subject to the rules, there is nothing to prevent the mover of the original motion from voting *against* it, either in its original or amended form.

(*j*) *Amendment to an amendment:* If permitted by the rules, the chairman may allow an amendment to an amendment which is already before the meeting—but it is always liable to cause confusion.

(*k*) *Voting on an amendment to an amendment:* If the chairman allows an amendment to an amendment, the usual practice is to vote upon the *second* amendment first; if it is adopted it is embodied into the first amendment, which is then put to the meeting and voted upon.

(*l*) *Voting on amendments:* Amendments are usually put to the vote in the order in which they affect the original motion, i.e. *not* in the order in which they were moved. But see later reference to the "popular" method of dealing with amendments.

(*m*) *Special business:* An amendment to a motion for the passing of a special form of resolution (e.g. a special or extraordinary resolution in the case of a limited company) should not be permitted—except to correct an error of grammar or spelling.

(*n*) *Equality of votes:* If the votes for and against an amendment are equal (and assuming that the chairman does not exercise a casting vote), it is deemed to have been rejected.

9. Procedures for dealing with amendments. Where several amendments are proposed, the alternative methods of dealing with them are as follows:

(*a*) *The "popular" method:* The procedure is:
(*i*) After each amendment has been discussed, *all* amendments are put to the vote *in the order in which they affect the original motion*, and not in the order in which they were moved.

(*ii*) *Substantive motion:* All amendments adopted by the meeting are then incorporated in the original motion, which is then put to the vote as a substantive motion.

(*iii*) *Amendments of the substantive motion* are permissible, unless the rules provide to the contrary—but such amendments must not merely re-introduce the original motion or any of the amendments already rejected by the meeting.

(*iv*) *If the substantive motion is rejected*, the original motion is *not* revived.

This procedure is exemplified below with the original motion worded as follows:

"That the common seal be and the same is hereby adopted as the common seal of the company, and that one key thereof be retained, when not in use, at the registered office of the company, and that the duplicate key be deposited with the company's bankers for safe custody, to be released only on written request." Amendments were proposed in the following order:

		Voting order
Amendment No. 1 That the words "in a sealed envelope" be inserted after the words "when not in use."	Accepted	2
Amendment No. 2 That the words "signed by one or more of the company's authorised signatories" be added at the end of the original motion.	Accepted	4
Amendment No. 3 That the words "an impression of which is affixed in the margin hereof" be inserted after the words "That the common seal."	Accepted	1
Amendment No. 4 That the words "the duplicate key" be deleted and the words "two duplicate keys" be substituted.	Defeated	3

The substantive motion reads as follows:

"That the common seal, *an impression of which is affixed in the margin hereof*, be and the same is hereby adopted as the common seal of the company, and that one key thereof be retained, when not in use, *in a sealed envelope* at the registered office of the company, and that the duplicate key be deposited with the company's bankers for safe custody, to be released only on written request, *signed by one or more of the company's authorised signatories.*"

(*b*) *The "parliamentary" method:* procedure:

(*i*) Each amendment must be in writing, and has to be submitted to the chairman of committees before the debate.

(*ii*) The chairman has power to select only representative and relevant amendments, i.e. in order to expedite the business of the committee the debate may jump from one selected amendment to another, omitting those in between which the chairman regards as repetitive, irrelevant or frivolous. (*See* Appendix III, reference to the "Kangaroo Closure.")

(*iii*) At the debate, the selected amendments must each obtain a seconder as they are put to the meeting.

(*iv*) The original motion is then linked with *each* of the amendments in turn, and a limited time is allowed for discussion on each amendment before it is put to the vote; thus there is no need to put a substantive motion to the meeting.

OTHER FORMS OF MOTION

10. Substantive motion

(*a*) The original motion, after discussion, may be altered by subsequent amendments.

(*b*) The form in which the motion is finally put to the meeting (after any amendments approved by the meeting have been incorporated in it) is known as the substantive motion.

11. Formal motions. These are procedural motions, intended to regulate the procedure and conduct of a meeting, with the principal objects of facilitating and expediting the business to be transacted at the meeting. The "Closure" and "Previous Question" are examples of formal motions. These and other formal motions are dealt with in the next chapter.

12. "Dilatory" motions. This is the term which is often used to describe the misuse of a formal (or procedural) motion, i.e. where it is being used for a dilatory purpose, with the object of impeding the progress of the meeting, or of preventing discussion on a motion before reasonable time has been given to it.

PROGRESS TEST 8

1. Distinguish between a motion and a resolution. Explain (*a*) dropped motion, (*b*) substantive motion. (**1, 2, 6, 10**)
2. What are the rules as regards (*a*) form, (*b*) presentation, and (*c*) disposal, of a motion? (**3, 4, 5**)
3. Draft a specimen motion for inclusion in the agenda of any organisation of which you are a member. In what ways might this motion subsequently be dealt with at the meeting for which it is intended? (**3, 4, 5**)
4. Discuss the effects of the case in *Re Horbury Bridge Coal Co.* (1879) on the subject of motions. (**3**)
5. What are the essentials of a valid amendment? (**8**)
6. What is an amendment? How does it differ from a "rider"? (**1** and Appendix III.)
7. Explain how a motion may be amended. Is an amendment to an amendment permissible? (**7, 8**)
8. In what circumstances, if at all, can a substantive motion be amended? (**9**)

CHAPTER IX

Formal (Procedural) Motions

USE OF FORMAL MOTIONS

1. Definition. A formal or procedural motion is one which concerns the form or procedure of the meeting at which it is proposed, and not the actual business for which the meeting was convened.

Consequently, no notice is required of such a motion, nor does it require to be in writing.

2. Purpose.

(*a*) Formal motions are designed to expedite and facilitate the business of a meeting.

(*b*) When used for their *intended* purpose, they can effectively terminate, defer or prevent discussion of business when it is a waste of time to continue with the business in hand. If, for example, a motion has already been moved, seconded and fully discussed, a formal motion might be used, for the benefit of the meeting, to interrupt discussion and take the sense of the meeting by putting the motion to the vote.

3. Dilatory motions. In practice, some of the formal motions are open to misuse. Where they are used frivolously, or with the object of curtailing discussion on the legitimate business of the meeting, they are usually referred to as "dilatory" motions.

4. The chairman's duty.

(*a*) The Chairman must, obviously, use his *discretion* in preventing formal motions from being used for a dilatory purpose.

(*b*) Thus, he may *reject a formal motion* if he considers it has been proposed frivolously or, for example, where it has apparently been proposed with the object of curtailing discussion on a matter which has not been given a reasonable time for discussion.

(*c*) Nevertheless, he must be careful about refusing a motion for *adjournment* of the meeting. Even though it may be moved for a dilatory purpose, he must bear in mind that the right to adjourn is primarily with the meeting. He is then faced with the problem—whether to refuse the motion, or to put the motion to the vote of the

IX. FORMAL (PROCEDURAL) MOTIONS

meeting, which will waste the time of the meeting and, no doubt, enable the mover of the motion to achieve *his* purpose.

NOTE: If the rules governing the meeting provide that the chairman "may" adjourn when so requested by the majority of members present, he is *not* bound to comply with that request if he considers it is not in the interests of the meeting to do so. See *Salisbury Gold Mining Co.* v. *Hathorn and Others* (1897).

5. Amendment. A formal motion cannot be amended; in some cases, however, a formal motion may be overridden by another formal motion, e.g. the "Previous Question" can be overridden by a motion for adjournment of the meeting.

TYPES OF FORMAL MOTION

6. The principal formal motions are usually worded as follows:

(*a*) "That the meeting proceed to the next business."
(*b*) "That the meeting postpone consideration of the subject."
(*c*) "That the question be now put"—usually referred to as the "Closure".
(*d*) "That the question be *not* now put"—usually known as the "Previous Question".
(*e*) "That the debate be adjourned."
(*f*) "That the meeting be adjourned."
(*g*) "That the recommendation be referred back to the committee."

These formal motions are dealt with more fully in the following paragraphs.

7. "That the meeting proceed to the next business."

(*a*) *Purpose:* to curtail discussion of a motion which is frivolous or time-wasting, and prevent the motion being put to the vote.

(*b*) *Disposal:*

(*i*) If *adopted*, the original motion is dropped at once without further discussion and no vote is taken, i.e. the meeting then proceeds to the next business. In this respect it has the same effect as the "Previous Question" motion.

(*ii*) If *rejected*, discussion on the original motion continues. In this respect it differs from the "Previous Question" motion.

(*c*) If the rules permit, the "next business" motion may be proposed again, having been rejected in the first instance, but usually only after a specified time limit of (say) half-an-hour.

8. "That the meeting postpone consideration of the subject."

(*a*) *Purpose:* If it is considered futile to commence discussion of a motion because of inadequate knowledge, e.g. where there has been delay in receiving reports from a committee, this formal motion may be used to postpone consideration of the original motion until later in the same meeting or, more likely, until a subsequent meeting.

The same motion may, however, be used *during* or *after* discussion of the original motion.

(*b*) *Disposal:*

(*i*) *If adopted*, discussion of the original motion is merely postponed, usually to afford time to obtain further information concerning it; that is, the motion is *not* "shelved".

(*ii*) *If rejected*, discussion on the original motion may be commenced or resumed.

(*c*) Before the "postponement" motion is put to the vote, the mover of the original motion is usually allowed the right of reply; that is, he is given the opportunity to state why (if he is still of that opinion) discussion on the original motion should commence or continue.

(*d*) If the "postponement" motion is rejected, it is usually permissible to move it again, but only after any time limit specified in the rules.

9. "That the question be now put", i.e. the "Closure" or "Gag'.

(*a*) *Purpose:* This is used to curtail prolonged discussion of either the original motion or of an amendment to it.

(*b*) *Disposal:*

(*i*) *If adopted*, the original motion (or amendment to it) is at once put to the vote, without further discussion. Moreover, the proposer of the original motion loses his right of reply.

(*ii*) *If rejected*, discussion on the original motion (or on the amendment to it) is resumed.

(*c*) The "closure" may be moved by the chairman or by any member; if moved by a member, the chairman must be careful not to accept it unless reasonable time has been allowed for discussion.

> NOTE: The above is the ordinary form of "closure", but reference will be made later to two additional forms of "closure" which are rarely used outside of the House of Commons, namely the "Guillotine" and "Kangaroo" forms of "closure".

10. "That the question be NOT now put", i.e. the "Previous Question".

IX. FORMAL (PROCEDURAL) MOTIONS

(*a*) *Purpose:* To get the meeting to decide whether the "previous question" (i.e. the original motion) shall be put to the vote at all, or whether it shall be "shelved" without any further discussion.

(*b*) *When moved:* As a rule, it can be moved only when the original motion is under discussion, usually at the close of a speech on the original motion.

NOTE: It cannot be moved on an amendment to the original motion.

(*c*) *Proposer:* It cannot usually be moved by one who had already spoken on the original motion.

(*d*) *Disposal:*

(*i*) *If adopted*, the original motion is dropped at once, without further discussion, i.e. it is "shelved" without being put to the vote, and cannot be moved again at that meeting.

(*ii*) *If rejected*, the original motion must be put to the vote at once, without further discussion.

NOTE: The mover of the original motion usually loses his right of second speech in either case.

(*e*) *How superseded:* Although it is not permissible to move an amendment to the "Previous Question", it can be superseded by a motion for adjournment of the meeting.

11. "That the debate be adjourned."

(*a*) *Purpose:* To adjourn discussion of a motion until later in the same meeting, or until a subsequent meeting, to give members time to consider the subject, or to await further information; alternatively, it may be used to defer debate on a relatively unimportant motion which has been unduly prolonged, in order to deal with a more important matter on the agenda.

(*b*) *Disposal:*

(*i*) *If adopted*, the subject under discussion is deferred until later in the same meeting (if time permits) or until the next meeting.

NOTE: The motion may, in fact, be worded to include the time or date to which the debate is to be adjourned.

(*ii*) *If rejected*, the debate on the subject in hand may be resumed.

(*c*) *The mover of the original motion* is usually given the right of reply, i.e. before the "adjournment" motion is put to the vote.

(*d*) *When the debate is resumed* at the same, or next, meeting, the person who successfully carried the "adjournment" motion is generally permitted to re-open the debate.

12. "That the meeting be adjourned."

(*a*) *Purpose:* This motion may be moved by the chairman or by any member at the close of any speech, or on concluding any business of the meeting, with the object of closing the meeting by adjourning it to a later date, for any one of the following reasons:

(*i*) because of unfinished business on the agenda, e.g. where a hall, in which the meeting is being held, was hired for a specified period;

(*ii*) because the business of the meeting cannot be conducted effectively owing to unruly behaviour of the members, and adjournment is necessary in order to allow tempers to cool;

(*iii*) because there has been an effective demand for a poll vote and, as this may take some considerable time, that part of the business is to be dealt with at the adjourned meeting.

(*b*) *Disposal:*

(*i*) *If adopted*, the unfinished business is resumed at the next ordinary meeting of the kind adjourned, unless the "adjournment" motion included a date for the adjourned meeting, or the chairman is permitted by the rules to fix the date.

(*ii*) *If rejected*, it is usually permissible to move the motion again after a reasonable time, or after any specified period set out in the rules.

(*c*) *The mover of the original motion* usually has the right of reply before the "adjournment" motion is put to the vote.

(*d*) As already stated, the "adjournment" motion may be used to supersede the "previous question" motion.

NOTE: Apart from the reasons for adjournment given above, the chairman may adjourn because of failure to muster a quorum or because of failure to keep a quorum (i.e. on a "count out"), but it might be argued that on each of these occasions there was, technically, "no meeting" and that the adjournment was merely a formality.

13. "That the recommendation be referred back to the committee."

(*a*) *Purpose:* Ostensibly, to refer the committee's recommendation back to it for further consideration, e.g. because part of the committee's recommendations are not acceptable to the appointing body. The motion is, however, sometimes used as a polite way of rejecting the committee's recommendations.

(*b*) *Disposal:*

(*i*) *If adopted*, the committee is given an opportunity to give further consideration to its original recommendations, and to

IX. FORMAL (PROCEDURAL) MOTIONS

submit new or amended recommendations, usually within a time limit imposed by the appointing body.

(*ii*) *If rejected*, it does not signify that the committee's recommendations are necessarily fully, or even partly, acceptable to the appointing body. If, after further discussion, they are to be adopted, a motion to that effect may be moved. It will probably include a vote of thanks for the committee's recommendations, unless a separate motion is moved for that purpose.

> NOTE: Although the "reference back" motion is often included with the formal (or procedural) motions, it may be argued that, strictly, it is neither formal nor procedural as it is not used to interrupt debate.

PROGRESS TEST 9

1. State the nature and purpose of a formal motion. (**1, 2**)
2. Explain the chairman's duty in respect of formal motions. (**4**)
3. In what forms are the following formal motions usually put to a meeting: (*a*) the "closure", (*b*) the "previous question"? What are the effects in each case of their being (*i*) carried, (*ii*) rejected? (**9, 10**)
4. Briefly describe the procedure following the application of the "guillotine" closure, and explain its purpose. (*See* Appendix I.)
5. What is the purpose and effect of the "kangaroo" closure? (*See* Appendix I.)

CHAPTER X

Summary of Procedure at a Meeting

Omitting the preliminaries, such as the chairman's opening address, reading of notice, adoption of minutes, etc., a typical meeting procedure might follow these lines:

1. Motion. A member puts forward a motion, either at the beginning or end of his speech.

> NOTE: If required by the rules, he has already submitted the motion in writing to the proper person, and within any specified time limit.

2. Seconding the motion. The chairman, having asked for a seconder (if required by the rules), the motion is seconded.

3. Discussion on the motion may follow, for which the chairman must allow reasonable time and opportunity to all who wish to speak.

4. Formal motion. At this stage, i.e. during discussion, a member may interrupt the proceedings by moving a formal motion, e.g. the "Previous Question" or the "Closure".

In this case, it has been assumed that discussion is resumed; that is, either:

(*a*) the chairman refuses to accept the "Previous Question" motion, on the grounds that it has been moved for a dilatory purpose; or

(*b*) the "Closure" motion having been put to the vote, is rejected.

5. Amendments. Arising out of the resumed discussion, one or more amendments may be moved and discussed.

> NOTE: During the discussion of an amendment, it is, of course, possible that a member may move a formal motion, e.g. the "Closure" or one of the other permissible formal motions,

X. SUMMARY OF PROCEDURE AT A MEETING

bearing in mind that the "Previous Question" cannot usually be moved on an amendment.

6. Amendments put to the vote. Assuming that the procedure is not interrupted by the adoption of a formal motion, the amendments are now separately put to the vote—in the order in which they affect the original motion.

7. Substantive motion. All amendments adopted, having been noted by the chairman and/or secretary, are then embodied in the original motion. Finally, the original motion, as amended, is put to the vote as a *substantive* motion.

8. Amendments to substantive motion. If permitted by the rules, one or more amendments may be moved to the substantive motion —so long as they do not merely reverse any of the earlier successful amendments, or introduce something which substantially changes the substantive motion or goes beyond the scope of the meeting.

CHAPTER XI

Adjournments

1. Definition. Adjournment is the act of extending or continuing a meeting for the purpose of dealing with unfinished business: *Scadding* v. *Lorant* (1851).

2. Notice of an adjourned meeting. Fresh notice of an adjourned meeting is *not* necessary: *Wills* v. *Murray* (1850), unless:

(*a*) specifically required by the rules, e.g. if the meeting is adjourned for (say) thirty days or more; or

(*b*) fresh business is to be introduced at the adjourned meeting; or

(*c*) the original meeting is adjourned *sine die*, i.e. without fixing a date for the adjourned meeting.

3. How a meeting may be adjourned.

(*a*) *Adoption of a formal motion* for adjournment of the meeting, i.e. passed by a simple majority of those attending and voting—unless there is an effective demand for a poll vote.

(*b*) *Action of the chairman:* Although the power of adjournment is strictly with the meeting, nevertheless there are occasions on which the chairman himself has power to adjourn, namely:

(*i*) *Where the rules give him express power* to adjourn, in any case, or for any specific purpose, stated in the rules.

(*ii*) *To take a poll vote.* His right to adjourn a meeting for the purpose of taking a poll vote arises out of common law: *R* v. *D'Oyly* (1840).

(*iii*) *When it is impossible to maintain order*, in which case he may adjourn without fixing a date for the adjourned meeting, or for only a short period to allow tempers to cool. (Even in these cases, however, he should attempt to get the consent of the meeting to the adjournment.)

(*iv*) *Failure to muster a quorum.* Here, although technically there is not a valid "meeting", the chairman must formally adjourn it to a new date, or proceed in any other way directed by the rules.

XI. ADJOURNMENTS

(v) *Where there is a "count out"*, i.e. where the quorum is not maintained; here again the chairman must formally adjourn, as there is no longer a valid meeting.

4. Important Court decisions on the subject of adjournment. The following cases are additional to those already referred to above:

(a) *Salisbury Gold Mining Co.* v. *Hathorn and others* (1897). If the rules provide that the chairman *may* adjourn a meeting when so requested by the majority of members present, there is an implication that he can use his discretion, and is *not* bound to carry out the wish of the majority if he does not think it is in the interests of the meeting to do so.

(b) *National Dwelling Society* v. *Sykes* (1894); also *Catesby* v. *Burnett* (1916). A chairman is not entitled to adjourn a meeting before the business of the meeting has been completed; if he does so without sufficient cause, upon his leaving the chair the meeting may appoint another chairman and continue the business for which the meeting had been convened.

(c) *Jackson* v. *Hamlyn and others* (1953) (*Gordon Hotels case*). An adjourned meeting is merely a continuation or extension of the original meeting.

NOTE: This case is perhaps better known in another connection, i.e. it established that proxies deposited between the original meeting and the adjourned meeting are not valid.

5. Postponement must be clearly distinguished from adjournment.

(a) *Postponement* is the action of deferring a meeting to a later date, even before the meeting is held; *adjournment* refers to the extension or continuation of a meeting which has actually been held.

(b) If a meeting has been properly convened, it cannot be postponed or cancelled by subsequent notice—unless the rules so provide: *Smith* v. *Paringa Mines* (1906). Thus, unless the rules permit postponement, the meeting must be held and, with the consent of the majority of those present and voting, formally adjourned.

(c) *If the meeting has not been properly convened*, e.g. where the notice is faulty as to date or place of the meeting; or if, for any reason, it is subsequently found to be impossible or impracticable to hold the meeting at the date or in the place originally stated in the notice, the following alternative procedures may be adopted:

(i) Give notice of the postponement to those entitled to

attend, by advertisement in the press and/or by post, explain the reason for the postponement, and at the same time (or subsequently) send a fresh notice in correct form, stating the re-arranged date; or;

(*ii*) Notify those entitled to attend by advertisement and/or post, explaining the circumstances and stating that, although the meeting will be held, in order to comply with common law, no business will be transacted; that is, the meeting will be held but adjourned immediately to a time and place to be arranged.

PROGRESS TEST 11

1. Explain the phrase "adjournment of a meeting" and the common law rule relating thereto. How is this common law provision sometimes modified by the regulations governing particular meetings? (**1, 2, 3**)

2. In what circumstances is the chairman of a meeting entitled (*a*) to refuse to accept an amendment, (*b*) to adjourn without consent of the meeting? (**2, 3**)

3. What do you understand by adjournment? In what circumstances may a chairman adjourn a meeting on his own responsibility? In what circumstances has he no option but to adjourn? When is notice of the resumed meeting required? Can a meeting once convened properly be postponed? (**1, 2, 3, 5**)

4. Enumerate the various ways whereby a meeting may be adjourned. Discuss the effects of any decided cases on the subject of adjournment and of the adjourned meeting. (**3, 4**)

5. Distinguish between adjournment and postponement of a meeting. What is the proper course to be adopted when it is desired to postpone a meeting after it had been properly convened? If the meeting has not been properly convened (e.g. if inadequate notice is given), what is the correct procedure? (**1, 5**)

CHAPTER XII

Minutes

THE TAKING OF MINUTES

1. Definition. Minutes may be defined as a written record of the business transacted at a meeting.

2. Contents. Although the contents will vary according to the kind of meeting, the following items are typical:

(*a*) *Heading:* This usually includes:
  (*i*) *Name* of the body, e.g. company, which held the meeting.
  (*ii*) *Kind of meeting*, e.g. annual general meeting.
  (*iii*) *Place* of the meeting.
  (*iv*) *Day and date* of the meeting. (The time is not usually stated.)

NOTE: Obviously, the name of the body concerned need not be shown in the minute book, but examination candidates ought to include it when drafting specimen minutes.

(*b*) *Names of those present*, including (where applicable) those "in attendance," i.e. those who are there by invitation, or *ex officio*, and not as members.

NOTE: The recording of names applies more particularly to board meetings and other comparatively small assemblies. In the case of large meetings, only the *number* present needs to be recorded, if at all.

(*c*) *Minutes of resolution:* Records of decisions taken and resolutions passed, e.g. *Resolved:* "That the Official Seal, an impression of which is impressed in the margin hereof, be and the same is hereby adopted as the Official Seal of the company."

(*d*) *Minutes of narration:* Records of items of business which do *not* require formal resolutions. Thus, the above minute of resolution might have been preceded by the following minute of narration: "The Secretary produced a design for the Official Seal of the Company."

(*e*) *Names of proposers and seconders:* Whether to record the names of proposers and (where necessary) seconders in the minutes is usually dependent upon the size or kind of meeting concerned; for example:

(*i*) *Board meetings and committee meetings:* Names of proposers and seconders are *not* usually recorded.

(*ii*) *General meetings:* In the case of large meetings, names of proposers and seconders *are* usually minuted.

(*f*) *Serial numbers:* Each item of the minutes is usually serially numbered. As will be explained later, this is particularly necessary in the case of loose-leaf minute books, where the numbers may run serially right through the whole of the book. The use of serial numbers, moreover, facilitates reference and, where applicable, the cross-indexing of minutes according to subject-matter.

(*g*) *Chairman's signature:* The chairman usually appends his signature at the next succeeding meeting, after that meeting has verified the accuracy of the minutes and passed a resolution to that effect.

NOTE: The chairman signing need not have been in the chair at the original meeting.

3. The essentials of good minute writing.

(*a*) *Authentic:* As the minutes may subsequently be required as evidence in a court of law, they must give a precise account of the proceedings of the meeting, and nothing more.

NOTE: The minutes of a meeting must not read like a report; thus, it is quite unnecessary to record the discussions and debates which preceded the passing of the various resolutions.

(*b*) *Complete:* The minutes must be complete, and in sufficient detail to enable a person who was not present at the meeting to understand fully what business was transacted.

(*c*) *Concise:* Minutes must be as concise as possible, but completeness must not be sacrificed for the sake of conciseness.

(*d*) *Free from ambiguity:* that is:

(*i*) Dates, numbers, amounts, quantities, etc., must be clearly stated.

(*ii*) Documents, such as share certificates, must be clearly identified, e.g. by number.

(*iii*) Officials and persons concerned in making decisions, giving or receiving instructions, etc., must be named or otherwise described, so as to indicate with certainty who is intended.

(*e*) *Past tense:* Minutes, being a record of what was *done*, i.e. decided, must be written in the past tense.

4. Specimen Minutes.

CRAFTS PROTECTION SOCIETY

Minutes of the Management Committee Meeting held at the Society's Head Office on Tuesday, 20th May, 19—.

Present: Mr. A. Moat (Chairman)
Mr. R. Cable
Mr. J. Snaith
Mr. G. Todd
Mr. M. Veitch

In attendance: Mr. E. Gilbert, General Secretary

1. *Minutes:* The minutes of the Management Committee Meeting held on 16th April, 19—, having been circulated to all members of the Committee, were taken as read, approved, and signed by the Chairman.

2. *Casual vacancy:* The Chairman having expressed the regrets of the Committee concerning the death of Mr. Martin Welsh, it was

Resolved: "That Mr. James Laing be and he is hereby appointed a member of the Management Committee, to fill the casual vacancy caused by the death of Mr. Martin Welsh."

3. *Correspondence:* The General Secretary read letters received from the Society's Midlands Branch Office, *viz.*

Letter No. 1456: Staff bonuses recommended, amounting to £985 were approved.

Letter No. 1467: Suggested improvements in office procedure were noted, but the General Secretary was instructed to write to the Secretary of the Midlands Branch for a detailed report of the suggested improvements together with figures of the cost involved.

4. *Applications:* The General Secretary read a list of 35 applications for membership of the Society, and it was

Resolved: "That the 35 applications for membership of this Society, numbered 1031 to 1035 both inclusive, be and they are hereby accepted."

The General Secretary was instructed to issue letters of acceptance forthwith.

5. *Resignations:* Letters of resignation from membership of the Society were read from: Ellis & Webb Ltd., Leeds, and Carson & Sons, Burnley, and the General Secretary was instructed to acknowledge and accept their resignations.

6. *Publicity:* The General Secretary produced a letter from the Society's publicity agent, requesting an increase in the sum

budgeted for the financial year ending 31st March, 19—, namely from £5,000 to £7,500.

It was decided to defer consideration of the matter until the next meeting of the Management Committee, and the General Secretary was instructed to write to the publicity agent to that effect.

7. *Contracts:* The quotations of several suppliers of office furniture were submitted by the General Secretary, and it was

Resolved: "That the quotation of Atlas Suppliers Ltd. dated 12th May, 19—, amounting to £455 for office furniture be accepted."

8. *The next meeting* of the Management Committee was fixed for 12 noon on Tuesday, 17th June, 19—, at the Head Office of the Society.

(Signed) ....
Chairman.

5. The Minute Book.

(*a*) *A bound minute book* is still favoured by many secretaries and has its advantages over the loose-leaf minute book in some respects:

   (*i*) The minutes are less liable to falsification and loss of the loose sheets.

   (*ii*) Many of the rather elaborate precautions required when using a loose-leaf minute book are unnecessary.

(*b*) *A loose-leaf minute book*, on the other hand, is perhaps more in keeping with modern methods; that is, the minutes are usually dictated (either to a shorthand-typist or into a dictating machine) by the secretary from his notes, typed on loose sheets and, subsequently, put into the loose-leaf binder which constitutes the minute book. As already indicated, the loose-leaf minute book is not without its disadvantages.

(*c*) *Its advantages* are as follows:

   (*i*) The tedious work of writing the minutes into the bound book is avoided.

   NOTE: It is, of course, possible to have the minutes typed on a sheet and pasted into the bound book, but the book soon becomes bulky and the additional thickness tends to put undue strain on the outside covers.

   (*ii*) At suitable intervals, the earlier sheets of minutes can be removed from the loose-leaf binder, and securely filed away in the safe or strong-room; thus, apart from saving space, there is a saving in cost as one loose-leaf binder replaces any number of bound books.

(*d*) *Precautions:* The usual precautions taken to prevent falsification of the records and removal of the sheets are as follows:

(*i*) A suitable locking device is incorporated in the spine of the book itself, the keys being kept by, say, the chairman and secretary.

(*ii*) Keeping the minute book itself in a safe or strong-room, preferably fire-proofed.

(*iii*) Blank sheets placed in the charge of the secretary or other responsible official.

(*iv*) Sheets numbered serially throughout the minute book.

(*v*) Each sheet initialled by the chairman at the time of signing the minutes of the last preceding meeting.

READING AND ALTERATION

6. Reading the minutes.

(*a*) *Not compulsory.* The reading of minutes at the next meeting is not compulsory, unless the rules specifically require it.

(*b*) *Often "taken as read".* In practice, with the consent of the meeting, they are often taken as read, particularly if copies of the minutes have been circulated to members prior to the meeting.

7. Approving the minutes.

(*a*) *After the minutes are read* (or taken as read), a motion is put to the meeting, recommending their adoption as a true record of the proceedings of the preceding meeting to which they refer; if approved, they are signed by the chairman.

NOTE: "Approval" is to be regarded merely as *verification* of the accuracy of the minutes; that is, a member who votes in favour of "approving" the minutes does *not* thereby indicate that he was necessarily in agreement with resolutions passed at the last meeting; nor does he "confirm" the minutes, as neither confirmation nor ratification is necessary.

(*b*) *Minutes as evidence:* Even after signature of the chairman, the minutes are only *prima facie* evidence; that is, they are not the only admissible evidence of the proceedings at the meeting to which they refer: *Re Fireproof Doors* (1916).

NOTE: It is, however, possible to include a provision in the regulations that (in the absence of fraud or bad faith) the minutes, having been signed by the chairman, shall be *conclusive* evidence: *Kerr* v. *Mottram* (1940).

8. Alteration of the minutes.

(*a*) *No erasures* should be made during preparation of the minutes, i.e. in the minute book itself or in the sheet to be inserted in a loose-leaf minute book. Any errors made should be ruled out and the substituted word or words neatly written or typed above or alongside.

(*b*) *Errors subsequently discovered*, i.e. at the next meeting, or at a later date, should be dealt with formally. In any case of doubt as to the accuracy of the minutes, an amendment may be put to the motion for their adoption; if the amendment is carried, the necessary alteration(s) must be made.

> NOTE: As a general rule, no alteration can be allowed after the minutes have been signed by the chairman; nevertheless, as already indicated, evidence may be brought to prove that the minutes are incorrect: *Re Fireproof Doors* (1916), unless the rules provide that the minutes, having been signed by the chairman, shall be conclusive evidence in the absence of fraud or bad faith: *Kerr* v. *Mottram* (1940).

PROGRESS TEST 12

1. What are minutes: State what information you would record therein and the safeguards you would introduce where the minute book is of the "loose-leaf" variety. (**1, 2, 5**)

2. What are the main contents of the minutes of a meeting? Distinguish between minutes and reports. (**2, 3** (*a*))

3. Draft minutes recording the following items of business at a meeting of the management body of a trade association: (*a*) Minutes; (*b*) Finance; (*c*) Applications for memberships; (*d*) Appointment of a public relations officer. (**2, 3**)

4. To what extent do the minutes of a meeting constitute legal evidence? How, and in what circumstances, can they be altered? (**7** (*a*), **8**)

PART TWO

DEFAMATION

CHAPTER XIII

Defamation

THE ACTION

1. Definition. Various acts concerned with defamation have not even attempted to define it, and those judges and authors who have made an effort to do so have not produced an entirely satisfactory definition. Perhaps the following is one of the best examples:

> "Defamation shall consist of the publication to a third party of matter which in all the circumstances would be likely to affect a person adversely in the estimation of reasonable people generally." (Faulks Committee Report.)

2. Defamatory "statements". These may be made about any natural person (human being) or artificial legal person (corporate body) and certain unincorporated associations which have the necessary personality recognised by law. This would include a partnership but not a trade union: *EETPU* v. *Times Newspapers Ltd* (1980). However, the officials of such unions could be defamed by innuendo (*see* **18**) when statements are made about the union itself.

> NOTE: It is the law that a statement which is defamatory of a group at large cannot be sued on by the individual members unless the individual member can show that the defamatory statement was understood as referring to him, e.g. a statement that all trade unionists are rascals does not allow any trade union member to bring an action for defamation.

Although a defamatory statement can be made in a variety of ways (e.g. in writing, verbally, pictorially or by gesture), legal action for defamation may be divided broadly into those for:

(*a*) Libel.
(*b*) Slander.

3. Libel. Legal action for libel may be taken:

(*a*) Where the defamatory statement was made in writing, in print, or some other *permanent* form.

NOTE: Since the passing of the Defamation Act 1952, the broadcasting of defamatory words "by wireless telegraphy" is now also to be regarded as publication in permanent form—provided it is broadcast for "general reception". It should also be noted that television is within the scope of the 1952 Act.

(*b*) Whether the plaintiff can prove actual damage or not, i.e. he need *not* have suffered any pecuniary loss.

4. Slander. Legal action for slander may be taken:

(*a*) Where the defamatory statement was made orally, or in some *transient* form of expression, e.g. slander may be expressed merely by gesture.

(*b*) Where the plaintiff can *prove* that he sustained actual damage. But this does not apply in all cases; thus it is *not* necessary for the plaintiff to prove that he suffered any actual pecuniary damage in the following cases:

(*i*) Slander imputing a crime for which he could be sentenced to imprisonment.

(*ii*) Slander imputing certain infectious or contagious diseases to the plaintiff.

(*iii*) Slander imputing unchastity or immorality of a woman or girl. (The Slander of Women Act 1891, s.1.)

(*iv*) Imputations in relation to the plaintiff's office, profession or trade.

(*v*) Imputations calculated to injure the plaintiff in his calling, even though the defamatory words were spoken of him otherwise than in the way of his office, profession or vocation.

NOTE: This, the last of these exceptions, was added by the Defamation Act 1952, s.2.

5. Libel and slander may be distinguished in the following respects:

(*a*) *Form:* Libel is defamation in a permanent form. Slander is defamation in some transient form.

(*b*) *Proof:* In the case of libel, proof of actual damage is *not* necessary, i.e. it is presumed in law that damage must result from the defamation. In the case of slander, actual damage must be proved, although, as stated above, there are exceptions.

(*c*) *Nature of offence:* Libel can be both a tort and a crime; that is, not only a civil offence but also a criminal offence. Slander, on the other hand, is not in itself a crime, though it may constitute a crime in certain circumstances, e.g. where it incites to murder or provokes a breach of the peace.

DEFENCES

6. Defences. In an action for defamation, certain defences are available to the defendant according to the circumstances and/or occasion. These are dealt with in **7–12** below.

7. Justification

(*a*) To succeed with this form of defence, the defendant must prove that the defamatory words complained of were true in substance and in fact.

(*b*) But the plea of justification must not be considered in a meticulous sense, and, so long as the defendant meets the sting of the charge, he is not bound to justify anything contained in the charge which does not add to its sting: *Edwards* v. *Bell* (1824).

(*c*) It is no longer necessary for the defendant to prove the truth of each distinct and several defamatory imputation, so long as he can prove that a substantial portion of the allegations were true, if the remainder, whose truth is not proven, are not such as will materially injure the plaintiff's reputation (Defamation Act 1952, s.5).

> NOTE: Justification is usually an expensive form of defence; moreover, if it fails, the damages awarded are often substantially higher than they might otherwise have been. It is not, therefore, surprising that the plea of justification is rarely used.

8. Fair comment. This is a defence which is available only on matters of *public* concern. It is a defence which protects defamatory criticism or expressions of opinion, and is available not only to newspapers but to every British subject.

But a plea of fair comment cannot succeed unless the following ingredients are present:

(*a*) *Public interest.* The matter commented upon must be of public interest, e.g. all matters of State and politics, local government, and the conduct of public officials, etc., are properly the subject of fair comment.

(*b*) *Truth.* The comment must be based on facts admitted or proved to be true, and relevant to the facts; thus, truth is vital, and an honest though mistaken belief that it is true is no defence: *Cooper* v. *Lawson* (1838); also *Silkin* v. *Beaverbrook Ltd.* (1958).

NOTE: The Defamation Act 1952 (s.6), renders it unnecessary to prove that *all* the facts were accurately stated, provided that the opinion expressed was "fair comment" having regard to the remaining allegations which are proved to be true.

(*c*) *Absence of malice.* The comment must not be made maliciously, i.e. it must not be "merely a cloak for malice": *Thomas* v. *Bradbury, Agnew & Co.* (1906); for example, malice may be inferred if there is undue publication.

(*d*) *Statement of opinion.* The comment must be an honest expression of the defendant's opinion, i.e. the inference which he draws from the facts; if, therefore, he does not indicate that what he says is merely his comment or opinion, and not a statement of facts, he cannot get protection from a defence of fair comment.

9. Absolute privilege. This provides a complete defence, even though the statement complained of was false or malicious. The circumstances or occasions on which a plea of absolute privilege is available may be classified as:

(*a*) *Parliamentary:* i.e. in respect of statements made by Members of Parliament in the House of Lords or in the House of Commons.

(*b*) *Statutory:* i.e. given by statute in respect of Parliamentary documents, newspaper reports of judicial proceedings and broadcast reports of judicial proceedings.

(*c*) *Judicial:* i.e. statements made in civil, criminal or military courts, also in certain tribunals exercising judicial functions.

(*d*) *Legal professional:* i.e. in respect of statements made between client and legal adviser.

10. Qualified privilege. If the plaintiff can prove that the defamatory statement complained of was made maliciously, e.g. by giving undue publication, a plea of qualified privilege is of no avail to the defendant. If, however, malice is not proven, qualified privilege extends to the following:

(*a*) *Fair and accurate reports of proceedings in Parliament,* appearing in a newspaper or elsewhere.

(*b*) *Fair and accurate reports of judicial proceedings* to which the public has access.

(*c*) *Fair and accurate reports of public meetings,* if publication is for the benefit of the public.

(*d*) *Statements made in discharge of a legal, moral or social duty,* to a person who has an interest in receiving such statements; thus, a former employer's reference concerning the character of a servant is protected by qualified privilege when given to a prospective employer.

NOTE: In *Blackshaw* v. *Lord* (1983) it was held that for this purpose a report of mere general interest to the public is insufficient. The public at large has to have a legitimate interest in receiving information contained in a report and the publisher has to have a corresponding duty to publish it to the public at large. Whether such legitimate interests exist depends on the particular circumstances. In this case the defendant had no duty to publish what was then mere rumour about the plaintiff even if it were fair and accurate comment.

(*e*) *Fair and accurate reports of proceedings of certain courts and legislatures* outside Great Britain, etc., contained in newspapers and certain periodicals.

NOTE: This was an extension of the statutory defence of qualified privilege conferred by the Defamation Act 1952 (s.7) on "newspapers" within the statutory definition and certain periodicals (*see* **13**).

11. Unintentional defamation. The *Defamation Act* (s.4) provides a remedy, which may avoid proceedings for libel or slander, where there has been unintentional defamation by publishers, printers and newspaper proprietors; thus:

(*a*) It provides that a person alleged to have published defamatory words of another person may avoid proceedings for libel or slander by:

(*i*) Showing that the words complained of were published *without intent to defame* the person making the complaint;

(*ii*) Showing that *reasonable care had been* exercised by his servants, agents and himself; and

(*iii*) *Offering to make amends*—by publishing (or joining in the publication of) a correction and apology.

(*b*) *If the offer is accepted* by the person aggrieved and performed, it will constitute a bar to further proceedings, though not against any other person jointly responsible for the publication.

(*c*) *If the offer is not accepted* by the person aggrieved, the defendant must *prove* in his defence:

(*i*) That the words complained of were published *innocently* in relation to the plaintiff;

(*ii*) That the *offer was made as soon as practicable*, i.e. after he had notice that the words were alleged to be defamatory of the plaintiff; and

(*iii*) That the *offer has not been withdrawn*.

(*d*) *An offer to publish a correction and apology* (or to join in publication with others) for the purpose of this section, must be accompanied by an affidavit, setting out the facts on which the defendant relies, to show that the words complained of were published without intent to defame, and without negligence.

NOTE: The affidavit must be carefully worded as, according to s.4(2), no evidence apart from the facts set out in the affidavit is admissible on behalf of the defendant.

(*e*) *In default of agreement* between plaintiff and defendant as to the form and manner to be adopted of publishing the correction and apology, s.4(4) provides that this may be decided by the court, whose decision shall be final.

12. Apology and payment into court. The Libel Act 1843 (also known as Lord Campbell's Act) provides a defence in an action for libel in a newspaper, i.e. by providing proof that an apology has been published or offered, and that payment has been made into court by way of amends. This has never been a popular form of defence, and as more recent legislation has provided the newspaper proprietors with more popular alternatives, it has become virtually obsolete.

SPECIAL RULES AS TO QUALIFIED PRIVILEGE

13. Protection given to newspapers. As already stated (*see* **10**), the Defamation Act (s.7) gives a *qualified* privilege in respect of reports published in a "newspaper" as defined in that Act.

The newspaper statements having qualified privilege are listed in a Schedule to the Act, and divided into two categories as follows:

14. Schedule: Part I—*Statements privileged without explanation or contradiction.* These can be summarised as:

(*a*) A fair and accurate report of any proceedings in public of:

(*i*) *The legislature* of any part of H.M. dominions outside Great Britain.

(*ii*) *An international organisation* of which the United Kingdom or H.M. Government in the United Kingdom is a member, or of any international conference to which that government sends a representative.

(*iii*) *An international court.*

(*iv*) *A court exercising jurisdiction* throughout any part of H.M. dominions outside the United Kingdom, or of any proceedings before a court-martial held outside the United Kingdom under the Naval Discipline Act 1957, the Army Act 1955, or the Air Force Act 1955.

(*v*) *A body or person appointed to hold a public inquiry* by the government or legislature of any part of H.M. dominions outside the United Kingdom.

(*b*) A fair and accurate copy of, or extract from, any *register* kept in pursuance of any Act of Parliament which is open to inspection by the public, or of any other document which is required by the law of any part of the United Kingdom to be open to inspection by the public.

(*c*) *A notice or advertisement* published by, or on the authority of, any court within the United Kingdom, or any judge or officer of such a court.

15. Schedule: Part II—*Statements privileged subject to explanation or contradiction* (i.e. if the defendant has been requested by the plaintiff to publish a reasonable letter or statement by way of explanation or contradiction, and has refused or neglected to do so, or has done so in a manner regarded as inadequate or unreasonable, the provisions of s.7 cannot be relied upon).

(*a*) A fair and accurate report of the decisions of any of the following associations:

(*i*) An association formed in the United Kingdom for the purpose of *promoting or encouraging the exercise of or interest in any art, science, religion or learning* ...

(*ii*) An association formed in the United Kingdom for the purpose of *promoting or safeguarding the interests of any trade, business, industry or profession* ...

(*iii*) An association formed in the United Kingdom for the purpose of *promoting or safeguarding the interests of any game, sport or pastime* ...

NOTE: The decisions referred to, and in respect of which a qualified privilege is given, relate to a person who is a *member* of, or subject by virtue of any contract to, the control of the association.

(*b*) A fair and accurate report of the *proceedings at any public meeting held in the United Kingdom*, for a lawful purpose, on a matter of public concern, whether admission be general or restricted.

(c) A fair and accurate report of the proceedings of any meeting in the United Kingdom of:
   (i) *Any local authority*, or committee of the same.
   (ii) *Any justice or justices of the peace*, acting otherwise than as a court exercising judicial authority.
   (iii) *Any commission, tribunal, committee or person* appointed for purposes of any inquiry by Act of Parliament, etc.
   (iv) *Any person appointed by a local authority to hold a local inquiry* in pursuance of any Act of Parliament.
   (v) *Any other tribunal, board, committee* or body constituted by an Act of Parliament.

> NOTE: The meetings referred to above must *not* be meetings to which representatives of newspapers and other members of the public are denied admission.

(d) *A fair and accurate report of the proceedings at a general meeting of any company* or association constituted, registered or certified by or under any Act of Parliament, or incorporated by Royal Charter, not being a private company within the meaning of the Companies Act 1948.

(e) *A copy, or fair and accurate report or summary, of any notice* issued for the information of the public by or on behalf of any government department, officer of state, local authority, or chief of police.

16. Loss of qualified privilege. The protection of s.7 will be lost:
   (a) If malice is proved by the plaintiff; or
   (b) If the matter published is prohibited by law; or
   (c) If the statement published is not of public concern, or not for the public benefit.

17. Interpretation of "newspaper". A "newspaper" is defined in the Act, s.7(5) as:

> "Any paper containing public news or observations thereon, or consisting wholly or mainly of advertisements, which is printed for sale and is published in the United Kingdom, either periodically or in parts or numbers, at intervals not exceeding 36 days."

INFERENCE OF DEFAMATION

18. Innuendo.

(a) *A statement may be defamatory by innuendo*, i.e. even though it may not appear directly to cast aspersion upon a person's private character, competence, or professional morals, it may have an indirect, hidden or extended meaning, commonly referred to as innuendo.

(*b*) The defamatory nature of such a statement need not be understood by everyone, i.e. the implication may be apparent to only a limited number of persons.

(*c*) The person purporting to have been defamed may not be specifically named in the statement; it is sufficient if there are some who could reasonably be expected to infer that the plaintiff was the person referred to.

(*d*) Thus, the plaintiff, in order to prove defamation by innuendo, may be required to show:

(*i*) That, although *prima facie* the statement complained of does not refer to him, it might reasonably, in all the surrounding circumstances, be understood to do so; or

(*ii*) That, although the words used, when taken out of context, were not defamatory, they would be likely to convey a defamatory meaning when published to persons with knowledge of the circumstances. For example, a newspaper advertisement introduced a caricature of a well-known amateur golfer, together with a limerick which included his name. It was held to be defamatory, as there was an inference that he had been paid for the advertisement, and, consequently, was not entitled to retain his amateur status: *Tolley* v. *Fry & Sons Ltd.* (1931).

PROGRESS TEST 13

1. Define defamation, and list the defences available to the defendant in an action for defamation. **(1)**

2. Explain briefly some of the effects of the Defamation Act 1952. **(3, 4, 5, 6, 13)**

3. "The greater the truth, the greater the libel." Explain.

PART THREE
COMPANY MEETINGS

CHAPTER XIV

Companies and Company Meetings

INTRODUCTION TO COMPANY LAW

1. Company law in the United Kingdom is contained in the Companies Acts 1948–81 as well as in a huge body of case law. The first of these, the 1948 Act, is a consolidating Act, bringing together earlier companies legislation to deal with the five structural pillars of company law in each of its parts. These are:
  (a) the incorporation of a company;
  (b) the share capital and debentures;
  (c) the registration of charges;
  (d) the management and administration of the company;
  (e) the winding up of the company.

Reforms, and in particular membership of the EEC, have meant further legislation, namely:
  (a) Companies Act 1967
  (b) European Communities Act 1972 (s.9)
  (c) Companies Act 1976
  (d) Companies Act 1980
  (e) Companies Act 1981

The provisions of these Acts in so far as they are relevant to meetings are dealt with in this section. Further changes in company law will follow as EEC directives are implemented in United Kingdom law. The most far reaching of these from the point of view of meetings is the Fifth EEC Directive on Company Structure and Administration.

NOTE: In this Part, unless otherwise indicated, section numbers refer to the Companies Act 1948.

TYPES OF COMPANY

2. Companies under the Companies Acts.

  (a) Companies may be registered under the Acts as follows:

(*i*) Companies limited by shares.

(*ii*) Companies limited by guarantee which have no share capital.

NOTE: There are also companies limited by guarantee which have a share capital but from 22nd December, 1980, no company may be formed as or become such a company.

(*iii*) Unlimited companies which may, or may not, have a share capital.

(*b*) *Limited Liability.* This means:

(*i*) *By shares*, each member's liability being limited to the amount, if any, which is unpaid (i.e. owing to the company) on his shares.

NOTE: This type of company is the most common and is used as a legal structure or "person" to carry on business.

(*ii*) *By guarantee*, each member's liability being limited to the amount he undertakes to pay to the assets of the company if and when it is wound up.

NOTE: This type of company is usually semi-charitable and non-profit making, e.g. a trade association or certain professional and educational bodies.

(*iii*) *Unlimited Companies* are companies not having any limit on the liability of their members and are consequently very few in number.

3. Public and private companies.

(*a*) The Companies Act 1980, s.1(1) states that "public company" means:

(*i*) a company limited by shares or limited by guarantee; and

(*ii*) having a share capital; and

(*iii*) the memorandum of which states that the company is to be a public company; and

(*iv*) in relation to which the provisions of the Companies Act as to the registration or re-registration of a company as a public company have been complied with.

NOTE: "Private Company" means a company that is not a public company.

(*b*) *Section 2 also requires:*

(*i*) that there are at least two subscribers (this was seven prior to the 1980 Act);

(*ii*) that the name of the company includes the words "public limited company" or an acceptable abbreviation such as "plc", or their Welsh equivalents;

(*iii*) that the company's memorandum is in a prescribed form which is set out in the 1980 Act (Sch. 1, Parts I and II)

(*c*) *Section 3 requires* that the amount of the share capital stated in the memorandum with which the company proposes to be registered must not be less than the authorised minimum (currently £50,000).

(*d*) *Section 4 requires* that requirements as to share capital are complied with before the company commences business.

NOTE: The registrar when satisfied that these requirements are complied with will issue a s.4 certificate which is conclusive evidence that the company is entitled to do business and exercise any borrowing powers.

4. Differences between public and private companies. Some of the more important changes are as follows:

(*a*) A public company may offer its shares to the public whereas it is a criminal offence for a private company to do so.

(*b*) When a company allots certain shares or securities there are strong pre-emption rights (1980 Act, s.17). That is, existing shareholders must first be given the right to take up these "new" shares. These pre-emption rules are stricter in the case of public companies. Private companies may exclude these rules by a provision in their memorandum or articles.

NOTE: Private companies will often have pre-emption clauses in their articles concerning the transfer (as opposed to allotment) of shares. Members are thereby required to offer their shares to other members before selling to an outsider.

(*c*) The disclosure requirements in relation to accounts etc. are more demanding for public companies.

(*d*) Additional requirements apply to distributable profits of public companies.

(*e*) Many of the rules relating to share capital are stricter for public companies.

LEGAL STATUS

5. The constitutional documents of registered companies.

(*a*) *The Memorandum of Association* is the more important of these and takes precedence over the *Articles of Association* where their wording conflicts. In law, a company has a personality of its own, separate and distinct from that of its members: *Salomon* v. *Salomon & Co. Ltd.* (1897). The basic characteristics of the company's particular corporate personality are identified in the memorandum.

Section 2 of the 1948 Act requires the memorandum of every company to state:

(*i*) its name;

(*ii*) the situation of the registered office (i.e. whether in England or Scotland);

(*iii*) its objects, and

in the case of the company limited by shares or by guarantee to have clauses stating:

(*iv*) that the liability of its members is limited; and

(*v*) the amount of the share capital or guarantee.

NOTE: The 1980 Act (s.1(1), 2(1)) requires further statements in the case of a public company, *see* **3** above.

(*b*) *The Articles of Association* are primarily concerned with the internal government of the company. They operate as a contract dealing with the relationship as between the company and its members and as between each member (s.20). This is very important from the point of view of meetings. The 1948 Act provides a series of specimen sets of articles (Schedule 1). The most important of these is Table A which is designed for companies limited by shares. Its provisions as relevant to meetings are dealt with in this Part. Part I applied to public companies prior to the 1980 Act, Part II to private companies. Part II was abolished by the 1980 Act and now Part I applies to both public and private companies.

Table A applies to companies if no other articles are adopted. However, companies may adopt different articles and/or exclude the provisions of Table A if they so desire. Table A articles will also deal with the powers and duties of directors and the relationship between the company in general meeting and the board of directors. That is, the articles will state the division of powers as between these two important organs.

6. The contractual capacity of companies.

(*a*) *Ultra vires.* Registered companies are artificial legal persons which can only do legally those things which they were incorporated to do as defined in their objects clause. These objects and the powers to fulfil them are contained in the Memorandum. If a company acts or contracts beyond the scope of these objects and powers it is said to be acting ultra vires. Generally any action which is ultra vires is null and void and neither the company nor the third party can sue on it except as provided by s.9(1) of the European Communities Act 1972.

This basically provides that an ultra vires contract may be:

(*i*) enforced against the company by the third party where the contract was decided upon by the directors and the third party acted in good faith which is presumed;

(*ii*) the company acting ultra vires cannot rely on s.9(1);

(*iii*) as between the company and the directors the operation of the ultra vires doctrine has not been affected.

(*b*) *Agency.* As artificial or "fictitious" persons, companies must act through the agency of human beings, normally their directors. The rules of agency are therefore variously adapted to apply as between the company as principal, directors in the role of agent and persons dealing with the company as third party. (Cf. *Royal British Bank* v. *Turquand* (1856), *Irvine* v. *Union Bank of Australia* (1877), *Freeman and Lockyer* v. *Buckhurst Park Properties Ltd.* (1964).) These rules may hold the company liable even where the director has acted beyond the scope of his authority (i.e. ultra vires his power but not beyond the company's).

(*c*) *Meetings and ratification.* It is important to distinguish between two very different situations:

(*i*) An act of the board or individual director which is ultra vires the company cannot be ratified by the members in general meeting: *Ashbury Carriage Co.* v. *Riche* (1875), *Rolled Steel Products Ltd.* v. *British Steel Corp.* (1982).

(*ii*) Where directors act beyond their powers under the articles but within the powers of the company their action may be ratified by the company in general meeting: *Bamford* v. *Bamford* (1970). The notice calling such a meeting should make it clear that the meeting has as its purpose the sanctioning of the directors' conduct, otherwise the resolution may be invalid because of lack of notice: *Kaye* v. *Croydon Tramways Co.* (1898). The director whose action is the subject of the resolution may use his votes in his own favour subject to the limitations of fraud on the minority.

NOTE: The director must have acted *bona fide* in the interests of the company. Ratification approving a prior performance of the board or director must be distinguished from an exercise of power by the general meeting where it validly exercises the relevant power itself. The latter is an issue of division of power between the company in general meeting and the board of directors.

COMPANY MEETINGS

7. The Division of power between the general meeting and board of directors.

(*a*) The Articles of a company will state the division of power between these two organs of the company. Table A (Art. 80) states:

"The business of the company shall be managed by the directors, who ... may exercise all such powers of the company as are not, by the Companies Acts 1948 to 1981, or by these regulations, required to be exercised by the company in general meeting, subject, nevertheless, to any of these regulations, to the provisions of the Companies Acts 1948 to 1981, and to such regulations, being not inconsistent with the aforesaid regulations or provisions, as may be prescribed by the company in general meeting; but no regulation made by the company in general meeting shall invalidate any prior act of the directors which would have been valid if that regulation had not been made."

This article is not drafted clearly and it is the subject of some debate. The majority view of the division of power is as follows:

"A company is an entity distinct alike from its shareholders and its directors. Some of its powers may, according to its articles, be exercised by directors, certain other powers may be reserved for the shareholders in general meeting. If powers of management are vested in the directors, they and they alone can exercise these powers. The only way in which the general body of shareholders can control the exercise of the powers vested by the articles in the directors is by altering their articles, or, if opportunity arises under the articles, by refusing to re-elect the directors of whose actions they disapprove. They cannot themselves usurp the powers which by the articles are vested in the directors any more than the directors can usurp the powers vested by the articles in the general body of shareholders": *John Shaw & Sons (Salford) Ltd.* v. *Shaw* (1935) (Greer L. J.).

In this case legal proceedings were instigated by the board of directors. The articles delegated the power of management, including the right to take such action, to them. The company in general meeting passed a resolution that the legal proceedings should be discontinued. This resolution was held to be of no effect. It was for the directors to determine whether or not legal action should be taken.

NOTE: Much depends upon the interpretation of the relevant articles. In a case where Article 80 applied it was stated:

"Under (Article 80) the majority of the shareholders within the company at a general meeting have a right to control the actions of the directors so long as they do not affect to control in a direction contrary to any of the provisions of the articles which bind the company": *Marshal Valve Gear Co.* v. *Manning* (1909). *Re Emmadart Ltd.* (1979) decided that Article 80 did not authorise a director, without the sanction of a resolution of the company in general meeting, to present a winding up petition on the ground of insolvency.

(*b*) *Default powers of the general meeting.* The general meeting does have power to act where:

(*i*) Directors act beyond their powers (but intra vires the company)—the company in general meeting may resolve to adopt their action:

"The ratifying of a particular contract which had been entered into by the directors without authority, and so making it an act of the company, is quite a different thing from altering the articles. To give the directors power to do things in future, which the articles did not authorise them to do, would be an alteration of the articles, but it is no alteration of the articles to ratify a contract which has been made without authority": *Grant* v. *U.K. Switchback Railways Co.* (1888).

(*ii*) There is a lack of quorum at board meetings.
(*iii*) There is a conflict with the board's duties to the company.
(*iv*) There is dissension between members of the board: *Baron* v. *Potter* (1914).

(*c*) *Circumstances in which the directors may only act with the sanction of members.* These include:

(*i*) Making a voluntary payment to a director in connection with his departure from office, other than a bona fide pension, 1948 Act, s.191, *Re Duomatic* (1969)

(*ii*) Under Table A (Article 79) borrowing money or giving security for debts in excess of the nominal value of the company's issued share capital.

(*iii*) Allotting shares, apart from the shares to be taken by the subscribers of the memorandum and shares allotted to an employees' share scheme, 1980 Act, s.14.

(*iv*) Allotting shares without first offering them to existing members (though the memorandum of a private company may exclude this provision), 1980 Act, ss.17 and 18.

(*v*) Making a fixed-term service contract with a director for a period of more than five years, 1980 Act, s.47.

(*vi*) Selling company property to a director or buying property for the company from a director if its value is above a certain limit which depends on the size of the company, 1980 Act, s.48.

8. The rule in *Foss* v. *Harbottle* (1843).

This is based on the principle of majority rule and relates to procedure and jurisdiction. When a wrong is done to the company it is for the company to determine (in accordance with its articles) whether to bring legal action. If the company in general meeting determines to ratify a wrong or breach of duty it is not for the court to interfere. Similarly where the directors have power under the articles to decide whether to take legal proceedings and decline in good faith to seek redress: *Shaw* v. *Shaw* (1935). There are exceptions to the rule:

(*a*) The rule does not apply where a company is engaged in or proposing to carry on an ultra vires act.
(*b*) Where a special majority (75 per cent) is required for certain action then it is not enough for directors to obtain ratification by virtue of an ordinary resolution.
(*c*) Where the act in question has infringed the so called personal rights of a shareholder.
(*d*) Where the company is committing a fraud on the minority.
(*e*) Where the interests of justice require it. This exception is subject to much doubt. *See Prudential Assurance Co. Ltd.* v. *Newman Industries (No.2)* (1982).

NOTE: The courts have not been consistent in their application of the rule in *Foss* v. *Harbottle*. In some cases relief has been granted but the rule has not been raised in defence e.g. *Salmon* v. *Quinn and Axtens* (1909). Sometimes the court has refused to intervene even though the rule was not cited in justification for them refusing. *See* also the 1980 Act, s.75.

9. Meetings as the forum and machinery of corporate democracy.

(*a*) *Artificial.* In terms of modern practice and reality the legislation and case law governing meetings is often artificial and dated. It has a certain Victorian "air" about it. As will be seen the general meetings of members represents the source of ultimate authority within the company structure. It passes as special resolutions those matters which most significantly affect the constitution of the company and elects the directors who in reality run the company. However, the meeting is increasingly less used as a forum of corporate democracy.
(*b*) *Public companies'* meetings are often poorly attended and

XIV. COMPANIES AND COMPANY MEETINGS

individuals who do not attend either vote in favour of the board's recommendations by proxy or remain passive. Large institutional shareholders (e.g. pension funds) tend to work behind the scenes rather than via the machinery of meetings. This helps to reinforce what is termed the managerial revolution, the separation of ownership and control. In terms of democracy within large companies it may have a detrimental effect. Modern company law recognises this problem to some extent. Both the 1980 and 1981 Acts and the Stock Exchange require an increasing number of matters to be submitted to members in general meeting for approval (*see* 7(*c*) above).

(*c*) *Small private companies* often operate on a much more informal basis. They are often treated as quasi partnerships by the court. In practice they may often forget the formalities of shareholders' and directors' meetings. The law recognises this and makes provision for it, as in Table A (Article 73A) and the case law on informal agreements. Nonetheless, the Jenkins Committee (1962) on Company Law Reform commented that members should take the trouble to get together and go through the procedure of holding a formal meeting as part of the legitimate price paid for the benefits of incorporation. Furthermore, whilst applying the principle on informal agreements in *Cane* v. *Jones* (1981) the judge commented, "I would also add that one of the most striking features of this case has been the almost total failure of all concerned to observe the simplest requirements of company law."

NOTE: Perhaps the nub of the issue is whether the limited company is the best form of legal vehicle for the small business. In the Gower proposals for "A New Form of Incorporation for Small Firms" an incorporated firm was suggested which would have simple rules about internal relations. These would enable them to operate internally with the same informality and absence of legal rules as apply to partnerships. But the price would be at least some reduction in the privileges of incorporation, e.g. limited liability.

(*d*) *Meetings on winding-up.* The Cork Report on Insolvency (1982) stated that the law of insolvency is now so unsatisfactory that unless fresh legislation is soon introduced it will fall into even greater decay and be regarded with contempt by society and those whose needs it is supposed to serve. The present procedure, including meetings, was described as cumbersome, complex, archaic and over-technical. The report's recommendations included:

(*i*) simplified procedures for debtors to make voluntary arrangements with their creditors;

(ii) that a process of liquidation of assets replace the present procedure for a creditor's voluntary liquidation.

(iii) A new unified jurisdiction known as the Insolvency Court.

(iv) For ailing companies a new provision to enable an administrator to be appointed with power to carry on the business concerned in order to avoid companies being forced into liquidation.

THE FUTURE

10. Industrial democracy and the EEC Fifth Directive. In many European countries (e.g. Germany) employees have some voice in the running of the company which employs them. The EEC Fifth Directive on the harmonisation of company law contains proposals which would provide employees with a voice in corporate decision making. Under these proposals company law would provide for both unitary and two-tier board structures. The latter system comprises of an executive board concerned with the day-to-day running of the company, which is answerable to a supervisory board. The supervisory board would have members' and workers' representatives. There is also provision for a works council to allow for grass roots participation in decision making by workers. The directive contains detailed proposals for the law of company meetings to facilitate these structural changes. However, it will probably be several years before they are enacted in United Kingdom law.

PROGRESS TEST 14

1. Categorise companies registered under the Companies Acts. **(2)**

2. Compare and contrast public and private limited companies. **(3, 4)**

3. Discuss meetings as the machinery of corporate democracy. **(7)**

4. Explain the rule in *Foss* v. *Harbottle* and its relationship to the division of powers between the company in general meeting and the board of directors. **(8)**

CHAPTER XV

The Agenda

CONVENING OF MEETINGS

1. The secretary's first duty in preparing for a meeting is to draw up a list of items of business to be dealt with at the meeting. These items constitute the agenda.

The agenda paper should set out the items of business in the order in which they are to be dealt with at the meeting. If they are set out in a logical order, it will be of great assistance to the chairman.

2. Form of agenda. The agenda prepared for company meetings may be in any of the following forms:

(*a*) *"Skeleton" form*, giving headings only of the items to be dealt with. This form of agenda is often included with, or forms part of, the notice convening the meeting.

(*b*) *Detailed form.* This gives much more detail of the business to be transacted at the meeting, and may even set out in draft form the resolutions to be submitted to the meeting.

(*c*) *The chairman's copy* of the agenda paper usually contains more detail than the copies issued to those entitled to attend the meeting. To enable him to make notes, a wide margin is usually provided on his copy.

NOTE: For more detailed treatment concerning the preparation of an agenda paper, together with specimens of both "skeleton" and detailed forms, *see* Chapter V.

3. Kinds of meeting. Notices may be required for various kinds of meeting. In the case of a company incorporated under the Companies Act 1948, or any previous Act affecting the class of registered company with which this section is concerned, the secretary may be authorised, at various times and in suitable circumstances, to convene meetings of the following kinds:

(*a*) *Annual general meetings* (s.131).
(*b*) *Extraordinary* general meetings.
(*c*) *Class meetings*, i.e. meetings of members holding a certain class of shares.

(*d*) *Directors'* (or Board) meetings.

(*e*) *Committee* meetings, principally meetings of committees appointed by the board, e.g. transfer committee, allotment committee, sealing committee, etc.

(*f*) *Meetings of creditors*, or classes of creditors, e.g. in connection with any form of reconstruction, or on winding-up the company.

(*g*) *Meetings of contributaries*, in the event of a winding up.

NOTE: Prior to the 1980 Act the first general meeting that a public company had to hold was the statutory meeting. This was repealed by the 1980 Act.

NOTICE

4. Persons entitled to receive notice of meetings.

(*a*) *Members.* Every member is entitled to have notice served upon him, unless the Articles provide to the contrary, for example, the Articles may exclude:

(*i*) the holders of cumulative preference shares, unless their cumulative dividend is in arrears for a specified period; or

(*ii*) members whose calls are in arrears; or

(*iii*) holders of non-voting shares.

(*b*) *Auditors.* The auditors of a company are entitled to receive notice of general meetings, which they have a right to attend. They also have a right to be heard at any general meeting which they attend on any part of the business of the meeting which concerns them as auditors. (Companies Act 1967, s.14(7).)

(*c*) *Legal personal representative(s)* of a deceased member, or the trustee in bankruptcy of a bankrupt member—if the deceased or bankrupt member himself would have been entitled to receive notice (Table A, Article 134).

NOTE: In the absence of provisions similar to those in Table A, Article 134, the legal personal representatives are *not* entitled to receive notice of meetings unless they have secured registration of the shares concerned in their own names: *Allen* v. *Gold Reefs of West Africa* (1900).

(*d*) *Joint holders.* Unless there is any provision to the contrary, notice of a meeting is effective if given to the joint holder first-named in the register of members (Table A, Article 132).

5. Waiver of notice.

(*a*) *Table A* (Article 51), and the articles of most companies, provide that *accidental* omission to give notice, or the non-receipt of notice by any person entitled to notice, shall *not* invalidate the proceedings at the meeting concerned. It is thought that this Article will not apply to auditors, since their right to receive notice is prescribed by statute (*see* **4**(b) above).

> NOTE: In *Re West Canadian Collieries Ltd* (1962), because some addressograph plates were accidentally mislaid, the company registrar failed to give notice of a meeting to nine shareholders who held 101 shares out of a total issued capital of 692,718 shares. This omission was excused by the court and the meeting was held to be valid. By implication, Article 51 would cover a situation where the whereabouts of a shareholder are unknown to the company, as where communications are returned from his old address and he does not notify the company of his new address.

"Accidental omission" will not cover the situation where notice is not sent because of a mistaken belief that a member is not entitled to attend: *Musselwhite* v. *Musselwhite & Son Ltd* (1962).

(*b*) *Table A* (Article 98) provides that it is *not* necessary to give notice of a meeting of directors to any director for the time being absent from the United Kingdom.

(*c*) *The Act* (s.133(3)) provides that a meeting called at *shorter* notice than that specified earlier in the same section or in the company's articles, shall not be invalidated on that account if the shorter notice is excused by *all* members entitled to attend and vote (in the case of an annual general meeting), and by a specified majority in the case of any other general meeting. (For what constitutes the specified majority, *see* **10**(*c*) below.)

> NOTE: Apparently there *must* be a notice, however short, but *written or verbal* consent to excuse the shorter notice is considered to be sufficient, and need not be given at the meeting concerned.

6. Contents of a notice. Apart from any special requirements of the Articles, the following are the most important contents.

(*a*) *Place* of the meeting.
(*b*) *Date, day and time* of the meeting.
(*c*) *Kind of meeting* to be held, e.g. annual general meeting, etc.
(*d*) *Business* of the meeting, indicating the nature of any "special" business to be transacted (*see* Table A definition of "special business" in **12** below).
(*e*) *Form of resolution* to be passed (e.g. where a special resolution or an extraordinary resolution is to be passed), with the precise wording of the resolution, in the case of special or extraordinary

resolutions. It appears that the special resolution passed at the meeting must be "the resolution" set out in the notice (s.141(2)). In *Re Moorgate Mercantile Holdings* (1980) it was confirmed that notice of a special meeting must contain the entire substance of the resolution. Where the company is under some obligation which requires the resolution to be passed, the notice must say so: *N.C. Securities* v. *Jackson* (1974).

(*f*) *Statements, given "reasonable prominence"*, to draw attention to the following:

(*i*) That a member is entitled to appoint a proxy (or more than one if permitted by the Articles) to attend and vote instead of him; and

(*ii*) That a proxy need *not* also be a member (s.136(2)).

NOTE: It is necessary to point out that s.136(2) refers only to notices calling a meeting of a company *having a share capital*.

(*g*) *Additional contents* (which may be embodied in the printed forms of notice), include:

(*i*) *The company's name*, which forms the heading of the notice.

(*ii*) *Date of the notice*, which may be assumed to be the date of posting.

(*iii*) *Signature*—usually the secretary's signature—which may be autographic, but quite often forms part of the printed notice; for example:

By Order of the Board,
A. Blank,

Secretary.

(*iv*) *An agenda*, in "skeleton" form. This may be on a separate sheet or, alternatively, it may form part of the notice.

(*h*) *Circulars and explanatory memorandum sent with notice*. These may be sent for various reasons, e.g.

(*i*) where a notice and proposed resolution are not self-explanatory. The circular will be read together with the notice in order to establish whether sufficient notice of the business to be conducted has been given (*Re Moorgate Mercantile Holdings* (1980)).

(*ii*) where the proposed business is other than routine, directors may send out a circular with the notice of meeting explaining why the steps to be taken at the meeting are necessary.

(*iii*) where the Companies Acts require the directors to circulate statements and representations, e.g. the directors are required to circulate a statement of not more than one thousand words prepared by the appropriate number of members who have requisitioned a meeting (s.140) and a director who is the subject of an intended s.184 resolution to dismiss him from office may require the company to send a copy of his representations to every member of the company to whom notice of the meeting is sent (s.184(3)).

(*iv*) A public *listed* company is obliged to send explanatory circulars to members in the case of major transactions (Acquisitions and Realisations Memorandum, para.5). Such a company must obtain the prior approval of the Stock Exchange to the contents of *all* circulars sent to members.

NOTE: In practice the explanatory statement or circular often forms the body of the document sent to members, with the notice of meeting contained in an appendix.

7. Service of notice.

(*a*) *The method* of serving notice is usually prescribed by the company's Articles and/or in the conditions of issue of its shares and debentures, e.g. notice by newspaper advertisement may be permitted in the case of holders of bearer securities, such as share warrants or bearer debentures.

(*b*) *The Act* (s.134) requires that notices shall be served in accordance with the provisions of Table A in so far as the company's articles do not make other provisions in that respect.

(*c*) *Table A* (Article 131) makes the following provisions:

(*i*) Notice may be given to any member either personally or by sending it to him by post at his registered address; or

(*ii*) If he has no registered address within the United Kingdom, notice may be sent to him at any address within the United Kingdom supplied by him to the company for the purpose.

(*iii*) Where a notice is sent by post, service is deemed to have been effected at the expiration of 24 hours after posting. Where it is intended to use second class post, it is advisable to amend Article 131 to provide that notice shall be deemed to be served 48 hours after posting.

(*d*) The Interpretation Act 1978, s.7 will apply where Table A has been excluded and the company's articles do not make other provision. It says that notice will be deemed to be effected at the time when the letter would be expected to be delivered in the ordinary course of post, provided it is properly addressed and prepaid.

(*e*) Table A (Article 50) empowers the general meeting to prescribe an alternative method of giving notice.

8. Clear days' notice.

Reference has already been made to the interpretation of "clear days" in relation to period of notice (*see* VI,7).

In the case of a company, however, the position is as follows:

(*a*) *First reference* should be made to the company's Articles.

(*b*) *If the Articles are silent*, Table A (Article 50) applies; that is, notice shall be exclusive of the day of service (or the day on which it is deemed to be served) and of the day for which it is given.

(*c*) *If the articles are silent and Table A is excluded*, then reference must be made to the Interpretation Act 1978, s.7 (*see* 7(*d*) above).

9. Authority to convene.

To ensure that a meeting is properly convened, it is necessary that it should be summoned by the person or persons having the necessary authority to do so.

(*a*) *The directors*, acting as a board, are usually empowered to authorise the convening of meetings, and the secretary issues the notices on their instructions. Table A (Article 49) states: "The directors may, whenever they think fit, convene an extraordinary general meeting...".

NOTE: By obtaining *individual* consents to convene a meeting from sufficient directors to form a quorum of the board, a secretary cannot convene a valid meeting: *Re Haycraft Gold Reduction and Mining Co.* (1900).

If, however, the secretary convenes a meeting without prior authority, the notice may be ratified by the board before the meeting is actually held: *Hooper* v. *Kerr* (1900).

(*b*) *Table A* (Article 98): Where Table A applies, a director may, and the secretary on the requisition of a director shall, at any time summon a meeting of the directors.

(*c*) *Where the Articles make no provision* as to the convening of meetings (or where, having made provision, there is no one capable of proceeding), two or more members holding not less than one-tenth of the issued share capital or, if the company has not a share capital, not less than five per cent *in number* of the members of the company may call a meeting (s.134(*b*)).

(*d*) *The Act* (s.132) makes provision for the requisitioning of an extraordinary general meeting by a specified minority of members, who may themselves convene the meeting if the directors fail to do so. (*See* further XXIII, Extraordinary General Meetings.)

(*e*) *The Department of Trade* has power to convene, or to order the convening of, a general meeting, where a company has failed to hold an annual general meeting (s.131(2)).

(*f*) *The court* has the power to call or direct the calling of a general meeting in the following circumstances.

(*i*) If for any reason it is impracticable to call or to conduct the meeting of the company in manner prescribed by the articles or the Act (s.135).

This was held to be sufficient to cover a case in which it was impracticable, owing to the terms of the articles and the state of the shareholding in the company, to get a quorum of thirteen members personally present. The court ordered a meeting of the company under s.135 on terms that the quorum should be five shareholders personally present: *Re Edinburgh Workmen's Houses Improvements Co. Ltd.* (1934).

NOTE: The application may be made to the court under s.135 by a director or any member of the company who would be entitled to vote at the meeting; alternatively, the court may act on its own motion.

(*ii*) Where a compromise or arrangement is proposed between the company and its members (s.206(13)).

(*iii*) Where a member of a company complains that the affairs of the company are being or have been conducted in a manner which is unfairly prejudicial. The court may, *inter alia*, regulate the conduct of the company's affairs for the future, require the company to do any act which it has omitted to do or to refrain from doing or continuing an act complained of, and authorise civil proceedings to be brought in the name and on behalf of the company (Companies Act 1980, s.75(4)).

(*iv*) The Court has an inherent jurisdiction to direct the calling of a meeting, e.g. to enable the company to determine whether an action brought in the company's name by a member should be continued: *Pender* v. *Lushington* (1877), cf *Newman Industries* v. *Prudential (No.2)* (1983).

(*g*) *A resigning auditor*, who considers that there are circumstances surrounding his resignation which should be brought to the attention of the members or creditors, may deposit with his resignation a requisition calling on the directors to convene a general meeting for the purpose of receiving and considering an explanation of those circumstances (Companies Act 1976, s.17).

(*h*) *Serious loss of capital.* On becoming aware of a "serious loss of capital" the directors of a *public* company are required to convene an extraordinary general meeting for the purpose of considering whether any, and if so what, measures should be taken to deal with the situation (Companies Act 1980, s.34).

NOTE: A serious loss of capital occurs where the value of net assets are half or less of the amount of the company's called up share capital. The meeting must be convened not later than 28 days from the earliest day on which a director is aware of the situation and for a date not later than 56 days from that date.

10. Period of notice.

(*a*) *Length of notice* for calling meetings must conform to the Articles, but any provision in a company's Articles requiring shorter notice than that required by s.133 is *void*.

(*b*) *The minimum notice* required by s.133 for general meetings of a company (other than an adjourned meeting) is as follows:

(*i*) *Annual general meeting:* Not less than 21 days' notice in writing.

(*ii*) *General meeting* held for the purpose of passing a special resolution: not less than 21 days' notice in writing.

(*iii*) *Any other general meeting:*
Not less than 14 days' notice in writing, in the case of a company other than an unlimited company.
Not less than 7 days' notice in writing, in the case of an *unlimited* company.

NOTE: At common law, notice is not required for an *adjourned* meeting: *Wills* v. *Murray* (1850). But the Articles usually provide that notice shall be given; in any case, Table A requires that notice shall be given if a meeting is adjourned for 30 days or more. The notice of the adjourned meeting must be the same as that given for the original meeting (Article 57).

(*c*) *A meeting called at shorter notice* than that specified in s.133 or in the company's Articles will *not*, however, be invalidated in the following cases:

(*i*) *An annual general meeting* will not be invalidated if *all* members entitled to attend and vote agree to excuse the shorter notice.

(*ii*) *Any other meeting* called at shorter notice will not be invalidated if there is agreement to excuse the inadequate notice by a majority in number of members entitled to attend and vote who together hold not less than 95% in nominal value of the shares giving the right to attend and vote; or holding not less than 95% of the total voting rights, if the company has no share capital (s.133(3)).

XV. THE AGENDA 93

NOTE: As already stated (*see* **3** above), there *must* be a notice, however short. But written or verbal consent to excuse the shorter notice is considered to be sufficient.

(*iii*) *A special resolution* may be validly passed without the usual 21 day period of notice where a majority in number (as stated in (*ii*) above) assent (s.141(2)). But the members must, in giving their consent, have knowledge of the special resolution which it is proposed to pass on a shorter period of notice. Similarly, s.133(3) will only be satisfied where the fact that a meeting is held on short notice is made known to those attending, *Re Pearce, Duff & Co.* (1960).

11. Special notice. In certain cases, the passing of a resolution in general meeting requires what s.142 describes as "special notice"; thus:

(*a*) *Section* 142 provides that notice of intention to move the resolution must be given *to the company* not less than 28 days before the meeting at which it is to be moved.

(*b*) The company must then give its members notice of the motion at the same time and in the same manner as it gives notice of the meeting; or

(*c*) If it is *not* practicable to give members the required notice (e.g. because of the time taken to get notices printed or to amend notices already printed), notice must be given by advertisement in the press, or in any other mode permitted by the Articles, not less than 21 days before the meeting.

(*d*) When special notice is required:

(*i*) *To remove a director*, by ordinary resolution, before the expiration of his period of office (s.184).

(*ii*) *To appoint an "over-age" director*, i.e. one who would otherwise have been ineligible, having attained the age of seventy (s.185).

(*iii*) *To appoint as auditor* a person other than a retiring auditor; or fill a casual vacancy in the office of auditor; or
reappoint as auditor a retiring auditor who was appointed by the directors to fill a casual vacancy; or
remove an auditor before the expiration of his term of office (Companies Act 1976, s.15).

12. Special business. Table A (Article 52) defines "Special Business" as: "All business ... transacted at an *extraordinary* general meeting, and also all that is transacted at an *annual* general meeting, with the *exception* of:

(a) declaring a dividend;
(b) the consideration of the accounts, balance sheets and the reports of the directors and auditors;
(c) the election of directors in place of those retiring; and
(d) the appointment of, and the fixing of the remuneration of, the auditors."

NOTE: Any business outside the scope of the ordinary business as defined in (a)–(d) above, is deemed special and its nature would have to be carefully set out in the notice convening the meeting. In practice, information on ordinary business is also given in some detail, for example, the dividend, if any, to be declared.

13. Practical aspects of preparing for meetings and the directors' report. These issues are dealt with in XXV and XXIX respectively after the rules relating to company meetings have been considered.

PROGRESS TEST 15

1. Describe the measures you would adopt in the preparation of an agenda for the annual general meeting of a public company, of which it may be assumed, you are the secretary. (**2**)

2. Draft a specimen agenda in sufficient detail to be of assistance to your chairman at the forthcoming annual general meeting of your company. (**2, 3**)

3. List the kinds of meetings that the secretary of a company may be required to convene. (**3**)

4. In preparing and issuing notices of general meeting of a company: (a) who, apart from members, are entitled to receive such notices; (b) what statements concerning proxies must be given "reasonable prominence"? (**6, 8**)

5. Who, apart from the directors, may convene, or order the convening of, a general meeting of a company? Explain the circumstances. (**8**)

6. Explain "special notice", and state when it is required. (**11**)

7. Draft the notice of an annual general meeting of a company at which the following business is to be transacted: (a) Presentation of accounts; (b) Re-election of a director aged 78 years; (c) Fixing of auditors' remuneration; (d) Increase of authorised share capital. (**3–11**)

CHAPTER XVI

Quorum

1. Definition. A quorum was defined, and the effects of absence or inadequacy of a quorum explained, in Chapter VII. It is now necessary to consider the quorum specifically in relation to company meetings.

2. The Articles of a company usually specify the number of members required to constitute a quorum.

3. Table A will, however, apply if the Articles do not make any other provision, namely:

(*a*) Two members present *in person or by proxy* are required as the quorum for any general meeting of a public or private company (Article 53).

NOTE: In this connection, Table A (Article 54) also provides the remedy where a quorum is not present, *viz*. "If within half-an-hour from the time appointed for the meeting a quorum is not present, the meeting:
  (*i*) if convened upon the requisition of members, shall be dissolved;
  (*ii*) in any other case it shall stand adjourned to the same day in the next week, at the same time and place or to such other day and at such other time and place as the directors may determine".
  (*iii*) for public companies registered before 22nd December 1980, Article 53 provided that *"three members present in person shall be a quorum"*, Article 54 provided *"if at the adjourned meeting a quorum is not present within half-an-hour from the time appointed for the meeting, the members present shall be a quorum."* These words were repealed by the 1980 Act, Sched.4.

(*b*) *Board meetings:* "The quorum necessary for the transaction of the business of the directors may be fixed by the directors, and unless so fixed shall be two" Table A (Article 99).

NOTE: If the Articles are silent and Table A excluded, a *majority* of directors must be present to constitute a valid quorum, *York*

Tramways v. *Willows* (1882) or where there is an established practice, the number who usually act at meetings, *Re Regents Canal Iron Co.* (1867). It has been held that power in the articles authorising the directors to determine the number which will form a quorum enables them to fix the number at one, *Re Fireproof Doors Ltd.* (1916).

4. The Act (s.134) makes the following provisions for the unlikely circumstances, where the Articles fail to fix a quorum and exclude Table A, namely "two members personally present shall be a quorum".

NOTE: It will be observed that Table A and the Act agree in respect of minimum numbers required. They are not, however, in agreement where proxies are concerned, as the Act requires two members *personally* present, whereas Table A permits proxies to be counted in the quorum.

5. Committee meetings. In most cases, the constitution of a committee is fixed by the Articles, or by the board of directors at the time of appointing the committee (*see* Table A, Articles 102–105). If, however, no provision is made for the fixing of a quorum, then *all* members of a committee must be present to constitute a valid quorum: *Re Liverpool Household Stores Ltd.* (1890).

6. One person may constitute a valid quorum. Reference was made (in II) to the cases of *Sharp* v. *Dawes* (1876) and *Re Sanitary Carbon Co.* (1877), in which it was decided that two persons at least are required to constitute a valid meeting.

Despite these decisions, however, there are several cases connected with company meetings in which *one* person may constitute a valid quorum, namely:

(*a*) *Class meeting.* Where one member holds *all* the shares of a particular class, e.g. preference shares, that one person alone would constitute a quorum for a "meeting" of shareholders of that particular class: *East* v. *Bennett Bros.* (1911).

(*b*) *Board or Committee meeting.* Where, as in Table A (Articles 98, 99 and 102) the directors have power to fix a quorum for board meetings, and to appoint and fix a quorum for committee meetings, they may decide that *one* director shall be a quorum for board or committee meetings. *Re Fireproof Doors Ltd.* (1916).

(*c*) *Adjourned meeting.* Where the pre-1980 Table A (Article 54) applies, and a meeting is adjourned because a quorum is not present within half-an-hour of the time appointed, *one* member alone would constitute a valid quorum at the adjourned meeting if no other member was present within half-an-hour of the time appointed.

NOTE: Table A stated that "the *members* present shall be a quorum," and this may appear to contradict what has been stated above. However, the Interpretation Act 1978, clearly provides that a reference to the plural includes the singular, and vice versa.

(*d*) *Meeting convened by Department of Trade.* If the Department of Trade, on the application of a member, convenes or directs the convening of a general meeting under s.131 (i.e. because the company has failed to hold its annual general meeting), *one* member of the company present in person or by proxy shall be deemed to constitute a quorum at that meeting.

(*e*) *Meeting convened by the court.* Where the court convenes or orders a meeting to be called under s.135 (i.e. because the company has found it impracticable for any reason to call a meeting of the company), *one* member of the company present in person or by proxy shall be deemed to constitute a quorum at that meeting.

7. Disinterested quorum.

(*a*) *At board meetings:*

(*i*) The quorum must be a "disinterested" one: *Re North Eastern Insurance Co.* (1919). Thus, unless the company's Articles permit, a director may not form part of the quorum at a board meeting held for the purpose of dealing with any contract or business in which he has a conflict of interests; nor is he entitled to vote as a director on such contract or business.

This is because of the general equitable duty to make full disclosure to the general meeting where a fiduciary (which includes a director) is in a position of conflict of interest. As a result a director may not contract with his company, or have any interest in any contract with his company without the prior approval of the general meeting.

Such a contract, lacking approval of the general meeting, is *voidable* at the instance of the company, *Aberdeen Rail Company* v. *Blackie Bros.* (1854), and the director is liable to account to the company for any profit he has made out of the transaction, *Boston Deep Sea Fishing Co.* v. *Ansell* (1888).

However, it is often impracticable and time-consuming to call a general meeting for such purposes. It is therefore usual to exclude the operation of the equitable rule by a clause in the articles. *See* Table A, Article 84, discussed in (*b*), below.

(*ii*) *Stock exchange regulations* do not permit a director to vote on any contract or arrangement or any other proposal in which he has a material interest.

NOTE: In his capacity as shareholder, a director *is* permitted to attend, form part of the quorum, and vote on any contract or business in which he has an interest, at a *general* meeting of the company.

In *North-West Transportation Co. Ltd.* v. *Beatty* (1887) it was stated that "every shareholder has a perfect right to vote upon any such question although he may have a personal interest in the subject matter". There are, however, limits to this, for example, the majority cannot by its controlling votes ratify an expropriation of the company's property (*Menier* v. *Hooper's Telegraph Works Ltd* (1874), cf *Cook* v. *Deeks* (1916)). The majority vote is also subject to the wider constraints of oppression or fraud on the minority.

(*b*) *Table A* Art 84(1)) requires a director to disclose his interest in any contract or proposed contract with the company, in accordance with the requirements of s.199 of the Act. Article 84(2) does not permit a director to be counted in a quorum, or to vote on any contract in which he is interested, at a board meeting, subject to the following exceptions:

(*i*) Any arrangement for giving any director any security or indemnity in respect of money lent by him to or obligations undertaken by him for the benefit of the company; or

(*ii*) Any arrangement for the giving by the company of any security to a third party in respect of a debt or obligation of the company for which the director himself had assumed responsibility in whole or in part under a guarantee or indemnity or by the deposit of a security; or

(*iii*) Any contract by a director to subscribe for or underwrite shares or debentures of the company; or

(*iv*) Any contract or arrangement with any other company in which he is interested only as an officer of the company or as holder of shares or other securities.

Therefore, for purposes (*i*)–(*iv*) above, a director may be counted in the quorum and vote.

(*c*) *Equitable rule excluded.* Article 84 (3) provides that any contract or arrangement entered into by or on behalf of the company in which any director is in any way interested:

(*i*) shall not be liable to be avoided by the company; and

(*ii*) the director concerned shall not be liable to account to the company for any profit realised by any such contract or arrangement.

This would appear to apply on a literal reading even if no disclosure has been made and the director has been counted in the quorum and voted on the contract. (But *see* (f), note, below.)

(*d*) *Disclosure of interest.* The Act (s.199) requires a director to disclose his interest in any contract or proposed contract of the company, i.e. he must declare the nature of his interest at a board meeting. In the case of a proposed contract, he must disclose his interest:

(*i*) at the board meeting at which the contract is first considered; or

(*ii*) at the next board meeting held after he became interested.

NOTE: The 1980 Act, s.60, extends the meaning of contract to include any transaction or arrangement, whether or not constituting a contract. Transactions within s.49 of the 1980 Act, namely loans, quasi-loans, guarantees and credit transactions to directors and certain connected persons are likewise included. The disclosure requirement of s.199(1) has thereby been considerably widened. (Cf s.63(3) of the 1980 Act.)

Failure to make such a disclosure makes a director liable on conviction on indictment to a fine and on summary conviction to a fine not exceeding the statutory maximum.

(*e*) *General notice.* To avoid the necessity of giving separate notice in respect of each individual contract in which he becomes interested, a director is permitted, under s.199(3), to give a *general* notice to the effect that

(*i*) he is a member of a specified company or firm, and that he is to be regarded as interested in any contract which may, after the date of the notice, be made with that company or firm.

(*ii*) he is to be regarded as interested in any contract which may, after the date of the notice, be made with a specified person who is connected with him (within the meaning of s.64 of the 1980 Act).

This general notice is deemed to be sufficient declaration of the interest in relation to any contract so made, but it will be of no effect unless either it is given at a meeting of the directors, or the director takes reasonable steps to secure that it is brought up and read at the next meeting of the directors after it is given.

(*f*) *Relationship between s.199 and Article 84.* Section 199(5) does not "prejudice the operation of any rule of law restricting directors of a company from having any interest in contracts with the company" therefore:

(*i*) compliance with s.199 does not, of itself, validate the contract, and (*ii*) the director must make disclosure to the general meeting unless the articles provide otherwise, and

(*iii*) Table A (Article 84) does provide otherwise as stated above.

NOTE: There is much academic debate about the relationship of s.194, Article 84 and s.205. Some cast doubts on the validity of parts of Article 84. However, there is no case law on the point, but many think that Article 84(3) must be read as subject to disclosure under Article 84(1).

(*g*) *Specimen minute.* A declaration by way of a general notice under s.199, made by a director concerning his interests may be minuted as follows:

"The secretary reported receipt of a letter from Mr. A.Charter (newly appointed director), in which, pursuant to s.199, he declared his interest in the following companies: Northern Quarries Ltd. (Chairman), British Steel Trust Ltd. (Director), London Carrying Co. Ltd. (Shareholder), New Plastics Ltd. (Shareholder). The contents of the letter were duly noted."

NOTE: If a matter before the board is one in which the *whole* of the directors are personally interested, it must be referred to a meeting of the members—unless there are no members other than the directors, in which event the latter may vote, and are deemed to vote as members: *Re Express Engineering Works* (1920).

8. Re Hartley Baird Ltd. (1955). This case merits special mention, as the decision of Wynn-Parry, J. appeared to contradict the decision in earlier cases, *thus:*

(*a*) *In Henderson* v. *Louttit* (1894) and other cases, which had hitherto been regarded as accepted authorities, it had been held that "where there is a quorum at the beginning of a meeting, such meeting cannot transact business after the members present have ceased to constitute a quorum"; in other words, that the quorum must be present for the *whole* meeting, and any business completed after the quorum ceased to exist is invalid.

(*b*) *In Re Hartley Baird Ltd.* (1955) the above decision was not followed, where:

(*i*) The company's articles stated that "No business shall be transacted at any general meeting unless a quorum is present *when the meeting proceeds to business*", i.e. following Table A (Article 53).

(*ii*) One member left before the vote was taken (on a motion for reduction of capital), so that the number present was less than that required for a quorum.

(*iii*) It was held that the resolution passed was *valid*.

NOTE: Wynn-Parry, J. contended that the article as worded was "clearly designed to save, by adjournment, a meeting properly convened but at which no quorum turned up ... but it did not meet the case where a quorum was present at the commencement of the meeting but ceased to be present when the meeting proceeded to vote."

PROGRESS TEST 16

1. Define (*a*) quorum, (*b*) "disinterested" quorum. (**1, 7**)
2. What constitutes a quorum for a general meeting of (*a*) a public company, (*b*) a private company, which has adopted Table A? (**3**)
3. Mention some circumstances in which *one* person may constitute a valid quorum of a meeting. (**6**)

CHAPTER XVII

Motions and Resolutions

GENERAL

1. Definitions. Although the words "motion" and "resolution" are often used indiscriminately—even in the Companies Act 1948— strictly speaking, they merit separate definitions:

(*a*) *A motion* is a proposition or proposal put forward for discussion and decision at a meeting, i.e. *before* it has been put to the vote.

(*b*) *A resolution* is the "acceptance" of the motion, i.e. *after* it has been put to the vote and agreed to by the necessary majority.

NOTE: It must be borne in mind, however, that the resolution in its final form may be different from the motion as it appeared in its original form as various amendments may subsequently have been put to the meeting and accepted. But as to special and extraordinary resolutions, *see* **2** below.

NOTICE

2. Notice and amendment of resolutions. An amendment may be validly put where it is within the scope of the notice calling the meeting. The freedom to amend resolutions will vary according to:

(*a*) *Whether the original resolution forms part of ordinary business.* As specific notice of ordinary business need not to be given where the articles distinguish between ordinary and special business, any amendment may be made to a resolution which is part of ordinary business, provided that it does not take the resolution outside the category of ordinary business.

(*b*) *Ordinary resolution.* There appears to be greater freedom in the amendment of an ordinary resolution.

(*c*) *Special or extraordinary resolutions.* No amendments of substance may be made to such resolutions. *See Re Moorgate Mercantile Holdings Ltd* (1980) discussed in **8** below.

As regards *ordinary and resolutions* and *special business* the test of sufficiency of notice is that it should enable a member to decide whether or not to attend to protect his interests. Accordingly an

XVII. MOTIONS AND RESOLUTIONS   103

amendment should not be allowed where it would affect a member's decision not to attend (*Betts* v. *MacNaughten* (1910)).

3. Form, presentation and disposal of a motion. These were dealt with in Chapter VIII, and the rules stated there need not to be repeated here, as they apply also to company meetings.

TYPES OF RESOLUTION

4. Kinds of resolution.

(*a*) There are three kinds of resolution referred to in the Act:
  (*i*) Ordinary resolutions.
  (*ii*) Extraordinary resolutions.
  (*iii*) Special resolutions.

(*b*) The kind of resolution required for any particular purpose is determined either by statute or by the Articles of the company concerned, but an *ordinary resolution* requiring a simple majority of votes cast, is adequate unless otherwise provided in the Act or in the Articles.

(*c*) The law also provides for an informal, unanimous resolution which does not have to be passed at a meeting to be valid, *see* **12** below.

5. Ordinary resolution.

(*a*) *When used.* This, the commonest form of resolution, is used for all routine business at *general* meetings, and for all business at board meetings.

(*b*) *Majority required.* It is passed by a *simple majority* of members entitled to vote, and actually voting, at a meeting of which proper notice has been given in accordance with the Articles.

  NOTE: The rule in *Foss* v. *Harbottle* (1843) has established a general principle that, where the majority passes an ordinary resolution which is within its powers to pass, the court will not normally intervene, i.e. the minority cannot normally object. For a brief discussion of the exception to this principle, *see* XIV, **8.**

6. Extraordinary resolution (s.141(1)).

(*a*) *Definition.* An extraordinary resolution is one "passed by a majority of not less than *three-fourths* of such members as, being entitled to do so, vote in person or, where proxies are allowed, by proxy, at a general meeting of which notice specifying the intention to propose the resolution as an extraordinary resolution has been duly given."

NOTE: A three-fourths majority means that at least three-fourths of those actually voting must vote in favour of the resolution before it is deemed to be passed. If, for example, there are at least 15 votes in favour out of a total of 20 votes cast, that would amount to a three-fourths majority.

(b) *When required.* Such a resolution is required only where either the Act or the Articles of a company so provide. The Act requires an extraordinary resolution in the following cases:

S.278: To wind up voluntarily, because the company cannot, by reason of its liabilities, continue its business.

S.303: To sanction the liquidator to compromise with creditors, debtors or contributories, in a members' voluntary winding up.

S.306: To make an arrangement with the company's creditors.

S.341: To dispose of the company's books and papers, when a company has been wound up, and is about to be dissolved.

(c) *The period of notice required* for a meeting at which an extraordinary resolution is to be passed is *not* specifically stated in the Act; therefore, it will vary according to the kind of meeting at which the resolution is to be passed, i.e.:

(i) 21 *days' notice* at least, if it is to be passed at the annual general meeting;

(ii) 14 *days' notice* at least, if it is to be passed at an extraordinary general meeting;

(iii) 7 *days' notice* at least, if it is to be passed at an extraordinary general meeting of an *unlimited* company.

NOTE: As aready stated, in XV, **10**, the Act provides that inadequate notice may be excused if, in the case of an annual general meeting, all members entitled to attend and vote agree, and in the case of any other meeting, a specified majority agree (s.133).

(d) *Contents of notice.* It appears that the principles in *Re Moorgate Mercantile Holdings* (1980) (discussed below at **8**) apply to extraordinary resolutions, since the notice requirements in s.141(1) for such resolutions is the same as that in s.141(2) for special resolutions.

(e) *Registration.* A copy of every extraordinary resolution must be filed with the Registrar within 15 days after it has been passed (s.143).

(f) *A copy of every extraordinary resolution* must be annexed to, or embodied in, every copy of the Articles issued after the passing of the resolution (s.143(2)).

NOTE: If Articles have *not* been registered, a copy of every extraordinary resolution must be forwarded to any member at his request on payment of 5p, or less if the company so directs (s.143(3)).

(*g*) *Stock exchange regulations.* In the case of a company whose shares are listed on the stock exchange, *four* copies of any extraordinary resolution must be delivered to the share and loan department of the stock exchange concerned.

7. Special resolution (s.141(2)).

(*a*) *Definition.* A special resolution is defined in the Act as "a resolution passed by the same majority as required for an extraordinary resolution at a general meeting of which *not less than* 21 *days'* notice specifying the intention to propose the resolution as a special resolution has been given."

NOTE: It will be observed that a special resolution differs from an extraordinary resolution only as regards the notice required, i.e. a special resolution requires at least 21 days' notice in *all* cases.

(*b*) *Inadequate notice* may be excused, i.e. if less than 21 days' notice is given, subject to compliance with the provisions of s.133.

(*c*) *When required.* A special resolution is required only where prescribed by the Act, and in any additional cases where the company's Articles so provide; that is, the Articles may demand a special (or extraordinary) resolution where an ordinary resolution would suffice for the purposes of the Act.

(*d*) *The Act requires a special resolution* for almost any alteration of the company's constitution or capital structure. These include the following purposes:

S.5: To alter the "objects" clause of the Memorandum of Association.

S.10: To alter the Articles of Association.

S.18: To change the name of the company.

S.23: To alter conditions in the Memorandum of Association.

S.60: To create reserve liability by rendering share capital incapable of being called up, except in the event of winding up.

S.65: To pay interest out of capital in certain cases.

S.66: To reduce share capital.

S.165: To apply to the Department of Trade for the appointment of inspectors to investigate the affairs of the company.

S.203: To alter the Memorandum of Association for the purpose of making the liability of directors unlimited.

S.204: To approve the assignment of office by a director.

S.222: To effect a winding up by the Court.

S.278: To effect a voluntary winding up, without assigning any reason.

S.287: To empower the liquidator, in a members' voluntary winding up, to transfer or sell the assets for shares in another company.

S.44 (Companies Act 1967): To re-register an unlimited company as a limited company.

S.30 (Companies Act 1976): To enable a company (already registered before the Act came into force with its registered office in Wales), within 12 months of the Act coming into force, to alter its Memorandum so as to provide that its registered office is to be situated in Wales.

S.5 (Companies Act 1980): To re-register a private company as public.

S.8: To allow an old public company to become a private company.

S.10: To re-register a public company as private.

S.18: To permit directors to disregard members' pre-emption rights on a new issue of securities, unless in the case of a private company, a general authority to disregard is contained in the company's articles or memorandum (s.17(9)).

S.43 (Companies Act 1981): To allow financial assistance for purchase of own shares by a private company.

S.47: To authorise an off market purchase of the company's own shares and for the assignment and release of the company's rights to purchase its own shares.

S.48: To authorise contingent purchase contracts of the company's own shares.

S.55: To authorise private companies to redeem or purchase shares out of capital.

(*e*) *Registration.* A copy of every special resolution must be filed with the Registrar within 15 days after it has been passed (s.143).

(*f*) *A copy of every special resolution* must be annexed to, or embodied in, every copy of the Articles issued after the passing of the resolution (s.143(2)).

NOTE: If Articles have *not* been registered, a copy of every special resolution must be forwarded to any member, at his request, on payment of 5p, or less if the company so directs (s.143(3)).

(*g*) *Stock exchange regulations.* In the case of a company whose shares are listed on the stock exchange, *four* copies of any special resolution must be delivered to the share and loan department of the stock exchange concerned.

8. The requirement that the special resolution as passed is substantially the same as that proposed.
In *Re Moorgate Mercantile Holdings Ltd* (1980) Slade J. summarised the principles relating to notices of, and the subsequent amendment of, special resolutions.

He said that:

(a) If a notice of the intention to propose a special resolution is to be a valid notice for the purpose of s.141(2), it must identify the intended resolution by specifying either the text or the entire substance of the resolution which it is intended to propose. In the case of a notice of intention to propose a special resolution, nothing is achieved by the addition of such words as "with such amendments and alterations as shall be determined on at such meeting".

(b) If a special resolution is to be validly passed in accordance with s.141(2), the resolution as passed must be the same resolution as that identified in the preceding notice. The phrase "the resolution" in s.141(2) means "the aforesaid resolution".

(c) A resolution as passed can properly be regarded as "the resolution" identified in a preceding notice, even though

(i) it departs in some respects from the text of a resolution set out in such notice (for example by correcting those grammatical or clerical errors which can be corrected as a matter of construction, or by reducing the words to more formal language) or

(ii) it is reduced into the form of a new text, which was not included in the notice, provided only that in either case there is no departure whatever from the substance.

(d) In deciding whether there is complete identity between the substance of a resolution as passed and the substance of an intended resolution as notified, there is no room for the court to apply the *de minimis* principle or a "limit of tolerance". The substance must be identical. Otherwise the condition precedent to the validity of a special resolution as passed, which is imposed by s.141(2), namely, that notice has been given "specifying the intention to propose the resolution as a special resolution", is not satisfied.

(e) It necessarily follows from the above propositions that an amendment to the previously circulated text of a special resolution can properly be put to and voted at a meeting, if, but only if, the amendment involves no departure from the substance of the circulated text, in the sense indicated in propositions (c) and (d) above.

(f) References to notices in the above propositions are intended to include references to circulars accompanying notices. Notices and circulars should ordinarily be treated as one document.

(g) All the above propositions may be subject to modification where all the members, or a class of members, unanimously agree to waive their rights to notice under s.141(2): (Cf s.143(4)(d)).

NOTE: In the case itself the notice stated the proposed resolution as "the share premium account of the company amounting to £1,356,900.48p be cancelled" whereas the resolution presented at the meeting stated "that the share premium account of the Company amounting to £1,356,900.48p be reduced to £321.97p". It was voted for unanimously by those present at the meeting. Nevertheless, on the principles stated above it was held not to have been validly passed in accordance with s.141(2). The same principles also apply to notices of special resolutions under the Building Societies Act 1962, s.69: *Nationwide Building Society* v. *Punt* (1983).

REGISTRATION AND CIRCULATION

9. Registration of copies of certain resolutions. The provisions of s.143 as to the filing with the Registrar of Companies, and members' entitlement to, copies of resolutions applies not only to special and extraordinary resolutions (referred to above), but also to the following:

(*a*) *Resolutions that have been agreed to by all members* of a company which would otherwise have required the passing of an extraordinary or special resolution.

(*b*) *Resolutions or agreements which have been agreed to by all members of a particular class* of shareholder, which would otherwise have required a particular majority.

(*c*) *Resolutions or agreements which bind all members of a particular class* of shareholder, though not agreed to by all of them.

(*d*) *Resolutions for the winding up of a company* voluntarily under s.278(1)(*a*).

(*e*) *Resolutions of the directors* of a company passed by virtue of s.8(3)(*a*) or 37(2) of the 1980 Act.

(*f*) *Any resolution, though ordinary*, which is stated to be subject to s.143, e.g. authority of company required for allotment of certain securities by directors, *see* s.14 of the 1980 Act.

10. Chairman's declaration.

(*a*) The chairman's declaration that an *extraordinary* or *special* resolution is carried is *conclusive* evidence of the fact, unless a poll is demanded; that is, without any need to prove the number or proportion of votes recorded for or against the resolution (s.141(3)).

(*b*) *Table A* (Article 58) makes a similar provision in respect of *all* resolutions. Thus:

"Unless a poll be so demanded, a declaration by the chairman that a resolution has, on a show of hands, been carried or carried unanimously, or by a particular majority, or lost, and an entry to that effect in the book containing the minutes of the proceedings of the company shall be conclusive evidence of the fact without proof of the number or proportion of the votes recorded in favour of or against such resolution."

(*c*) *Exceptions.* Nevertheless, the chairman's declaration may be set aside, e.g.

(*i*) Where the chairman's declaration is, on the face of it, incorrect: *Re Caratal New Mines* (1902); or

(*ii*) Where, because there was no apparent opposition, the chairman neglected to put the motion to the vote: *Citizens' Theatre Ltd.* (1946).

11. Circulation of resolutions and statements.

(*a*) *Shareholders' rights.* Section 140 gives shareholders the following important rights:

(*i*) *To introduce resolutions* for consideration at the company's *annual* general meeting; or

(*ii*) *To circulate statements* concerning any resolution to be proposed at *any* general meeting of the company.

(*b*) *The requisition to the company* must be made in writing by:

(*i*) *Any number of members*, representing not less than one-twentieth of the total voting rights of all members having a right, at the date of the requisition, to vote at the meeting to which the requisition relates; or

(*ii*) *Not less than* 100 *members* holding shares in the company on which there has been paid up an average sum per member of not less than £100.

(*c*) *Time and place for deposit of the requisition.* A copy of the requisition, signed by the requisitionists (or two or more documents which among them contain the signatures of all the requisitionists) must be deposited at the registered office of the company:

(*i*) *Not less than six weeks* before the meeting, in the case of a requisition requiring notice of a resolution; and

(*ii*) *Not less than one week* before the meeting, in the case of any other requisition, i.e. one requiring circulation of a statement.

(*d*) *The company must comply with the requisition;* that is, by giving notice of any resolution to those entitled to receive notice of the next annual general meeting, or by circulating any statement submitted by the requisitionists, *provided that:*

(*i*) Any statement submitted by the requisitionists does not exceed 1,000 words; and

(*ii*) The requisitionists tender with their requisition a sum reasonably sufficient to meet the company's expenses in giving effect thereto.

(*e*) The company is not bound to circulate a statement if, on application by the company or any aggrieved person, the court is satisfied that the rights conferred by s.140 are being abused to secure needless publicity for defamatory purposes.

NOTE: There is *no* right of appeal to the court against giving notice of a resolution submitted by the requisitionists.

RESOLUTION WITHOUT MEETING

12. Valid resolutions without holding a meeting.

(*a*) *Table A (Article 73A)* provides that "...a resolution in writing signed by all the members for the time being entitled to receive notice of and to attend and vote at general meetings (or being corporations by the duly authorised representatives) shall be as valid and effective as if the same had been passed at a general meeting of the company duly convened and held". This is stated to be subject to the provisions of the Companies Acts but would appear to extend to extraordinary and special resolutions.

(*b*) *A line of cases has also developed the doctrine that* "... where a transaction is intra vires the company and honest the sanction of all members of the company, however expressed is sufficient to validate it, especially if it is a transaction entered into for the benefit of the company". (Astbury J. in *Parker & Cooper Ltd.* v. *Reading* (1926).)

This principle applies even if the members do not meet together in one room or place, but all of them merely discuss and agree to it one with another separately. Hence it does not matter whether that assent (which may be oral only) is given at different times or simultaneously.

(*c*) *The principle has been extended* to cover acts requiring special or extraordinary resolutions. In *Cane* v. *Jones* (1981) it was said that s.10 (special resolution to alter articles) is merely laying down a procedure whereby *some* only of the shareholders can validly alter the articles. The principle was applied to an agreement between all the shareholders of the company which had the effect of removing the chairman's casting vote under the articles, even though there had been no meeting and no special resolution. In *Re Shankey Contracting Ltd.* (1980) it was held that with such unanimous consent an extraordinary resolution can be passed without any meeting being held. The principle is best stated by Buckley J. in *Re Duomatic Ltd.* (1969) "Where it can be shown that all shareholders *who have a right to attend and vote at a general meeting* of the company assent to some matter which a general meeting of the company could carry into effect, that assent is as binding as a resolution in general meeting would be".

(*d*) *Limits to the principle.* In *Re Duomatic*, Buckley J. doubted that the principle would apply to approval of the company under s.191 for payments to directors for loss of office. Nor would the principle or Table A (Article 73A) be appropriate for an ordinary resolution to alter the capital of the company under s.61 since that section "must be exercised by the company in general meeting". Presumably the principle might apply to a "class" decision where shareholders of a class unanimously but orally assent to a variation of their class rights (*see* XXIV).

PROGRESS TEST 17

1. Distinguish between a motion, a resolution, and a substantive motion. What are the main rules to be followed in drafting a resolution? (**1**)

2. Give one example in each case of business which may be transacted by the passing of the following types of resolution: (*a*) ordinary resolution; (*b*) ordinary resolution of which special notice has been given; (*c*) special resolution; and (*d*) extraordinary resolution. Draft the resolution for the business you have selected in (*b*). (**4, 5, 6**)

3. Define "special resolution", and describe the procedure necessary for its passing. Enumerate some of the purposes for which a special resolution may be passed. (**6**)

4. Distinguish between ordinary, extraordinary and special resolutions. (**4, 5, 6**)

5. When may a "resolution" be validly passed without a meeting being held for that purpose? (**12**).

CHAPTER XVIII

Voting

1. Methods of voting. The methods most commonly used at company meetings are:

(*a*) *Show of hands*, i.e. one person one vote. This is the "common law method" of voting: *Re Horbury Bridge Coal Co.* (1879)

(*b*) *Poll:* A method of voting which gives the right to record votes proportionately to, say, shares or stock held.

NOTE: The other methods of voting, namely ballot, division and acclamation are seldom used at company meetings.

2. Table A makes the following provisions as to method of voting and members' voting rights:

(*a*) *At general meetings*, a motion put to the vote shall be decided *on a show of hands* in the first place (Article 58).

(*b*) *But a poll may be demanded*, on or before declaration of the result of the show of hands, by:

(*i*) the chairman;

(*ii*) at least *two* members present in person or by proxy (prior to amendment of Article 58 by the 1980 Act, the number was three);

(*iii*) any member, or members, present in person or by proxy and representing *not less than one-tenth of the total voting rights* of all members having the right to vote at the meeting; or

(*iv*) a member, or members, holding shares on which an aggregate sum has been paid up equal to *not less than one-tenth of the total sum paid up* on all shares conferring the right to vote at the meeting (Article 58).

(*c*) *On a show of hands*, every member present *in person* is entitled to one vote, i.e. a proxy has *no* power to vote on a show of hands (Article 62).

(*d*) *On a poll:*

(*i*) Every member is entitled to *one vote for each share of* which he is the holder (Article 62).

(*ii*) Votes may be given *either* personally or by proxy (Article 67).

112

XVIII. VOTING

NOTE: It is quite common for the articles to give some shares weighted votes, e.g. in *Rights and Issues Investment Trusts* v. *Stylo Shoes* (1964) management shares had a right to eight votes per share and this was validly increased to sixteen votes per share, and in *Bushel* v. *Faith* (1970), the right of directors to have weighted votes on a resolution to dismiss them was upheld.

3. The Act (s.134) makes the following general provisions, to be applied where a company makes no provisions on the subject of voting in its Articles Table and A is excluded:

(*a*) In the case of a company originally having a share capital, every member is entitled to *one vote for each share* held, or for each £10 of stock held.

(*b*) In any other case, every member is entitled to *one* vote.

NOTE: It will be observed that the method of assessing voting power referred to in (*a*) above can only be applied *when a poll is taken*, since on a show of hands each member is, of course, entitled to only *one* vote.

4. Voting at board meetings.

(*a*) *The conduct of board meetings.* Board meetings are usually informal in character; nevertheless, the Articles may regulate the proceedings.

(*b*) *In practice*, however, the directors are often allowed to regulate their own meetings.

(*c*) *Table A* (Article 98) on the subject of board meetings provides that:

(*i*) "The directors may meet together for the despatch of business, adjourn, and otherwise regulate their meetings as they think fit."

(*ii*) "Questions arising at any meeting shall be decided by a majority of votes."

(*iii*) "In case of an equality of votes, the chairman shall have a second or casting vote."

PROGRESS TEST 18

1. Explain the difference between a show of hands and a poll, when voting takes place at a company meeting. (**1, 2**)

2. In the case of a company which has adopted Table A, who has the right to demand a poll, and when? (**2**)

CHAPTER XIX

Polls

1. A common law right. Although voting must be by show of hands in the first place, there *is* a common law right to demand a poll: *R* v. *Wimbledon Local Board* (1882). In practice this right is often either excluded or restricted by the relevant regulations.

2. The Act (s.137) makes it quite clear that, so far as companies are concerned, there *is* a right to demand a poll. It provides:

(*a*) That any provision in a company's Articles is *void* which would exclude the right to demand a poll, *except:*
  (*i*) on a motion to elect a chairman; or
  (*ii*) on a motion for adjournment of the meeting.

(*b*) That any article is rendered void which seeks to make ineffective a demand for a poll made:
  (*i*) by not less than five members entitled to vote at the meeting; or
  (*ii*) by a member or members representing not less than one-tenth of the total voting rights of all members entitled to vote at the meeting; or
  (*iii*) by a member or members holding shares conferring a right to vote at the meeting, being shares on which an aggregate sum has been paid up equal to not less than one-tenth of the total sum paid up on all the shares conferring that right.

(*c*) That a proxy is entitled to demand, or join in the demand for a poll.

3. Table A. The provisions of Table A (Article 58) on the subject of demanding a poll were stated in XVIII, **2** and should be compared with those of s.137 of the Act, stated above.

4. Procedure on taking a poll. After an effective demand for a poll the following procedures are undertaken:

(*a*) *Time, place and method to be adopted.* Usually, the chairman has power to decide when, where and how the poll is to be taken. *Table A* gives him this power, but with certain exceptions, namely:

(*i*) on a motion for election of a chairman;
(*ii*) on a motion for adjournment of the meeting.

NOTE: In these two cases, the poll must be taken "forthwith" (Table A, Article 61).

(*b*) *Chairman's announcement.* The chairman, having made his decision, announces the time and place for taking the poll, and explains the method to be adopted.

(*c*) *If the demand for a poll had been anticipated*, so that voting slips and/or polling lists are already available, he may decide (or be compelled by the Articles) to take the vote at once.

(*d*) *If, on the other hand, the poll will entail much preparatory work* (or if he considers other business of the meeting to be more pressing), he will probably decide that the poll shall be taken at a later date, and make an announcement to that effect.

(*e*) *Appointment of scrutineers.* When the poll is taken, the chairman usually appoints scrutineers. Where opposition parties are known to exist and are easily identifiable, he may select one or more scrutineers from each party, or permit each party to appoint its own scrutineers.

(*f*) *Voting slips are issued* to all members and (where applicable) proxies present, on which they will record:
  (*i*) Vote *for* or *against*.
  (*ii*) Number of votes to which they are entitled.
  (*iii*) Signature.

(*g*) *Voting slips are collected*, entered on polling lists (either by polling clerks or the scrutineers themselves) and checked by the scrutineers.

(*h*) *As an alternative* to the issue of voting slips, the members may proceed to tables suitably arranged and lettered (within the hall or in an adjoining room), and themselves sign a polling list, after indicating in a separate column the number of shares and/or amount of stock held. In that case, separate polling lists are provided for votes cast "for" and "against" the motion as in the following specimen:

Polling List
BLANK COMPANY LIMITED

In Favour

At a poll taken at an Extraordinary General Meeting of Blank Company Limited held at the Registered Office of the Company, London Wall, London E.C.2, on .... 19.. at ... a.m./p.m., the undersigned voted *In Favour* of the following Special Resolution.

"That the capital of the company be reduced from £1,000,000 divided into 1,000,000 Ordinary Shares of £1 each fully paid up, to £500,000 divided into 1,000,000 Ordinary Shares of 50p each fully paid up, by repaying to the Ordinary Shareholders the sum of 50p per share."

No. of Shares (or Stock held)	Signature	No. of Shares (or Stock held)	Signature

(i) *After checking and counting the votes* cast "for" and "against" the motion, the scrutineers will report the result to the chairman. If the meeting is a large one, the scrutineers usually present their report in writing, stating the number of votes cast "for" and "against" the motion. Such a report is illustrated below:

BLANK COMPANY LIMITED

We, the undersigned, having been appointed scrutineers at a poll taken upon the undermentioned Special Resolution at an Extraordinary General Meeting of Blank Company Limited, held at the company's Registered Office, London Wall, London E.C.2, on .... 19.. at ... a.m./p.m., hereby report the result of the poll.

Resolution

"That the capital of the company be reduced from £1,000,000 divided into 1,000,000 Ordinary Shares of £1 each fully paid up, to £500,000 divided into 1,000,000 Ordinary Shares of 50p each fully paid up, by repaying the Ordinary Shareholders the sum of 50p per share."

Votes IN FAVOUR of the Resolution   _____
Votes AGAINST the Resolution   _____
                                                 _____

Dated this .... day of .... 19..

                    _____
                    _____ } Scrutineers

(j) *The chairman announces the result* of the poll, and may or may not state the number of votes cast "for" and "against" in accordance with the usual practice of the company concerned.

NOTE: It should be borne in mind that on taking a poll, *proxies* must be included, but on a show of hands (unless otherwise stated in the Articles) they must be excluded from the reckoning: *Ernest v. Loma Gold Mines* (1897).

PROGRESS TEST 19

1. What are the rights of members of a company to demand a poll? (**1, 2**)

2. Is there a right at common law to demand a poll? The Articles of a company may exclude the right to demand a poll in two exceptional cases. What are the permitted exceptions? (**1**)

CHAPTER XX

Proxies

1. Definition. The word "proxy" is often used indiscriminately to refer to either:

(*a*) A *document* in writing by which one person authorises another to attend a meeting (or meetings) and to vote on his behalf; or

(*b*) A *person* authorised in such a document to act for the appointor, i.e. in the present context, to attend a meeting (or meetings) and to vote on behalf of the appointor.

APPOINTMENT OF PERSON AS PROXY

2. At common law, there is *no* right to appoint a proxy: *Harben* v. *Phillips* (1883).

3. The Act (s.136) overrides common law, i.e. it empowers any member entitled to attend and vote at a meeting of a company *having share capital:*

(*a*) To appoint any other person (whether a member or not) as his proxy, to attend and vote instead of him; and

(*b*) in the case of a proxy appointed to attend and vote on behalf of a member of a *private company*, the proxy is also given the right to speak at the meeting(s) concerned.

4. However, unless the articles otherwise provide:

(*a*) The power to appoint a proxy is *not* given to a member of a company *having no share capital.*

(*b*) A member of a *private* company can appoint only *one* proxy to attend on the same occasion—whereas it is implied (s.136(2)) that a member of a public company having share capital can appoint one or more proxies.

(*c*) A proxy is not entitled to vote except on a poll (s.136(1)).

THE PROXY DOCUMENT

5. Deposit of proxies. Section 136(3) provides that Articles may not require a proxy, or other document for the purpose, to be deposited more than 48 hours before a meeting or adjourned meeting. (This provision ensures that the convenors of the meeting are given at least 48 hours in which to check proxy forms before the meeting is due to start.)

Table A (Article 69) accordingly provides that the instrument appointing a proxy must be deposited with the company:

(*i*) not less than 48 hours before the time for holding the meeting or adjourned meeting, or

(*ii*) in the case of a poll, not less than 24 hours before the time appointed for the taking of the poll, and in default, the instrument of proxy shall not be treated as valid.

> NOTE: Reference to the deposit of proxies usually appears as a footnote in the notice of the meeting, and may be worded as follows: "Proxies must be lodged at the Company's Registered Office not less than forty-eight hours before the time of the meeting." Additionally (as already stated in IX, **6**, where applicable, the footnote will give "reasonable prominence" to the fact that a member is entitled to appoint a proxy, and that the proxy need not be a member (s.136(2)).

6. Issue of proxy forms. An invitation issued at the *company's* expense to some only of its members, requesting them to appoint as proxy a person (or persons) specified in the invitation is *prohibited*, unless:

(*a*) the proxy form was made available to *every* member on written request; or

(*b*) where it had been sent to a member at his written request (s.136(4))

> NOTE: Although it is common practice to send proxy forms along with notices of meetings, this section is designed to prevent directors from sending proxy forms, at the company's expense, only to members from whom they might expect support. Any director who does so becomes liable to a fine not exceeding £100.

7. Form of proxy.

(*a*) *Form.* The Articles usually set out the form of proxy to be used, and may or may not require attestation of the appointor's signature.

(b) *Table A* (Article 68) provides that:

(i) A proxy must be in writing, signed by the appointor or his attorney duly authorised in writing. (Attestation is not required.)

(ii) If the appointor is a *corporation*, it must be under seal or signed by a duly authorised officer or attorney.

(c) *Table A* (Article 70) provides a speciment of an ordinary proxy form, which is to be followed as closely as circumstances permit. This is worded as follows:

.... Limited
I/We .... of ...., in the county of ...., being a member/members of the above-named company, hereby appoint ....
of ...., or failing him, ...
of .... , as my/our proxy to vote for me/us on my/our behalf at the (annual or extraordinary, as the case may be) general meeting of the company, to be held on the .... day of .... 19. ., and at any adjournment thereof.
Signed this .... day of .... 19. .

(d) *Two-way proxy*. The stock exchange regulations require that the use of "two-way" proxy forms shall not be excluded. Such a form of proxy enables a member, through his proxy, to vote "for" or "against" a motion. Table A (Article 71) affords this facility, and provides a specimen in the following form, to be followed as closely as circumstances permit:

....Limited
I/We .... of ...., in the county of ...., being a member/members of the above-named company, hereby appoint ....
of .... or failing him, ...
of .... , as my/our proxy to vote for me/us on my/our behalf at the (annual or extraordinary, as the case may be) general meeting of the company, to be held on the .... day of .... 19. ., and at any adjournment thereof.
Signed this .... day of .... 19. .

This form is to be used $\dfrac{\text{*in favour of}}{\text{against}}$ the resolution.
Unless otherwise instructed, the proxy will vote as he thinks fit.
*Strike out whichever is not desired.

(*e*) *A special proxy* is one which is valid for *one* meeting only and at any adjournment thereof. It is now free of stamp duty.

(*f*) *A general proxy* is valid for more than one meeting. In this case, the proxy form requires a 50p stamp.

REVOCATION AND REJECTION

8. Revocation of proxy. Subject to the provisions of the Articles, a proxy may be revoked by:

(*a*) *Death or insanity of the appointor*, and receipt by the company of notice to that effect *before* the meeting to which the proxy relates (Table A, Article 73).

(*b*) *The appointer himself attending* and exercising his vote at the meeting, in which case the proxy is automatically revoked (*Cousins* v. *International Brick Co.* (1931)).

(*c*) *Deposit of a notice of revocation* within any specified time limit.

(*d*) *Deposit of a new proxy form* in favour of another person, within any specified time limit.

(*e*) *Transfer of the share(s)* in respect of which they prox is given, and receipt by the company of notice to that effect before the meeting.

(*f*) *Verbal intimation to the chairman* prior to the commencement of the meeting.

9. Rejection of proxies.

(*a*) On receipt of proxy forms deposited before a meeting, it will be the secretary's duty (or that of some other responsible person appointed for the purpose) to examine them carefully, and to reject any received *after* the specified time for deposit.

(*b*) He must also reject any which do not conform to requirements for any of the following reasons:

(*i*) *Form unsigned or (where required by the Articles, in the case of a corporation) unsealed.*

(*ii*) *Signature not attested*, i.e. where attestation is required by the Articles.

(*iii*) *Inadequately stamped*, i.e. in the case of a general proxy.

(*iv*) *Alterations* of a major character have not been initialled.

(*v*) *Incomplete*, deficient, or in any way contrary to the form and content required by the Articles.

NOTE: The proxy form may be signed in blank, so long as it is filled in by the time it is used. If it is returned to the company, signed by the member but without inserting the name of a proxy, the board has an implied authority to complete it: *Ernest v. Loma Gold Mines* (1897).

(c) *Methods of dealing with rejected proxies.* Practice appears to differ between companies at this point; if time permits, it is only reasonable to return proxies for amendment. If, however, this is not possible, or if amended proxy forms are not received within the specified time limit, those finally rejected are the subject of an announcement by the chairman, who may also explain the reasons for rejection.

VALIDITY OF PROXY

10. Dealing with valid proxies. In order to expedite work at the coming meeting, and in anticipation of an effective demand for a poll, it is usual to number serially the valid proxies after they have been checked and passed, and to list them alphabetically.

11. Validity of proxies at "adjourned" meetings.

(a) As already stated in **5**, s.136(3) refers to the lodgment of proxies "forty-eight hours before a meeting or *adjourned* meeting ..." from which it can be assumed that, in general, a proxy deposited after the original meeting but before the adjourned meeting is valid—provided that it is lodged in the form and within the time prescribed by the Articles.

(b) Nevertheless, an "adjournment" to take a poll is *not* an adjournment such as would permit the deposit of *fresh* proxies during the interval between the original meeting and its "adjournment," as the latter is merely an extension or enlargement of the original meeting: *Jackson v. Hamlyn and others (Gordon Hotels Case)* (1953).

12. Corporate representatives Section 139 provides:

(a) *Appointment.* A corporation may appoint a natural person to act as its representative:

(i) at any general meeting or class meeting of a company of which it is a member;

(ii) for creditors' meetings held in pursuance of the Act or the provisions of a debenture or trust deed.

Appointment is by resolution of the directors or other governing body of the corporation. The latter would include the liquidator of the appointing company, where it is in liquidation, provided the liquidator is in effective control.

(*b*) *Advantages*. These stem from the fact that a corporate representative has the same rights at a meeting as if he were registered with the shares held by his appointing corporation. Therefore he may:

(*i*) be counted in the quorum;
(*ii*) speak at the meeting
(*iii*) vote on a show of hands,

and there is no need to notify the company of the appointment of a representative before the meeting. Proof of appointment may, however, be required subsequently by the company.

The appointing corporation may appoint a proxy rather than a representative. Such a proxy is in the same position as if he had been appointed by an individual member.

NOTE: The term corporation means any corporate body whether or not a company within the meaning of the Companies Acts.

PROGRESS TEST 20

1. What do you understand by the term "proxy", and what are the usual rules relating thereto? (**1–9**)

2. On what grounds are proxies deposited before a meeting liable to be rejected? What is the procedure for dealing with (*a*) proxies which have been rejected, (*b*) proxies which have passed inspection? (**9**)

3. The Act requires that every notice calling a meeting of a company must give "reasonable prominence" to certain information relating to proxies. Draft a footnote to a notice to meet this requirement. (**5**)

CHAPTER XXI

Minutes

1. Minutes and minute writing were covered, and specimen minutes illustrated in XII. Everything stated there can be applied to the minutes of company meetings.

2. The minute book.

(*a*) *A statutory requirement.* Section 145 requires every company to keep minutes of all proceedings at *general* meetings, also of board meetings and (where applicable) of meetings of managers, in books kept for that purpose.

(*b*) *Location.* The minutes of *general* meetings must be kept at the company's registered office (s.146).

(*c*) *Inspection and copies* (s.146):

(*i*) The minutes of *general* meetings must be open to the inspection of any member, without charge, during business hours, and for not less than two hours each day.

(*ii*) Any member is entitled to be furnished with a copy of the minutes within seven days after making a request, at a charge not exceeding 2½p per 100 words.

(*iii*) The court has power to compel immediate inspection and to direct that copies be provided, in the case of refusal. The Act also imposes penalties on the company and every officer in default.

NOTE: It will be observed that members are not entitled under s.146 to inspect the minutes of board meetings; hence the usual practice of keeping *separate* minute books for general meetings and board meetings.

(*d*) *Loose-leaf minute books.* Companies are permitted to use loose-leaf minute books, s.436 stating, "Any register, index, minute book or accounting records required by this Act to be kept by a company may be kept either by making entries in a bound book or by recording the matters in question *in any other manner.*" But penalties are imposed for failure to take adequate precautions against falsification. For usual precautions, see XII.

(*e*) *The Stock Exchange (Completion of Bargains) Act 1976, s.3* states that minutes and other records may now be kept "otherwise than in legible form" as long as the recording is capable of being reproduced in legible form. This obviously covers computers and, with the increasing use of word processors, is likely to become more important as a method of keeping minutes.

3. Minutes as evidence of proceedings.

(*a*) Section 145(2) states that minutes kept in accordance with s.145(1), if purporting to be signed by the chairman of the meeting at which the proceedings were conducted, or by the chairman of the next succeeding meeting, shall be evidence of the proceedings.

(*b*) *The usual practice* is for the secretary to make notes at the meeting and for the minutes to be subsequently written up in the book. They are then normally signed by the chairman at the beginning of the next general meeting.

(*c*) *The minutes are prima facie evidence only* and therefore may be contradicted by conflicting evidence. Thus the absence of any reference to a resolution in the minutes is evidence that it was not brought before the meeting, but contrary evidence may be addressed to prove that it was passed at the meeting: *Re Fireproof Doors* (1916).

(*d*) *The Articles may provide that the minutes shall constitute conclusive evidence of the proceedings.* Where this is the case, their accuracy can only be questioned where bad faith or fraud is alleged; *Kerr* v. *Mottram* (1940), or where there is an error on the face of the minutes: *Re Caratel (New) Mines* (1902).

(*e*) *Amendments* may be made by the chairman before he signs the minutes. Such amendments must be initialed by him. Nothing should be erased as this may give rise to a suspicion of falsification. The minutes should not be altered once they have been signed, any further amendment being made by an entry in the minutes of a subsequent meeting.

PROGRESS TEST 21

1. What are the provisions of the Act as to (*a*) location, (*b*) inspection, and the taking of copies, of minutes of a company's meetings? (**1**)
2. What are the advantages and disadvantages of loose-leaf minute books? (**4**)
3. Is a company permitted to use a loose-leaf minute book? If so, what precautions are necessary to safeguard its contents? (**2**)
4. Discuss minutes as evidence of proceedings. (**3**)

CHAPTER XXII

The Annual General Meeting

1. The purpose of the annual general meeting.

The purpose and importance of general meetings is discussed in XIV, **9**. However, it is now proposed to make some specific comments about the annual general meeting:

(*a*) *It is a forum of last resort*, in that it enables directors to give an account of their stewardship of the company, especially in relation to the latest profit and loss account and the dividend proposed. They must also submit themselves to re-election and answer questions. The annual general meeting is wisely treated with respect by most boards of directors who normally prepare for it with care and who ought to be ready for the unexpected or difficult question.

(*b*) *In the case of public companies*, particularly those listed on the stock exchange, wide press coverage is given to the preliminary announcement of the years figures. Such publicity is required by the Stock Exchange Listing Agreement as soon as possible after the draft accounts have reached final audit stage (para. 3(*b*)). This often precedes the annual general meeting by two months. At the meeting shareholders are therefore more interested in hearing the latest trading position of the company rather than reviewing the accounts of the previous period. Other points follow from this:

(*i*) *Institutionaly shareholders* do not often take any active part in the proceedings of the annual meeting, preferring to apply pressure behind the scenes where a company is ailing or the board proposes a course of action with which the institutional shareholder disagrees.

(*ii*) *The meeting often becomes a social event* for small shareholders who may be more interested in the security of their investment than in the welfare of the company. It is easier for such shareholders to realise their investment by sales than to mount an *effective* challenge to the board at the meeting.

(*c*) *In the case of private companies*, the annual general meeting is one of the minimum requirements for the privileges of incorporation and limited liability. It ought therefore to be adhered to in principle and practice. It can profitably be used to assess the performance of the company and shareholder directors. (*See* the comments in *Cane* v. *Jones*, XVII, **12.**)

2. When held. Section 131(1) provides that *every* company must hold an annual general meeting:

(*a*) in each year, in addition to other meetings held in that year; and

(*b*) in any case, not more than 15 months after the previous annual general meeting.

3. The first annual general meeting need not, however, be held in the year of a company's incorporation, nor in the following calendar year, so long as it is held *within* 18 *months of incorporation* (s.131(1)).

4. Notice. The notice convening the annual general meeting must expressly state that the meeting is to be an "annual general meeting" (s.131(1)).

NOTE: As already stated in XV, **10**, the minimum period of notice required is 21 days (s.133).

5. Business of the meeting. The main purpose of the annual general meeting is to transact *ordinary* business, which may be specified in the Articles as, for example:

(*a*) To consider (and approve) the directors' and auditors' reports, the accounts and balance sheet.
(*b*) To sanction the dividend (if any) recommended by the directors.
(*c*) To appoint (or re-appoint) directors.
(*d*) To appoint and fix remuneration of the auditors.

NOTE: Other business may, however, be transacted at the annual general meeting, provided its nature is clearly stated in the notice.

6. Default. The Department of Trade may call (or direct the calling of) a general meeting of the company, on the application of any member, if default is made in holding an annual general meeting in accordance with the Act (s.131(2)).

NOTE: A general meeting so held is deemed to be (or it may be resolved at the meeting to be) treated as the annual general meeting in respect of which there had been default.

7. Preparation for an annual general meeting. This is dealt with in XXXV.

PROGRESS TEST 22

1. What is the usual business of a company's annual general meeting? **(4)**
2. When must a company hold its first and subsequent annual general meetings? **(1, 2)**
3. In what circumstances has the Department of Trade power to call (or direct the calling of) a company's general meeting? **(5)**
4. Define the statutory rights available to members in regard to the giving of notice of a resolution at an annual general meeting and the statutory requirements in connection therewith. **(9)**

CHAPTER XXIII
Extraordinary General Meetings

1. **Power to call** an extraordinary general meeting:

(*a*) *The directors* may call an extraordinary general meeting at any time to transact business which cannot conveniently be held over until the next annual general meeting, subject to their giving adequate notice.

(*b*) *Two or more members* holding not less than one-tenth of the issued share capital (or not less than 5% in number of the members of the company, if it has not a share capital), may call a meeting (s.134).

NOTE: This will apply only where the company's Articles do not make other provisions.

(*c*) *Requisitionists* may themselves convene an extraordinary general meeting under (s.132, if the directors fail to comply with their requisition. (*See* **3** below.)

(*d*) *The court* has power under s.135 to order the calling of a general meeting, if the company has found it impracticable to do so; this it may do either of its own motion or on the application of a director or of any member who would be entitled to vote at the meeting.

(*e*) *Table A* (Article 49) provides:

(*i*) *The directors* may, whenever they think fit, convene an extraordinary general meeting.

(*ii*) *The members* shall have power to requisition an extraordinary general meeting in accordance with the provisions of s.132.

(*iii*) *Any director or any two members* may convene an extraordinary general meeting, if at any time there are not sufficient directors within the United Kingdom capable of acting to form a quorum; the meeting to be convened as nearly as possible in the same manner as that in which meetings may be convened by the directors.

2. **Notice required.** Ordinarily an extraordinary general meeting requires not less than 14 days' notice in writing (s.133), but exception must be made in the following cases:

(*a*) 21 *days' notice* at least is required if it is intended to pass a *special* resolution;

(*b*) 7 *days' notice* at least is required, in the case of an *unlimited* company.

NOTE: For the passing of a *special* resolution, 21 days' notice is the minimum requirement in *all* cases, i.e. it applies to both limited and unlimited companies.

3. Members' power to requisition under s.132.

(*a*) *Despite anything in the Articles* to the contrary, members are entitled to requisition the convening of an extraordinary general meeting if:

(*i*) The requisition is made by members holding *not less than one-tenth of the paid-up capital* carrying voting rights at the company's general meetings; or, if the company has no share capital, not less than one-tenth of the total voting rights of the members at general meetings (s.132(1)).

(*ii*) *The requisition sets out the objects of the meeting*, and is deposited at the company's registered office. (s.132(2)).

NOTE: The requisition may consist of several documents in like form, signed by one or more of the requisitionists.

(*b*) *If the directors fail to comply;* that is, if they do not, within 21 days from deposit of the requisition, convene an extraordinary general meeting, the requisitionists (or a majority of them as regards voting rights) may themselves convene a meeting as nearly as possible in the same manner as required by the Articles. In that event:

(*i*) The meeting must be held *within three months* from the date of deposit of the requisition.

(*ii*) *The requisitionists may claim* from the company any reasonable expenses incurred through the directors' default.

(*iii*) *The company may retain the expenses* out of fees or other remuneration for services due to the directors in default (s.132(3)–(5)).

(*c*) *In Re Windward Islands Enterprise (UK) Ltd.* (1982) it was held that the 21 day period refers to the time by which the directors must have decided to convene the extraordinary general meeting. Provided the meeting has been so convened it need not be held within this period. This will prevent the requisitionists themselves convening a meeting under the above procedure. In this case the directors had validly convened a meeting, within 21 days, but for more than 3 months from the date of deposit of the requisition, as Nourse J. explained:

> "Section 132 produces an open-ended state of affairs in that the section in no way prevents the company from calling the meeting for a date to say 6 months ahead or even longer. That oddity, in regard to a section whose evident purpose was to protect minorities, was commented on, and a recommendation was made by . . . the Jenkins Committee. However, that recommendation has not been implemented."

NOTE: If it can be shown that the directors are trying to frustrate the aims of the requisitionists by calling the meeting at some distant date the court might exercise its inherent jurisdiction and order an earlier meeting.

4. Auditor's right to requisition under Companies Act 1976 (s.17). Where an auditor's notice of resignation contains a statement that there are circumstances connected with his resignation which he considers should be explained to the company, he may call on the directors to convene an extraordinary general meeting to enable him to do so.

PROGRESS TEST 23

1. What is an extraordinary general meeting, and who has a statutory right (*a*) to convene, (*b*) to requisition, such a meeting? **(1, 3)**

2. What is the prescribed minimum notice required for the convening of an extraordinary general meeting of (*a*) a limited company, (*b*) an unlimited company? How is this affected, if at all, if the meeting is to be held for the purpose of passing a special resolution? **(2)**

CHAPTER XXIV

Class Meetings

PURPOSE OF MEETING

1. When held. Class meetings are held principally in connection with the variation of rights and privileges attached to different classes of shares, usually by the holders of a class of shares likely to be adversely affected.

2. Variation of class rights.

(*a*) The power to vary class rights is usually given in the Articles or (more rarely) Memorandum, and in the conditions of issue. In that case, the holders of the shares affected must be given an opportunity to meet as a class to consider the effects of the alterations.

(*b*) Thus, the company's Articles may also provide for the holding of meetings of particular classes of shareholders, and for the majority required at such meetings to bind members of the class concerned.

3. Table A (Article 4) will apply, if the Articles make no provision as to variation of class rights; that is:

(*a*) If at any time the share capital is divided into different classes *the rights attaching to any class of shares may be varied:*

(*i*) by the holders of *three-fourths* of the issued shares of that class, *by consent in writing*; or

NOTE: By this method, no meeting is required and the majority required apparently does not take account of the amount paid up on the shares concerned.

(*ii*) by *extraordinary resolution*, passed at a separate general meeting of the holders of the shares of that class.

4. Protection of the minority (s.72).

(*a*) Even where provision *is* made for the variation of class rights, s.72 gives some protection to a minority of shareholders of a particular class, in the following terms:

(*i*) If the Memorandum or Articles authorise the variation of class rights, "subject to the consent of any specified proportion of the holders of the issued shares of that class, or the sanction of a resolution at a separate meeting of the holders of those shares. . ."; and

(*ii*) If the rights of that class *are* varied in the manner prescribed, then application can be made to the court with 21 days to have the variation cancelled, by the holders of not less in the aggregate than 15 per cent of the issue shares of that class, being persons who did not consent to, or vote in favour of, the variation.

NOTE: The application must be made within 21 days after the date on which the consent was given or the resolution was passed, as the case may be.

(*b*) The application can be made by one or more of the shareholders entitled to apply; they may be appointed in writing to apply on behalf of the others.

(*c*) If application *is* made to the court within 21 days by the specified minority, the variation of the class rights does not become effective unless and until it receives the confirmation of the court; the court may, however, decide to cancel the proposed variation.

(*d*) In all cases the court's decision to confirm or cancel the variation shall be final.

NOTE: Apparently the court cannot take a middle course, except with the consent of both parties.

(*e*) A copy of the court order, setting out its decision, must be filed with the Registrar within 15 days after the making of the order. The company and every officer of the company are liable to a fine in case of default.

(*f*) In s.72, "variation" included abrogation.

NOTE: The weakness of s.72 was that it only applied where there was already some procedural provision to protect class rights on a proposed variation. It did not apply where there was no Article 4 or equivalent. This meant that it did not apply when it was most needed. Partly to remedy this situation, s.32 of the 1980 Act lays down comprehensive rules for the variation of class rights (*see* **5** below).

METHODS OF VARIATION

5. Variation of rights attached to special classes of shares. Section 32 of the Companies Act 1980 has effect with respect to the variation (including abrogation) of the rights attached to any class of shares where a company's share capital is divided into different classes. It lays down the following procedures:

(*a*) (*i*) *Where class rights are attached in documents other than the memorandum* (e.g. the articles or terms of issue), and
 (*ii*) *no variation procedure is contained in the memorandum or articles*.
those rights may be varied only if:
 (*iii*) the holders of three-quarters in nominal value of the issued shares of the class in question consent in writing to the variation; *or*
 (*iv*) an extraordinary resolution passed at a separate general meeting of the holders of that class sanctions the variation, and
 (*v*) any additional requirement (howsoever imposed) is complied with (s.32(2)).

NOTE: The procedure in (*a*)(*iii*) and (*iv*) above is the *statutory variation* procedure. Section 32(8) also applies s.72 of the 1948 Act to this type of situation, even though there is no provision for the variation of class rights in that section.

(*b*) (*i*) *Where class rights are attached in documents other than the memorandum* (as in (*a*) above), and
 (*ii*) *a variation procedure is contained in the articles at the time of the company's original incorporation or is later added,*
those rights may be varied as follows:
 (*iii*) If the variation is connected with the giving, variation or renewal of an authority for the purposes of allotment of certain securities by directors (s.14 of the 1980 Act) or with a reduction of share capital (s.66 of the 1948 Act) then the variation can be effected if the *statutory variation procedure* is followed (*see* (*a*)(*iii*) and (*iv*)); and
 (*iv*) any additional requirements of the memorandum are complied with (s.32(3)).
If the variation is not so connected:
 (*v*) it may only be effected by means of the procedure set out in the articles (s.32(4) and Table A (Article 4)).

(*c*) (*i*) Where class rights are attached by the *memorandum*, and
 (*ii*) no variation procedure is contained in the memorandum or articles or *if contained in the articles otherwise than on incorporation* (s.32(4)),
class rights may be varied either:
 (*iii*) by means of a scheme or arrangement (s.206 of the 1948 Act); or

(*iv*) all the members of the company must agree to the variation (s.32(5)).

NOTE: This requirement cannot be overridden by an alteration of the articles because s.32(7) says that an alteration relating to class rights shall itself be treated as an alteration of class rights.

(*d*) (*i*) Where class rights are attached by the *memorandum*, and
(*ii*) a variation procedure is contained in the *memorandum*, those rights may be varied as follows:
(*iii*) If the variation is connected with the giving, variation or renewal of an authority for the purposes of allotment of certain *securities by directors* (s.14, 1980 Act) or with a reduction of share capital (s.66, 1948 Act) then the variation can be effected if the statutory variation procedure is followed (*see* (*a*)(*iii*) and (*iv*)), and
(*iv*) any additional requirements of the memorandum are complied with.

If the variations are not so connected:
(*v*) they may only be effected by means of the procedure set out in the memorandum (s.23(2) of the 1948 Act)

(*e*) (*i*) Where class rights are attached by the *memorandum*, and
(*ii*) there is *express prohibition on variation in the memorandum then*
(*iii*) no variation can be effected except by means of a scheme of arrangements (s.23, 206 of the 1948 Act).

NOTE: Section 32 of the 1980 Act makes no provision for this situation and therefore s.23(2) of the 1948 Act applies. This prevents alteration of the memorandum where the memorandum itself prohibits the alteration of class rights. The only way to vary the rights would be by a Scheme of Arrangement under s.206 of the 1948 Act, which requires court sanction. The only alternative to such a scheme is a reconstruction under s.287 of the 1948 Act, but this would involve the winding up of the company.

(*f*) (*i*) Where class rights are attached by the memorandum, and
(*ii*) a variation procedure is contained in the Articles which dates from the times of original incorporation, those rights may be varied:
(*iii*) as in (*b*)(*iii*) and (*a*)(*iii*) and (*iv*), except that any additional requirements of the *Articles* must be complied with in addition to the statutory variation procedure (s.32(3)).

When not connected with allotment of securities or reduction of capital variation may only be effected:
(*iv*) by means of the procedure set out in the Articles (s.32(4) and Table A (Article 4)).

CONDUCT OF MEETING

6. Provision as to meetings. Section 32(6) provides that the following sections of the 1948 Act:

S.133 (length of notice for calling meetings);
S.134 (general provisions as to meetings and votes);
S.140 (circulation of members' resolutions);

and the provision of the Articles applying to general meetings; shall, where relevant, apply to shareholders' meetings concerned with the variation of class rights, except that:

(*a*) *The necessary quorum* shall be two persons holding or representing by proxy at least one-third in nominal value of the issued shares of the class in question; and

(*b*) *At an adjourned meeting* the necessary quorum shall be one person holding shares of the class in question or his proxy; and

(*c*) *A poll* may be demanded by any holder of shares of the class in question present in person or by proxy.

7. Voting in good faith. In *Re Holders Investment Trust* (1971) the resolution for class consent to a variation of rights was of no effect because the majority (who held more than one class of share) had voted with their interests in another class in mind, not with a view to the interests of the class whose rights were being varied. There is a general rule that those voting at a class meeting must vote bona fide (in good faith) for the interests of that class as a whole. Similarly, those voting at any members' meeting must vote bona fide for the interests of the company as a whole.

8. What amounts to a variation of class rights. This is a matter of company law and as such outside the scope of this book. Briefly, however, the general rule is that the class rights must literally be varied. It does *not* amount to a variation of rights for a class where other shares are altered to join that class, even though the voting strength of existing class shareholders is weakened. Anything that merely affects the enjoyment of class rights, e.g. voting, without actually varying them will not amount to a variation: *Greenhalgh* v. *Arderne Cinemas* (1946), *White* v. *Bristol Aeroplanes Ltd.* (1953).

PROGRESS TEST 24

1. What is a "class" meeting, and what protection does the Act give to a minority of shareholders of a particular class if their rights have been varied? **(1, 4)**

2. A company's Articles provide for the alteration of class rights

by resolution of a three-fourths majority, passed at a meeting of the class of shareholders concerned. Such a resolution is passed at a meeting of the company's preference shareholders, permanently reducing the preference dividend from 7½ per cent to 6 per cent. What remedy does the Act provide for the protection of the minority in such a case? **(4)**

CHAPTER XXV

Board Meetings

1. Purpose.

(*a*) An incorporated body, such as a limited company, must act through properly appointed agents, i.e. the directors, "by whatever name called" (s.455).

(*b*) The directors are responsible for managing the company's affairs and deciding matters of policy.

(*c*) Their decisions are made and their will expressed at board meetings; nevertheless, there are matters which are required (by the Act and/or the Articles) to be decided by the company in *general* meeting.

BUSINESS AT BOARD MEETINGS

2. The first board meeting. Some or all of the following items of business are likely to be included in the agenda of the first board meeting, which should be held as soon as possible after appointment of the first directors and receipt of the company's Certificate of Incorporation.

(*a*) *Certificate of Incorporation.* The secretary will produce the Certificate of Incorporation, and its receipt will be recorded.

(*b*) Appointment of the first directors. Record the appointment of the first directors.

NOTE: The first directors have already been adequately appointed, having been named as such in a statement in prescribed form, signed by the subscribers to the memorandum, and containing a consent signed by each person named: Companies Act 1976, (s.21).

(*c*) *Appointment of chairman.* The person appointed will usually also take the chair at general meetings of the company.

(*d*) *Appointment of secretary.* Record the appointment of the first secretary (or joint secretaries) and fix the terms of his (or their) appointment(s).

NOTE: The first secretary (or joint secretaries) have already been adequately appointed, having been named as such in a statement in prescribed form, signed by the subscribers to the memorandum, and containing a consent signed by each person named: Companies Act 1976 (s.21).

(*e*) *Appointment of the company's solicitors.*

(*f*) *Appointment of the company's brokers.* In the case of a public company, this appointment would be necessary if it was the company's intention to apply to the stock exchange for permission to deal.

(*g*) *Appointment of the company's bankers.* The resolution passed for this purpose will usually be in the form required by the bank concerned.

(*h*) *Appointment of the company's auditors.* A public company intending to offer its shares in a prospectus may make such an appointment at this early stage, as they will wish to include the names of the auditors in the prospectus.

(*i*) *Common seal.* Submit and adopt a design for the company's common seal, and lay down rules for its use and custody, unless already included in the Articles.

(*j*) *Raising capital.* Determination of the method (or methods) to be adopted for obtaining capital. If the company is offering its shares to the public, the principal methods are by prospectus, offer for sale and stock exchange "placing".

> NOTE: A company registered as a public company on its original incorporation must have allotted share capital, the nominal value of which is not less than the authorised minimum (currently £50,000): Companies Act 1980 (s.4).

(*k*) *Prospectus or equivalent document.* If the previous item (*j*) is applicable, prepare and/or consider draft prospectus or equivalent document, submitted by the secretary or solicitor.

(*l*) *Underwriting contract.* If it is intended to underwrite the share issue, consider the terms of the draft underwriting contract, submitted by the secretary or solicitor.

(*m*) *Purchase agreement.* Where applicable, i.e. if the company has been formed to acquire another business, execute the purchase agreement.

> NOTE: It must, however, be borne in mind that any contract made by a public company at this state is provisional only, i.e. until it obtains its "trading certificate" entitling it to commence business: Companies Act 1980 (s.4.).

(*n*) *Instructions to the secretary.* Formal instructions will be given to the secretary at this stage, e.g. to deal further with the appointment of the company's bankers, and to submit application to the stock exchange for permission to deal.

3. Business at subsequent board meetings may be divided into these concerned with:

(*a*) *Policy making*, i.e. considering and making decisions affecting the broad policy of the company. These are principally matters which are likely to be handled by the *full* board, and not delegated to committees, e.g.:

(*i*) *Development of the company's business*, consideration of the additional capital required, and how it is to be acquired.

(*ii*) *Acquisition of another company* or of a controlling interest in it; preliminary discussion will begin at board level.

(*iii*) *Receiving reports* of various committees, and making decisions based on recommendations submitted, or on information provided, by committees.

(*b*) *Routine business*. In the case of a large public company, much of the routine business is delegated to separate standing committees, which will attend to the following:

(*i*) *Transfers*. Approval (or rejection) of transfers submitted for registration.

(*ii*) *Sealing of documents*, such as share certificates.

(*iii*) *Finance*. Routine financial matters rather than high finance.

(*iv*) *Budgetary control*, and other controls given over to committees within certain limits.

(*v*) *Personnel*. Appointments (up to certain levels), resignations, salary increases, welfare, etc.

CONDUCT OF BOARD MEETINGS

4. Conduct. Regulations affecting the conduct of board meetings are usually set out in a company's Articles and (as in Table A) they frequently give the directors the power to regulate their own meetings in most respects.

Table A makes the following provisions on the subject of board meetings (Articles 98–106):

(*a*) *The directors* may meet, adjourn and otherwise regulate their own meetings, as they think fit (Article 98).

(*b*) *Chairman:*

(*i*) The directors may elect a chairman for their meetings and determine the period for which he is to hold office.

(*ii*) In case of an equality of votes, the chairman shall have a second or casting vote (Articles 98, 101–103).

(c) *Quorum:*

(i) The quorum of a board meeting may be fixed by the directors, and unless so fixed the quorum shall be two (Article 99).

(ii) If there is a vacancy in the body of directors, the continuing directors may act. Where the vacancy reduces the number of directors below that required for a quorum, the continuing directors or director may act for the purpose of restoring the quorum, or to summon a general meeting of the company, but for no other purpose (Article 100).

(iii) A director shall not vote in respect of any contract in which he is "interested" and if he does vote his vote shall not be counted; nor shall he be counted in the quorum present at the meeting (Article 84).

NOTE: These prohibitions are, however, subject to various exceptions (*see* XVI, 7).

(d) *Convening meetings:*

(i) A director may summon a board meeting at any time, and the secretary must do so on the requisition of a director.

(ii) It is not necessary to give notice of a board meeting to any director for the time being absent from the United Kingdom (Article 98).

(e) *Voting.* All decisions at board meetings are to be made by a majority of votes (Article 98).

(f) *A resolution in writing*, signed by *all* the directors for the time being entitled to receive notice of a meeting of the directors, shall be as valid and effectual as if it had been passed at a meeting of the directors duly convened and held (Article 106).

NOTE: Such a resolution should, nevertheless, be recorded in the minutes. Although the Act does not give members the right to inspect the minutes of board meetings, the auditors may wish to do so as part of their normal duties.

(g) *Committees.* The directors have power to delegate any of their powers to committees (Article 102).

(h) *Attendance at board meetings.* Every director present at any meeting of directors or committee of directors must sign his name in a book to be kept for that purpose (Article 86).

(i) *Validity of acts.* Where it is *afterwards* discovered that there is a defect in the appointment of directors or of any person acting as such, then any acts done by them at meetings are as valid as if they had been duly appointed or were qualified (Article 105). *See* s.108 and *Morris* v. *Kanssen*, below at 5(*b*)(*iii*).

5. If no corresponding provision is made by the Articles (and assuming Table A is excluded), the decision arrived at in the following cases will apply:

(*a*) *Chairman.*
(*i*) The appointment of a chairman without specifying the duration of such appointment does not entitle him to hold office until he ceases to be a director, as the remaining members of the board may remove him at any time, and appoint another of their number as chairman: *Foster* v. *Foster* (1916).

(*ii*) The chairman has *no* casting vote: *Nell* v. *Longbottom* (1894).

(*b*) *Quorum.*
(*i*) A board meeting need not necessarily be held in a boardroom; it can be held under informal circumstances, but the casual meeting of the only two directors of a company cannot be treated as a valid board meeting, if either of them objects: *Barron* v. *Potter* (1914).

(*ii*) A disinterested quorum is essential for a board meeting: *Yuill* v. *Greymouth Point Elizabeth Railway Co.* (1904).

(*iii*) The board must be properly constituted; if, therefore, acts are done as directors by persons who have not been validly elected, they do *not* bind the company: *Garden Gully Quartz Mining Co.* v. *McLister* (1875).

> NOTE: If, however, the defect in the appointment or qualification of the director(s) is only discovered *afterwards*, s.180 provides that their acts shall be valid. But in *Morris* v. *Kanssen* (1946) this was interpreted as applying to a defective appointment and not to where there had been no appointment at all. Therefore a mere slip or procedural defect in the appointment of a director is covered by s.108. In this case it was held that s.108 did not cover an originally valid appointment which had been vacated by reason of a statutory provision (s.182(3)) requiring qualification shares to be taken up within two months. See also Table A (Article 105) above at **4**(*i*).

(*iv*) A majority of directors will constitute a valid quorum for a board meeting: *York Tramways* v. *Willows* (1882).

(*c*) *Convening meetings.*
(*i*) Reasonable notice of board meetings is necessary, unless they are held on regular dates at a fixed time and place: *Compagnie de Mayville* v. *Whitley* (1896); nevertheless, it is, of course, advisable to send reminders to the directors, even if meetings are held on regular dates.

(*ii*) A director cannot waive his right to notice; failure to give notice to a director will render proceedings at a board meeting void, even though he indicates that he will not be able to attend and does not require notice: *Re Portuguese Consolidated Copper Mines* (1889); *also Rex* v. *Langhorne* (1836).

6. Directors' attendance book.

(*a*) Although it is often the practice at board meetings to pass around an attendance sheet for signatures of directors present, it is perhaps preferable to follow Table A provision (Article 86), i.e. by providing a *book* for the purpose.

(*b*) In this way, the secretary can produce signed evidence in a convenient form, to establish which of the directors were actually present at any particular board meeting.

> NOTE: It should be borne in mind that a director does not make himself responsible for the business transacted at a meeting merely by voting at a subsequent meeting for approval of the minutes: *Burton* v. *Bevan* (1908).

7. Small Private Companies.

Sometimes the number of directors of such companies may fall to one. Table A (Article 99) for example fixes the quorum for a board meeting at two. As a result, there may be a problem in passing a board resolution. This may be solved in one of the following ways:

(*a*) *The remaining director* may act for the purpose of increasing the number of directors to that required for a quorum, or to summon a general meeting of the company, but for no other purpose. Table A (Article 100).

(*b*) *A resolution in writing*, signed by all the directors for the time being entitled to receive notice of a meeting of the director, shall have the same effect as a resolution passed at a meeting of the directors (Article 106).

(*c*) *The Articles* may provide for a quorum of one or alternatively not state the number for a quorum and give directors power to fix a quorum for board meetings. This is a debateable solution because of the majority view that it is impossible to have a meeting of one. (*See* II.)

PROGRESS TEST 25

1. What are the regulations affecting the conduct of board meetings as provided in Table A, in respect of: (*a*) quorum; (*b*) voting; (*c*) resolutions in writing? (**4**)

2. In relation to board meetings, explain the decisions arrived at in any *three* of the following cases: (*a*) *Foster* v. *Foster* (1916); (*b*) *Nell* v. *Longbottom* (1894); (*c*) *Barron* v. *Potter* (1914); (*d*) *York Tramways* v. *Willows* (1882); (*e*) *Yuill* v. *Greymouth Point Elizabeth Railway Co.* (1904). (**5**)

CHAPTER XXVI

Committee Meetings

APPOINTMENT AND PURPOSE

1. Appointment.

(*a*) *If permitted by the Articles*, directors may delegate their powers and duties to committees, and such committees may then have power to bind the company by their decisions, so long as the act *intra vires*.

NOTE: It may be questioned whether the authority of the Articles *is* necessary if a committee is appointed merely to consider or investigate a particular problem, and then to report back to the board, usually with their recommendations. Obviously, it is advisable, and safer, not to put the matter to the test, and to ensure that the Articles give the necessary power before making such an appointment.

(*b*) *Table A* (Article 102) permits the directors to delegate any of their powers to committees, consisting of such member or members of their body as they think fit; and provides that a committee so formed:

(*i*) must conform to any regulations that may be imposed on it by the directors;

(*ii*) may elect its own chairman; or, if no such chairman is elected (or, if at any meeting the chairman is not present within five minutes after the time appointed for holding the same), the members present may choose one of their number to be chairman of the meeting (Article 103);

(*iii*) may meet and adjourn as it thinks proper;

(*iv*) may decide questions arising at any meeting by a majority of votes of the members present; and

(*v*) in the case of an equality of votes, the chairman shall have a second or casting vote (Article 104).

NOTE: It will be observed that where a company is regulated by Table A, Article 102, directors may delegate their powers to a committee of *one*.

2. Quorum. If there is no quorum fixed, either by the Articles or by the directors, *all* members of a committee will constitute a valid quorum of that committee's meetings: *Re Liverpool Household Stores* (1890).

3. Powers. When delegating work to a committee, it is essential that the powers of the committee should be clearly defined in writing, i.e. either in the Articles or in the separate resolution by which the committee is appointed.

NOTE: So long as the committee acts within the scope of its authority, the board and the company will be bound by its actions. A committee cannot delegate powers to a sub-committee unless specifically authorised to do so.

4. Advantages of the committee system.

(*a*) *Specialised knowledge can be applied* to the business for which the committee is appointed; thus the work can be done more thoroughly and more quickly.

(*b*) *The duties of the directors* can be more evenly distributed, i.e. amongst various committees to which routine work is delegated.

(*c*) *Business delegated to a committee* can be considered in greater detail than would be possible at a full board meeting.

(*d*) *Fewer full board meetings* are required, and these are conducted more expeditiously and yet more effectively.

(*e*) *More time is allowed*, at those board meetings which are necessary, for deciding questions of policy, i.e. without prolonging the meetings on routine matters which are being handled by appropriate standing committees.

5. Disadvantages of the committee system. As with any "system", it must be properly applied, and unless due care is taken the committee system may be found to have the following disadvantages:

(*a*) *The authority of the Board* (or of any other appointing body) may be weakened, i.e. by delegating too much of its power to committees and the consequent loss of control.

NOTE: To avoid this state of affairs, the chairman of the board is usually also an *ex officio* member of all committees. Moreover, it is also necessary to ensure that the powers of all committees are clearly defined.

(*b*) *Delays may occur*, e.g. where a dilatory committee fails to report back to the board by a specified date.

NOTE: This, too, is a fault which arises out of loss of control, and is not a valid criticism of the system. Here again, the remedy may lie in the chairman of the parent body acting as *ex officio* member of all committees.

(c) *Weak management may "hide behind" a committee*, e.g. when making a decision which is likely to be unpalatable.

NOTE: This is primarily a criticism of the management concerned rather than of the committee system, although it does, no doubt, provide a weak management with the necessary opportunity.

(d) *A committee often tends to be dominated* by an overbearing member; therefore, the committee's decisions or recommendations are, in fact, those of that one person alone.

NOTE: Although this may, undoubtedly, be true in a few cases, it is not a valid criticism of the system but of those members of a committee who are weak enough to allow it to happen.

TYPES OF COMMITTEE

6. Classification. Committees may be classified according to:

(a) *The power they exercise:* i.e.
   (i) Those *having* power to bind the parent body.
   (ii) Those *without* any power to bind the parent body; or
(b) *The function and/or duration* of the committee, i.e.
   (i) *Executive committees*, possessing wide powers of authority.
   (ii) *Standing committees*, which are relatively permanent and appointed to do a routine task.
   (iii) *Ad hoc committees*, appointed for a particular task only.

7. Descriptions of the principal forms of committee.

(a) *Executive committee.* In a general way this describes any committee having the power to act, generally or specifically. It is, however, more commonly used to describe a body with power to govern or administer; in that sense, therefore, it might be applied to, say, a management committee, or any such committee having plenary power, i.e. full power of authority.

NOTE: It may be argued that the board of directors is itself a "committee" (appointed by the shareholders), to the extent that it governs or administers.

(b) *Standing committee.* Such a committee is formed for a specified purpose (or purposes) and, being permanent, its role is to deal with routine business delegated to it at, say, weekly or monthly meetings. Transfer committees, sealing committees, finance committees and allotment committees are typical.

(c) *Ad hoc committee.* This is formed for a particular task only, i.e. not for the purpose of dealing with routine business (*ad hoc* = "for this"); thus, an *ad hoc* committee might be appointed to investigate the possibility, and to advise on the inauguration of, a superannuation scheme. It might equally be described as a "fact-finding" or "special" committee. Such a committee is relatively short-lived; that is, having achieved its purpose and reported back to the parent body, it then ceases to exist.

(d) *Sub-committee.* A committee may, if it has the necessary power, appoint one or more of its members to a sub-committee, which may be either a form of standing committee, e.g. where it is to relieve the parent committee of some of its routine work; or an *ad hoc* committee, formed to make a specific investigation.

(e) *Joint committee.* Such a committee may be formed for the purpose of coordinating the activities of two (or more) committees, e.g. a committee consisting of representatives from both employers' and employees' committees. It may be a permanent committee or a special committee, formed to consider one particular problem.

PROGRESS TEST 26

1. What do you understand by (*a*) standing committees, (*b*) *ad hoc* committees? Enumerate the advantages of the committee system. Have you any criticisms of the system to offer? (**4, 5, 7**)

2. Describe the committee system of carrying out the work of a society or association, dealing (*inter alia*) with (*a*) purposes and powers, (*b*) chairman, (*c*) notices of meetings. (**1, 3**)

3. Classify the various kinds of committee. In what respects can committees be used to assist the board of directors of a large public company? (**6, 7**)

4. The committee system is said to have many weaknesses. Enumerate some of the criticisms which are often levelled at it, and state your arguments for or against their validity. (**5**)

CHAPTER XXVII

Meetings in a Winding Up by the Court

HOW A WINDING UP IS EFFECTED

1. Methods of winding up. According to s.211, a company may be wound up:

(a) by the court—which may be called a compulsory winding up;
(b) voluntarily—either as:
  (i) a *members'* voluntary winding up; or
  (ii) a *creditors'* voluntary winding up;
(c) subject to the supervision of the court.

2. The secretary as liquidator. Although this section is concerned with the meetings held in a winding up by the court, it is not suggested that the company secretary is ever likely to be appointed liquidator in this form of winding up, nor in a winding up subject to court supervision. He may, however, be appointed liquidator in a *members'* voluntary winding up and (though very rarely) in a creditors' voluntary winding up.

PROCEDURE

3. Brief outline of procedure in a winding up by the court. In addition to giving some information concerning the purpose, procedure and regulations affecting the various meetings required to be held in a winding up by the court, it may be helpful also to outline the winding up procedure in order to indicate the points at which the meetings are held (*see* **4–11** below).

4. Winding up petition.

(a) *The petition is presented* to the appropriate court, i.e. by the company itself, any creditor or creditors, any contributory or contributories, the Department of Trade, or the official receiver.

NOTE: Section 213 defines a "contributory" as "every person liable to contribute to the assets of a company in the event of its being wound up", and for the purpose of determining a final list, the term may also include persons *alleged* to be contributories.

(b) *The Registrar fixes time and place* for the hearing of the petition.

(c) *The hearing is advertised* in the *London Gazette* and in a newspaper circulating in the district in which the company's registered office is situated.

(d) *The petitioner (or his solicitor) attends before the Registrar*, merely to satisfy him that all requirements of the winding-up rules have been satisfied.

(e) *The court may appoint the official receiver* (or any other person) to be provisional liquidator—usually where the assets are in jeopardy (s.238).

(f) The court may, on application of the company or any creditor or contributory, *stay or restrain any legal proceedings* against the company (s.226).

5. Hearing of the petition.

(a) *This may be attended by the company*, any creditor and any contributory.

(c) *The court may make a compulsory winding-up order*, dismiss the petition, adjourn the hearing, or make an interim order, etc., as it thinks fit (s.225).

6. If the petition is successful, i.e. where the court makes a compulsory order for winding up:

(a) A copy of the winding-up order must be filed forthwith with the Registrar of Companies (s.230).

(b) Any transfer of shares or any disposition of the company's property made after commencement of the winding up are void, unless the court orders otherwise (s.227).

(c) No actions can be commenced or proceeded with against the company, without leave of the court (s.231).

(d) The official receiver becomes provisional liquidator, and continues to act until another liquidator is appointed.

(e) The court may appoint a special manager, e.g. if the business of the company is to be carried on.

NOTE: The commencement of the winding up (referred to above) dates back to the time of *presentation* of the petition for winding up. If, however, the winding up began as a voluntary winding up, the commencement of the winding up dates back to the passing of the resolution for voluntary winding up.

7. The official receiver as provisional liquidator:

XXVII. MEETINGS IN A WINDING UP BY THE COURT 151

(*a*) *Takes control* of all books and papers of the company immediately the winding-up order is made.

(*b*) *Serves notice* on the directors and secretary, ordering them to submit to him a statement of affairs, containing particulars of the company's assets, debts and liabilities, and particulars of the company's creditors (s.235).

(*c*) *Sends a preliminary report* to the court, as soon as possible after receipt of the statement of affairs (s.236). A further report may be necessary if fraud is suspected, e.g. in formation of the company.

> NOTE: The statement of affairs must normally be submitted to the official receiver within 14 days of the appointment of a provisional liquidator, or of the date of the winding-up order, or within such extended time as the official receiver or the court may for special reasons appoint.

(*d*) *Convenes the first meetings of creditors and contributories*, which will now be considered in some detail.

8. The first meeting of creditors and contributories. Although the Act provides for the convening of these meetings, they are governed by the Companies (Winding-Up) Rules 1949, as regards procedure. The combined requirements of the Act and the winding-up rules may be summarised as follows:

(*a*) *Convening the meetings.* Section 239 requires the official receiver to summon separate meetings of the creditors and contributories of the company.

(*b*) *When required to be held.* Unless the court otherwise directs, the meetings are to be held:
    (*i*) within *one month* after the date of the winding-up order; or
    (*ii*) within *six weeks* after the date of the winding-up order; if a special manager has been appointed; and
    (*iii*) on dates fixed by the official receiver (Rule 121).

(*c*) *Notices.* The winding-up rules as to the giving of notices are as follows:
    (*i*) The official receiver shall forthwith give notice of the dates fixed by him for the meetings to the Department of Trade, who shall gazette the same (Rule 122).
    (*ii*) The meetings are to be called by giving not less than *seven days'* notice in the *London Gazette* and in a local paper; also by post to every creditor and contributory (Rule 129).
    (*iii*) The notices (which may follow the forms provided in the Appendix to the Rules) must state a time within which the creditors

are required to lodge their proofs, in order to entitle them to vote at the first meeting (Rule 124).

(*iv*) The official receiver must also give seven days' notice to each of the officers of the company who, in his opinion, ought to attend the first meetings of creditors and contributories. These notices may be delivered personally or sent through the post, as may be convenient (Rule 125).

> NOTE: Every officer who receives such a notice has a duty to attend; if he fails to do so, the official receiver must report such failure to the court.

(*v*) As soon as practicable, the official receiver must send to each creditor and each contributory a summary of the company's statement of affairs and (where applicable) a statement of the causes of the company's failure (Rule 126).

(*vi*) Unless the court orders otherwise, the proceedings and resolutions passed at a meeting of creditors or contributories will not be invalidated on the grounds that some of the creditors or contributories have not received the notice sent to them (Rule 136).

> NOTE: The court might be expected to set aside this rule where a substantial creditor was not represented at the meeting.

(*d*) *Place.* The meetings must be held at a place which, in the opinion of the person convening them, is most convenient for the majority of creditors or contributories, but the respective meetings may be held at different times or places, or both, if it is considered expedient (Rule 131).

(*e*) *Chairman.* The chair is taken by the official receiver himself, or by his nominee.

> NOTE: Rule 133 states, "Where a meeting is summoned by the official receiver or the liquidator, he or someone nominated by him shall be chairman of the meeting" but, at subsequent meetings, "the chairman shall be such person as the meeting by resolution shall appoint". This rule does not apply to a creditors meeting in a creditors' voluntary winding up under s.293.

(*f*) *Quorum.* The quorum required at the respective meetings is at least three creditors or three contributories, entitled to vote (or *all* creditors or *all* contributories, if the number does not exceed three), before any business can be validly transacted, except for the purpose of:

(*i*) election of a chairman;
(*ii*) proving of debts; and
(*iii*) adjournment of the meeting (Rule 138(1)).

XXVII. MEETINGS IN A WINDING UP BY THE COURT

NOTE: In the absence of a quorum within half-an-hour from the time appointed for the meeting, the meeting shall be adjourned to the same day in the following week at the same time and place (unless the chairman fixes some other time and place), but the day appointed must be not less than seven or more than twenty-one days from the date of the original meeting (Rule 138(2)).

(*g*) *Resolutions.* A resolution is deemed to be passed:

(*i*) *At a meeting of creditors*, when a majority in number and value of the creditors, present personally or by proxy and voting on the resolution, have voted in favour of the resolution;

(*ii*) *At a meeting of the contributories*, when a majority in number and value of the contributories present personally or by proxy and voting on the resolution, have voted in favour of the resolution—the "value" of the contributories being based on the number of votes conferred on each contributory by the company's regulations (Rule 134).

NOTE: The official receiver must file with the Registrar a certified copy of every resolution passed (Rule 135).

(*h*) *Proxies.* The rules concerning proxies are briefly summarised:

(*i*) A creditor or a contributory may vote either in person or by proxy (Rule 146).

(*ii*) Two forms of proxy are permitted, i.e. general and special forms, which must be sent to the creditors and contributories along with the notice summoning their respective meetings (Rule 148).

(*iii*) A proxy intended for use at the first meetings of creditors or contributories must be lodged with the official receiver not later than the time mentioned in the notice convening the meeting (Rule 154(1)).

NOTE: The time stated must be not earlier than 12 noon of the day but one before, and not later than 12 noon of the day before that on which the meetings are to be held, unless otherwise directed by the court.

(*iv*) The holder of a proxy may not vote in favour of any resolution which would, directly or indirectly, place himself, his partner or employer in a position to receive any remuneration out of the estate of the company, otherwise than as a creditor rateably with the other creditors of the company (Rule 153).

(*v*) No person shall be appointed a general or special proxy who is a minor (Rule 154(3)).

(*vi*) A creditor or contributory may appoint the official receiver to act as his general or special proxy (Rule 152).

(*i*) *Adjournment.*

(*i*) As stated above (*see* (*f*) Quorum (*iii*)), provision is made for formal adjournment where there is a failure to muster a quorum.

(*ii*) The chairman may also, with the meeting's consent, adjourn it from time to time and from place to place. But it must be held at the same place as the original meeting, unless the resolution for adjournment specifies another place, or the court orders that it be held in another place (Rule 137).

(*j*) *Minutes.* The chairman must ensure that proper minutes are drawn up and entered in a minute book, and he (or the chairman of the next ensuing meeting) must sign them.

A list of creditors and contributories present at their respective meetings must also be kept in the prescribed form (Rule 145).

NOTE: The main purposes of the meetings are:

(*i*) To enable those attending to hear the official receiver's statement, and to ask any questions relating to it.

(*ii*) To decide whether to apply to the court to appoint a liquidator, in place of the official receiver.

(*iii*) To determine whether to apply to the court to appoint a committee of inspection at act with the liquidator (s.252).

(*iv*) To decide who are to be members of the committee of inspection, if one is to be appointed.

9. Appointment of liquidator(s).

(*a*) *Following the decisions* made by the creditors and contributories at their respective meetings; the court may:

(*i*) Appoint a liquidator, and so give effect to the decisions of the meetings.

(*ii*) Decide the difference, if the meetings do not agree, and act as it thinks fit; or

(*iii*) Decide *not* to appoint a liquidator, so that the official receiver will continue in the office of liquidator (s.239).

(*b*) *If the court appoints a liquidator*, i.e. to replace the official receiver:

(*i*) He must notify his appointment to the Registrar of Companies.

(*ii*) He must also give security in prescribed manner to the Department of Trade. (The bond of an approved guarantee society is usually acceptable.)

NOTE: Until he complies with these two requirements, he cannot act as liquidator (s.240).

(*iii*) His appointment must be gazetted by the Department of Trade, and advertised by the liquidator himself in manner prescribed by the court, after he has given the required security.

10. Appointment of a committee of inspection (s.252).

(*a*) If the meetings decide to apply to the court to appoint a committee of inspection to act with the liquidator, the court may make the appointment.

(*b*) If, however, the meetings do *not* agree, the matter may be determined by the court.

(*c*) *If the court appoints a committee of inspection:*
  (*i*) It will consist of creditors and contributories, or their attorneys.
  (*ii*) No statutory number is fixed for the committee, but the respective numbers of creditors and contributories may be determined at the meetings—or by the court, if the meetings fail to agree.

(*d*) *The function of the committee* is to assist and, to some extent, control the liquidator; but the directions of creditors and contributories will prevail over those of the committee (s.246).

(*e*) *Meetings* of the committee of inspection:
  (*i*) The committee must meet at least once a month—but the liquidator, or any member of the committee, may call a meeting as and when necessary.
  (*ii*) At such meetings, a majority of the committee constitutes a quorum.
  (*iii*) Resolutions are passed by a majority of members present.

(*f*) *If no committee of inspection is appointed*, its place may be taken (on the application of the liquidator) by the Department of Trade, whose powers may be excercised by the official receiver.

11. Subsequent procedure.

(*a*) *Duties of the liquidator.* Following his appointment, the principal duties of the liquidator are to collect and realise the company's assets, pay its debts, and distribute any balance among the contributories.

(*b*) *Powers.* To enable him to carry out his duties, the liquidator is given wide powers under s.245, although some of them can be exercised only with the sanction of the court or of the committee of inspection.

(*c*) *Meetings.* He also has the power, subject to the provisions of the Act and the control of the court, to summon, hold and conduct meetings of the creditors and contributories, for the purpose of ascertaining their wishes in all matters relating to the winding up

(Rule 127). These meetings are referred to in the winding-up rules as Liquidator's meetings of creditors and contributories. Other meetings may, however, be convened, namely:

(*i*) Court meetings of creditors and contributories, directed to be held by the court, under s.346; and

(*ii*) Meetings summoned by the liquidator at such times as the creditors or contributories *by resolution* may direct, or when requested *in writing* to do so by one-tenth in value of the creditors or contributories, as the case may be (s.246(2)).

(*iii*) The above meetings are also governed by the winding-up rules. This is stated in Rule 128 as follows:

"Except where and so far as the nature of the subject matter or the context may otherwise require, the rules as to meetings hereinafter set out shall apply to *first* meetings, *court* meetings, *Liquidator's* meetings of creditors and contributories, and voluntary liquidation meetings, but so nevertheless that the said rules shall take effect as to first meetings subject and without prejudice to any express provisions of the Act, and as to court meetings subject and without prejudice to any express directions of the court."

NOTE: The relevant winding-up rules affecting notices, place of meetings, chairman, quorum, resolutions, proxies, adjournment and minutes, have already been stated earlier in this chapter (*see* 8 "The first meetings of contributories") and are not repeated here.

PROGRESS TEST 27

1. What business is usually dealt with at the separate meetings of creditors and contributories held after the making of a winding-up order? (**8**)

2. How, and by whom, is a committee of inspection appointed in a compulsory winding up? Describe the committee's constitution, powers and duties. (**10**)

3. When, and for what purposes, are the first meetings of creditors and contributories held in a winding up by the court? (**8**)

4. In connection with a compulsory winding up, explain briefly (*a*) committee of inspection; (*b*) provisional liquidator; (*c*) statement of affairs; (*d*) first meetings of creditors and contributories. (**7, 8**)

CHAPTER XXVIII
Meetings in a Voluntary Winding Up

HOW A WINDING UP IS EFFECTED

1. A voluntary winding up enables a company to wind up without many of the formalities of a winding up by the court and, in the case of a creditors' voluntary winding up, the company and its creditors can settle their affairs without any petition to the court.

2. Circumstances in which a company can be wound up voluntarily: A company may be wound up voluntarily in the following circumstances, as provided in s.278:

(a) When the period (if any) fixed for the duration of the company by the Articles expires, or the event (if any) occurs on the occurrence of which the Articles provide that the company shall be dissolved; and the company in general meeting has passed a resolution requiring the company to be wound up voluntarily, e.g.

Resolved: That the ten-year period fixed for the duration of the Company, in its Articles of Association, having expired, the Company be wound up; and that Mr. Albert Blank of 6, West Street, London E.C.1, be and he is hereby appointed liquidator for the purpose of the winding up.

NOTE: An *ordinary* resolution is adequate in this case, unless another form of resolution is required by the Articles.

(b) If the company resolves by *special resolution to be wound up voluntarily*, e.g.

Resolved: That the Company be wound up voluntarily, and that Mr. Albert Blank of 6, West Street, London E.C.1, be and he is hereby appointed liquidator for the purpose of the winding up.

NOTE: In this case, i.e. where the company is wound up voluntarily without assigning any reason for so doing, a *special* resolution is required.

(c) If the company resolves by *extraordinary* resolution that it cannot, by reason of its liabilities, continue its business, and that it is advisable to wind up, e.g.

Resolved: That the Company, being unable by reason of its liabilities to carry on its business, be wound up voluntarily, and that Mr. Albert Blank of 6, West Street, London E.C.1, be and he is hereby nominated as liquidator for the purpose of the winding up.

NOTE: The liquidator is merely "nominated" in this case as the creditors at their meeting also have power to nominate a liquidator.

PROCEDURE

3. Notice of the resolution to wind up voluntarily must be advertised in the *London Gazette* within 14 days after the passing of the resolution (s.279). Failure to do so renders the company and every officer in default liable to fines.

NOTE: A copy of the resolution must be filed with the Registrar within 15 days after it was passed (s.143). *See* XVII, **5, 6,** and **7**.

4. Commencement of the winding up (s.280). A voluntary winding up is deemed to commence at the time of the passing of the resolution which authorised it. As from the commencement of the winding up there are various important consequences:

(*a*) *Business.* The company ceases to carry on its business, except for the purpose of its beneficial winding up. Nevertheless, the corporate state and powers of the company continue until it is dissolved (s.281).

(*b*) *Transfers of shares* after commencement of the winding up are *void*, unless to, or with the consent of, the liquidator.

(*c*) *Status of members.* Any alteration in the status of the members made after commencement of the winding up shall be *void* (s.282).

(*d*) *A statement* that the company is being wound up must be made on every invoice, order for goods or business letter issued by or on behalf of the company or the liquidator on which the company's name appears (s.338).

NOTE: Section 338 applies to *all* forms of winding up, and the company and any person wilfully authorising or permitting the default are liable to a fine of £20.

(*e*) *Company's servants.* The winding up may operate as a dismissal of the company's servants; if, for example, the company is insolvent. In any case, however, the liquidator may continue to employ the company's servants under a new contract of employment.

NOTE: The provisions in the Act for stay of proceedings does *not* apply in the case of a voluntary winding up; nevertheless, the court may stay proceedings if the liquidator can show the necessity for it.

FORM AND PROCEEDINGS

5. Forms of voluntary winding up. There are two forms of voluntary winding up:
   (*a*) A *members'* voluntary winding up, i.e. a solvent winding up; and
   (*b*) A *creditors'* voluntary winding up, i.e. an insolvent winding up.

6. The proceedings in a members' voluntary winding up are summarised in the following table, and compared with the relevant proceedings in a *creditors'* voluntary winding up:

Members' Voluntary Winding Up	Creditors' Voluntary Winding Up
(*a*) *Statutory Declaration of Solvency.* The directors of the company (or, if there are more than two, a majority of them) may, at a board meeting, make a declaration of solvency (as required by s.283), which is filed with the Registrar.	(*a*) *Not applicable.* In this case, the form of winding up is determined by the company's *inability to make a declaration of solvency.*
(*b*) *General meeting of the company* (held not more than 5 weeks after making statutory declaration:	(*b*) *Company must summon two meetings:*
(*i*) to pass a resolution for winding up (either ordinary or special according to circumstances);	(*i*) *A general meeting:* to pass an extraordinary resolution for winding up, and to *nominate* a liquidator.
(*ii*) to *appoint* a liquidator, and fix his remuneration (s.285).	(*ii*) *A creditors' meeting* (on the same or following day): to present a statement of the company's affairs, to *nominate* a liquidator, and (if desired) to appoint a committee of inspection.
However, the statutory declaration is of no effect	

Members' Voluntary Winding Up

unless made within 5 weeks immediately preceding the date of passing the winding up resolution, or on that date, but before the passing of that resolution. It must also embody a statement of the company's assets and liabilities as at the latest practicable date before the making of the declaration. The declaration must be delivered to the Registrar within fifteen days of the date on which the winding up resolution was passed, otherwise the company and every officer in default will be liable to a fine.

(*c*) *Notice of liquidator's appointment.* Within 14 days after his appointment, the liquidator gives notice of his appointment:

(*i*) in the *London Gazette*; and
(*ii*) to the Registrar of Companies (s.305).

(*d*) *Notice of winding-up resolution.* The company must give notice of the resolution within 14 days after it was passed, in the *London Gazette* (s.279).

(*e*) *The liquidator's duties.* In general, these are to wind up the company's affairs and to distribute its assets, but, in order to carry out such duties he seeks and/or exercises powers in the following ways:

Members' Voluntary Winding Up

(*i*) *Without sanction*, to settle lists of contributories, and to make calls.

(*ii*) *With the sanction of an extraordinary resolution:*
(1) to pay any class of creditors in full;
(2) to compromise or make arrangements with creditors (s.303).

Creditors' Voluntary Winding Up

(*i*) *Without sanction*, to settle lists of contributories, and to make calls.

(*ii*) *With the sanction of the court* or committee of inspection (or meeting of creditors, if no committee of inspection):
(1) to pay any class of creditors in full;

XXVIII. MEETINGS IN A VOLUNTARY WINDING UP

Members' Voluntary Winding Up	Creditors' Voluntary Winding Up
	(2) to compromise or make arrangements with creditors (s.303).
(*iii*) *To summon general meetings* of the company, as he thinks fit, in order to obtain sanction by special or extraordinary resolutions (s.303 (*e*)).	(*iii*) *To summon meetings of creditors*, for the purpose of ascertaining their wishes in all matters relating to the winding up (Rule 127).
NOTE: If the liquidator is of the opinion that the company will *not* be able to pay its debts in full within the period stated in the declaration of solvency, he must forthwith summon a meeting of creditors and lay before the meeting a statement of assets and liabilities (s.288).	
(*iv*) *To summon general meetings* of the company at the end of the first and each succeeding year of the liquidation, and to lay his accounts before the members (s.289).	(*iv*) *To summon general meetings and creditors' meetings* at the end of the first and each succeeding year of the liquidation; and to lay his accounts before the respective meetings (s.299).

(*f*) *At the conclusion of the winding up:*

(*i*) *To summon a general meeting* of the company, by one month's notice in the *London Gazette* (s.290).	(*i*) *To summon a general meeting and a creditors' meeting*, by one month's notice in the *London Gazette* (s.300).
(*ii*) To lay his accounts before the meeting.	(*ii*) To lay his accounts before the respective meetings.
(*iii*) *To send a copy of his accounts*, within one week of holding the final meeting, to the Registrar, with a return of the holding of the meeting (s.290(3)).	(*iii*) *To send a copy of his accounts*, within one week of holding the final meetings, to the Registrar, with a return of the holding of the meetings (s.300(3)).

(g) *Three months after registration of the liquidator's return* (referred to in (*f*)(*iii*) above), the company is deemed to be *dissolved (ss.290 and 300).*

NOTE: The court has power to *defer* the date of dissolution on application of the liquidator or of any other interested person (ss.290 and 300).

7. Regulations governing meetings in a members' voluntary winding up. So long as the winding up proceeds in the form of a *members' voluntary wind up,* the meetings, being company meetings, are based almost entirely on the requirements of the Act and/or Articles of the company concerned, but the winding-up rules are or may become applicable in certain respects:

(*a*) *The general meeting* held for the purpose of passing the winding-up resolution will be convened by:

(*i*) 21 *days' notice* at least, if a *special* resolution is to be passed (s.141).

(*ii*) 14 *days'* notice at least, if an *ordinary* resolution is to be passed.

(*b*) *Subsequent general meetings* of the company, including any convened by the liquidator to obtain sanction to pay any class of creditors in full, or to make any compromise or arrangements with creditors, by *extraordinary* resolution under s.303, will require 14 days' notice at least.

(*c*) *The final general meeting* of the company must be summoned by the liquidator in the *Gazette*, giving *one month's* notice, and specifying time, place and object of the meeting (s.290).

(*d*) *Meeting of creditors in case of insolvency* (s.288). If the liquidator is of the opinion that the company will *not* be able to pay its debts in full within the period stated in the statutory declaration of solvency:

(*i*) He must convene a meeting of creditors, and lay before them a statement of the company's assets and liabilities.

(*ii*) This meeting must be summoned by at least *seven days'* notice of the time and place, such notice to be given in the *Gazette*, in a *local paper*, and to every creditor by *post* (Winding Up Rule 129).

NOTE: Where s.288 has effect, the winding up will then proceed as though it were a *creditor's* voluntary winding up and *not* as a members' voluntary winding up (s.291).

8. Regulations governing meetings in a creditors' voluntary winding up. These may be summarised as follows:

Meetings of the company

These are governed by the provisions of the Act and/or the company's Articles:

(a) *The general meeting* convened by the company for the purpose of passing the *extraordinary* resolution for winding up requires at least *seven days' notice*—unless the Articles require longer notice (s.293(1)). Failure to give such notice will not itself invalidate any resolution passed or thing done at that meeting (s.293(7)).

NOTE: In *Saxton Ltd.* v. *Miles Ltd.* (1982) it was held that this operated to validate a resolution for a voluntary winding up passed at a meeting convened for the purpose, even though there had been a failure to give notice under s.292(1), provided the resolution was otherwise valid. Since the short notice had been waived by all the members of the company, the resolution was effective.

Reference has already been made to the fact that a creditors' voluntary winding up might develop out of a members' voluntary winding up under s.288, in which case the extraordinary resolution referred to above will not be necessary (*see* **7**)).

Meetings of the creditors

These are governed by the Act and/or Articles of the company, and subsequently by the Winding Up rules 127–156:

(a) *The creditors' meeting*, convened by the company for the same day (or next following day) as the general meeting (referred to opposite), will require at least *seven days' notice*, i.e. the notices must be sent through the post simultaneously with the sending of notices of the general meeting of the company (s.293(1)(*a*), (*b*).

NOTE: The creditors must also be notified by advertisement in the *Gazette* and in two local newspapers circulating in the district where the registered office is situate (s.293(2)).

Meetings of the company	Meetings of the creditors
(b) *Subsequent general meetings*, i.e. following the liquidator's appointment, will be convened by him and held in accordance with the provisions of the Act and/or the company's Articles. This applies, for example, to the meetings he must convene at the end of each year of the winding up under s.299, or may call under s.303.	(b) *Subsequent meetings* of creditors are convened and held in accordance with the Winding Up Rules 127–156. NOTE: These rules are not repeated here, as the most important of them were set out in **8** in relation to meetings of creditors and contributories in a winding up by the court.
(c) *The final general meeting of the company is summoned by the liquidator at the conclusion of the winding up by one month's notice in the Gazette* (s.290).	(c) *The final meeting* of creditors is summoned by the liquidator at the conclusion of the winding up by one month's notice in the *Gazette* (s.290).

9. Proposals for reform. These are discussed in XIV, **9**(*d*).

PROGRESS TEST 28

1. In what circumstances, and by what forms of resolution respectively, may a company be wound up voluntarily? (**2**)

2. When is a voluntary winding up deemed to commence? What important consequences follow its commencement? (**4**)

3. List some of the important points of comparison between a members' and a creditors' voluntary winding up? (**6**)

CHAPTER XXIX

Directors' Report

Important changes were introduced by the Companies Act 1967 as regards the content of the directors' report: in particular, ss.16 to 19 of that Act (as amended by the 1980 and 1981 Acts) require additional information to be included in the directors' report.

The essential contents of a directors' report are summarised below.

STATUTORY REQUIREMENTS

1. State of the company's affairs, required by s.157(1) of the 1948 Act. It requires that a report by the directors must be attached to every balance sheet before the company in general meeting, containing:

(*a*) a fair review of the development of the business of the company and its subsidiaries during the financial year ending with the balance sheet date)
(*b*) the position of the company at the end of that financial year;
(*c*) dividend (if any) recommended;
(*d*) amount (if any) to be carried to reserves.

NOTE: The remainder of s.157 was repealed by the 1967 Act, and subsequently amended by s.13(1) of the 1981 Act.

2. Names of directors. Section 16(1) of the 1967 Act requires the directors' report to state:

(*a*) the names of all persons who, at any time during the financial year, were directors of the company;
(*b*) the principal activities of the company and of its subsidiaries, and any significant changes in those activities during the year.

3. Change in fixed assets. Section 16(1)(*a*) requires:

(*a*) Particulars of any *significant* changes in the fixed assets of the company, or of its subsidiaries, which have occurred in the financial year.

(*b*) In the case of *interests in land*, if the market value at the end of the year differs substantially from the amount at which it is included in the balance sheet and the difference is, in the opinion of the directors, of such significance as to require that the attention of members or debenture holders should be drawn to it, the difference must be indicated with such degree of precision as is practicable.

NOTE: This requirement is inapplicable to banking and discount companies, insurance companies and shipping companies (as referred to in Part III of Sched. 8A to the 1948 Act): s.16(2) (as saved by the 1981 Act, Sched. 2, para. 5(4)).

4. Directors' interests in shares or debentures. Section 16(1)(*e*) requires this information, already shown in the Register of Directors' Interests, to be shown also in the directors' report. It applies to such interests in the company, its subsidiary or holding company or fellow subsidiary. It is, however, necessary to show only their respective interests at the beginning and end of the year; there is no need to show the intervening transactions.

Alternatively, this information may be given by way of notes to all accounts, instead of in the directors' report (s.16(4A)).

5. Other material facts. Section 16(1)(*f*) makes provision for:

(*a*) Particulars of any important events affecting the company and its subsidiaries which have occurred since the end of the company's financial year.

(*b*) An indication of likely future developments in the business of the company and its subsidiaries.

(*c*) An indication of the activities (if any) of the company and its subsidiaries in the field of research and development.

6. Health, safety and welfare. Section 16(1)(*g*) requires information about the arrangements in force for securing the health, safety and welfare at work of the employees of the company and of its subsidiaries and for the protection of other persons against risks to health or safety in respect of the activities at work of employees.

NOTE: This subsection was added by the Health and Safety at Work, etc. Act 1974, s.79.

7. Employee consultation arrangements. Section 16(1)(*h*) provides that, where a company had an average weekly number of at least 250 employees during the financial year, the report must contain a statement describing the action that has been taken during the financial year to introduce, maintain or develop arrangements aimed at:

(*a*) providing employees systematically with information on matters of concern to them as employees;
(*b*) consulting employees or their representatives on a regular basis so that the views of employees can be taken into account in making decisions which are likely to affect their interests;
(*c*) encouraging the involvement of employees in the company's performance through an employees' share scheme or by some other means;
(*d*) achieving a common awareness on the part of all employees of the financial and economic factors affecting the performance of the company.

NOTE: This provision was inserted by the Employment Act 1982, s.1.

8. Acquisition of company's own shares. Section 16A provides that where shares in any company:

(*a*) are purchased by the company or are acquired by the company by forefeiture or surrender in lieu of forfeiture or in pursuance of s.35(2) of the 1980 Act;
(*b*) are acquired by the company's nominee or by any other person with financial assistance from the company in circumstances in which the company has a beneficial interest in the shares subject to s.37(1)(*c*) or (*d*) of the 1980 Act; or
(*c*) are made subject to a lien or other charge taken by the company and permitted by s.38(2)(*a*), (*c*) or (*d*) of the 1980 Act, the directors' report shall include:

(*a*) the number and nominal value of shares so acquired or purchased and where such acquisition is by purchase the consideration paid and reason for the purchase;
(*b*) the maximum number and nominal value of shares so acquired or charged (whether in the year to which the report relates or not) which were held during the year;
(*c*) the number and nominal value of shares so acquired or charged which were disposed of or cancelled during the year and, where disposed of for value, the consideration in each case, and
(*d*) the amount of the charge in each case where the shares have been charged (s.16A(2)).

NOTE: In stating the number of shares the percentage of called up share capital which those shares represent must also be expressed.

9. Turnover and profitability. Section 17 (which will now only apply in exceptional circumstances) requires that if the company (and its subsidiaries, in the case of a group) carries on two or more classes of business which, in the directors' opinion, differ substantially from each other, the directors' report must state:

(*a*) The proportions in which turnover for the year (so far as stated in the accounts) is divided among those classes.
(*b*) The extent, expressed in monetary terms, to which (in the directors' opinion) the business of each class contributed to, or restricted, the profit or loss of the company for that year, before taxation.

NOTE: If the company has subsidiaries, the same information must be given where the company and its subsidiaries between them carry on business of two or more classes. Section 17 will only apply when the accounts include group accounts (s.16(1) of the 1981 Act). This information will normally be given in the accounts and the notes thereto.

10. Number of employees and remuneration paid. Section 18 requires the directors' report to state:

(*a*) the average number of employees in each week in the year;
(*b*) the aggregate remuneration paid or payable to employees.

NOTE: If the company has subsidiaries, the same information must be given in respect of their employees. Again, s.18 will only apply when the accounts include group accounts (s.16(1) of the 1981 Act). Such information will normally be given in the accounts and notes thereto.

11. Political and charitable contributions. Section 19 requires:

(*a*) Where the company has given more than £200 during the financial year for political or charitable purposes, the directors' report must state the amount of each gift.
(*b*) Where contributions have been given for political purposes, the report must also state the name of each person to whom money has been given for such purposes exceeding £200 in amount, the amount of each contribution and the identity of any political party to which a donation or subscription in excess of £200 was made and the amount given.

NOTE: The above does not apply to a wholly-owned subsidiary incorporated in Great Britain; nor does it apply unless the total given by company and subsidiaries between them exceeds £200.

13. Auditors' responsibility. Section 23A provides that, in preparing their report on the accounts, the auditors are under a duty to consider whether the information given in the directors' report relating to the financial year in question is consistent with their accounts. If they are of the opinion that it is not, they must state that fact in their report.

NOTE: This provision was inserted by s.15 of the 1981 Act.

STOCK EXCHANGE REQUIREMENTS

Companies subject to stock exchange regulations are required to include in, or to circulate with, each annual directors' report and audited accounts or chairman's statement, the following information (Listing Agreement, para. 10). It will be noted that some of the items are additional to, while other are identical with, statutory requirements, though expressed in a different way.

13. General points.

(a) A statement by the directors as to the reasons for any significant departure from standard accounting practice.
(b) An explanation when trading results differ materially from any published forecast made by the company.
(c) If the company or, as the case may be, the group, trades outside the United Kingdom, a statement showing a geographical analysis of its trading operations.
(d) If the company has subsidiaries, a list giving for each the name of the principal country in which each subsidiary operates.

14. Borrowings of the company or group. A statement at the end of the financial year showing the aggregate amounts repayable:

(a) in one year or less, or on demand;
(b) between one and two years;
(c) between two and five years;
(d) in five years or more.

15. Interests in associated companies. If the company or, as the case may be, the group has interests in associated companies, a list giving for each:

(a) Its *name and country* of operation.
(b) Particulars of its *issued share and loan capital* and the total amount of its reserves.

(*c*) The *percentage of each class* of share and loan capital attributable to the company's interest (direct and/or indirect).

16. A statement of persons holding or beneficially interested in any *substantial part of the share capital* of the company and the amounts of the holdings in question, together with particulars of the interests of each director ... in the share capital of the company and, otherwise than through the company, any of its subsidiaries, distinguishing between beneficial and other interests.

17. Taxation

(*a*) A statement showing whether or not the company is a close company for taxation purposes and any change in that status since the end of the financial year.

(*b*) A statement of the amount of interest capitalised by the company (or group) during the financial year, with an indication of the amount and treatment of any related tax relief.

18. Particulars of any arrangements whereunder any director has waived or agreed to waive any emoluments.

19. Particulars of any contract of significance in which a director of the company is or was, for stock exchange purposes, materially interested or, if there has been no such contract, a statement of that fact.

PART FOUR

LOCAL AUTHORITY MEETINGS*

CHAPTER XXX

The Structure of Local Government

1. Organisation. The Local Government Act 1972, s.1, which came into effect on 1st April, 1974, divided England (apart from Greater London) into administrative counties and then subdivided these counties into districts. At the time of writing the administrative counties are of two types: metropolitan, and non-metropolitan, although legislation is being processed which will abolish metropolitan counties.

All districts have the same functions but two types have special features:

(*a*) certain districts may be given the status of "borough" by Royal Charter under the Act (s.245);

(*b*) certain districts may be subdivided into parishes or, in Wales, communities. These are mainly rural areas, although the parish council (community council in Wales) may resolve that they shall have the status of "town" (s.245).

The structure in Greater London is regulated by the London Government Act 1963 which is incorporated in Sched. 2 of the Local Government Act. This created a two-tier system consisting of the Greater London Council as the first tier and thirty-two inner and outer boroughs as the other.

2. Local authorities. Section 270 defines local authorities and these are:

(*a*) county councils;
(*b*) Greater London Council;
(*c*) district councils;
(*d*) London borough councils;
(*e*) parish councils;
(*f*) community councils (in Wales).

* All references in this section relate to the Local Government Act 1972 unless otherwise indicated.

This section also defines "principal areas", these being the areas represented by (a)–(d) above and therefore these are the "principal councils".

3. Parish and community meetings. Every parish in England and every community in Wales must call a meeting at least once every year and this may be attended by all local government voters of that parish or community. These meetings are not within the definition of a "local authority".

4. Functions of local authorities. These are wide, varied and constantly changing, but can be said to be concerned with provision of services for the residents of the authority's area. The provision of these services obviously requires decision making to take place and on the face of it such decisions are made at council meetings of local authorities. However, in practice, much of the decision making is done in committees and the advice and reports of such committees are heavily relied on. Nevertheless, the final legal decision which gives authority for the acts of the authority can only be made at a properly convened and constituted meeting of a local authority.

PROGRESS TEST 30

1. What are local authorities? (**2**)
2. What are principal authorities? (**2**)
3. How can districts be subdivided? (**1**)

CHAPTER XXXI

Principal Council Meetings

TYPES OF MEETING

Part I, Sched. 12 of the Local Government Act 1972 makes the following provisions.

1. Annual meeting. There is a statutory requirement to hold an annual meeting in every year.

(*a*) In a year where elections of councillors takes place this meeting should be held on the eighth day after the day of retirement or within twenty-one days after the day of retirement.

(*b*) In any other year the council may fix any day in March, April or May to hold this meeting.

(*c*) The council may fix the hour of the meeting but if this is not done the meeting shall take place at 12 noon.

2. Other meetings. In every year the council may hold other meetings as they decide necessary.

3. Extraordinary meetings. These may be called:

(*a*) at any time by the Chairman himself;

(*b*) by the Chairman within seven days of the receipt of a requisition signed by five members of the council;

(*c*) by any five members where the Chairman refuses to call a meeting or fails to call a meeting after seven days when he has received a requisition signed by five members.

NOTE: The above rules vary slightly for the Greater London Council.

CONDUCT OF MEETINGS

4. Notice of meetings.

(*a*) A council meeting must be duly convened by a summons given or sent at least three clear days before the meeting to every member of the council.

(*b*) This summons should be left at or sent by post to the place where the member normally resides or left at or sent by post to any other place upon the direction of the member in writing to the proper officer of the council.

(c) The summons should contain an agenda which should not contain the item "any other business". Part I, Sched. 12(5) states:

> "Except in the case of business required by or under this or any other Act to be transacted at the annual meeting of a principal council and other business brought before that meeting as a matter of urgency in accordance with the council's standing orders, no business shall be transacted at a meeting of the council other than specified in the summons relating thereto".

(d) In addition to the summons a notice of the time and place of the meeting must be published at the offices of the council.

(e) If the meeting is called by members (see 3(c) above) it must be signed by those members and specify the business to be transacted.

(f) Failure to serve the summons on a member does not affect the validity of the meeting.

5. The chairman.

(a) The chairman of the council shall preside when he is present.

(b) If the chairman is not present the vice-chairman shall preside.

(c) If both the chairman and vice-chairman are absent a councillor chosen by the members present shall preside.

6. Quorum.

(a) No business shall be transacted at a meeting of a principal council unless one quarter of the whole number of members is present, except where

(b) more than one third of members become disqualified at the same time. Then the quorum should be decided by reference to the number of members qualified rather than the whole number of members. This should continue until the number of members qualified rises to not less than two-thirds of the whole number.

7. Procedure at meetings.

(a) The major statutory provision in relation to procedure is that all matters coming before a council meeting are to be decided by a majority of members present and voting. In the case of an equality of votes, the person presiding at the meeting shall have a second or casting vote.

(b) The general rules of debate and procedure at council meetings are regulated by standing orders made by that council. Model standing orders for the use of local authorities are available and these may be adopted or amended for use by the council or the council may draft its own original standing orders. In any case the section on meetings would probably include the following rules:

(*i*) for order of business;
(*ii*) for motions (with and without notice);
(*iii*) restricting length and content of speeches;
(*iv*) relating to amendments;
(*v*) relating to suspension of debate;
(*vi*) rescission of resolutions;
(*vii*) appointment of committees and sub-committees;
(*viii*) adjournment of meetings;
(*ix*) suspension of standing orders.

(*c*) As standing orders are subject to the Act any standing order made by a council which is inconsistent with the Act will be *ultra vires* and void. The statutory provision referred to in 7(*a*) above means that even if a council has no regulation in its standing orders relating to their suspension, this suspension will still be possible at any time by a simple majority vote of the council.

3. Minutes. Minutes must be kept and the rules relating to them in Sched. 12, para. 41 can be summarised as follows:

(*a*) The minutes must be signed at the same or next meeting by the person presiding.

(*b*) The minutes must be kept in a minute book or kept on looseleaf paper, in which case each leaf must be numbered consecutively and initialled by the persons presiding at that or the next meeting.

(*c*) Until the contrary is proved, a meeting for which proper minutes are kept is deemed to have been properly convened and held, and all the members present at the meeting shall be deemed to have been duly qualified.

PROGRESS TEST 31

1. What are the rules relating to annual meetings? (**3**)
2. What other meetings may be held by principal councils? (**2, 3**)
3. What form must the notice of meetings take? (**4**)
4. How is the procedure at meetings regulated? (**7**)
5. Could a meeting which fails to muster a quorum be presumed to be valid? (**6, 8**)

CHAPTER XXXII

Parish and Community Council Meetings

TYPES OF MEETING

Part II, Sched. 12 of the Local Government Act 1972 makes the following provisions.

1. Annual meeting. There is a statutory requirement to hold an annual meeting in every year.

(*a*) In a year where elections of councillors takes place this meeting should take place either on or within fourteen days of the date at which the elected councillors take office.

(*b*) In any other year the meeting must take place in the month of May.

(*c*) The council may fix the time of the meeting but if this is not done the meeting shall take place at 6.00 p.m.

2. Other meetings. Additionally, a parish council must hold at least three other meetings every year whilst a community council must hold such meetings as the council deem necessary

3. Extraordinary meetings. These may be called:

(*a*) at any time by the chairman himself;
(*b*) by the chairman within seven days of the receipt of a requisition signed by two members of the council;
(*c*) by any two members where the chairman refuses to call a meeting or fails to call a meeting when he has received a requisition signed by two members.

CONDUCT OF MEETINGS

4. Place of meeting. The meetings of these councils may be held either within or without the council's area but must not be held in premises licensed for the sale of intoxicating liquor, except in cases where no other suitable room is available for such meetings, either free of charge or at a reasonable cost (Sched. 12, parags. 10 and 26).

5. Notice. The rules relating to notice are as for principal councils (*see* XXXI, **4**), except that the notice should be displayed in a conspicuous place in the parish.

6. Quorum. The rules relating to quorum are as for principal councils (see XXXI, **6**), except that the figure is fixed at one-third of the whole number of members and the quorum cannot be less than three members.

7. Voting. Voting at these meetings is by show of hands unless provided otherwise in the standing orders. Any member of the council may requisition the voting of each member to be recorded. As with principal councils, the person presiding has a second or casting vote if there is an equality of votes.

PROGRESS TEST 32

1. Where can parish and community meetings be held? (**4**)
2. What differences are there in the rules for principal councils and parish councils with regard to annual and other meetings? (XXXI, **1, 1**)
3. How is the quorum fixed at parish and community meetings? (**6**)
4. What is the procedure for voting at these meetings? (**7**)

CHAPTER XXXIII

The Committee System

MEMBERSHIP AND TYPES OF COMMITTEE

1. Appointment. Any local authority may appoint a committee or sub-committee to discharge their functions or to advise them on any matter relating to the discharge of their functions unless the function is one which should be discharged by the whole council (s.102), e.g. the levying of a rate or the borrowing of money (s.101).

2. Membership. Persons who are not members of the local authority may be co-opted to serve on the committee but at least two thirds of the members must be members of the authority. The term of office of co-opted members must be fixed by the council, whilst members of the authority cease to be members of committees when their membership of the authority ends.

NOTE: The finance committee must consist exclusively of members of the appointing authority (s.102).

3. Types of Committee.

(*a*) *Standing committees.* These are constituted for the whole of the council's year to administer a particular service as environmental health and housing.

(*b*) *Ad hoc committees.* These special committees are appointed to deal with a specific task and its term of office is over when the task is completed.

(*c*) *Statutory committees.* The authority is required to appoint certain committees and these are listed in s.101(*a*). An authority must not reach a decision on any business which is the proper concern of a statutory committee until it has received a report or recommendation from that committee. These committees include education, police and social services.

(*d*) *Sub-committees.* If the volume of work to be carried out by a committee is large it may decide to delegate some part of its function to a sub-committee. Where standing sub-committees exist the council may delegate duties directly.

CONDUCT OF COMMITTEE MEETINGS

4. Standing orders and committees. The practice here is not standardised; some authorities apply the rules for meetings to committees and sub-committees, some choose to adopt them with some relaxation of the procedural requirements. However, in many cases the authority abandons the standing orders completely in order to achieve a less formal and more productive approach.

5. Minutes of committee meetings. The rules relating to the keeping of minutes referred to in XXXI, **8** above apply to committees and sub-committees. Additional rules are:

(*a*) any minute properly made and signed is presumed to deal with matters within the authority of the committee unless proved otherwise;

(*b*) minutes of a committee or sub-committee are not open to public inspection unless they have been laid before the council for approval (*Williams* v. *Manchester Corporation* (1897).

PROGRESS TEST 33

1. What are the main kinds of committee and what are their functions? (**3**)

2. How are committees appointed and who can be members? (**1, 2**)

3. What rules govern the procedure at committee and sub-committee meetings? (**4**)

4. What records are required for committees and sub-committees? (**5**)

CHAPTER XXXIV

Disqualification From Voting

1. Section 94 states that where a member of a local authority has a pecuniary interest, whether direct or indirect, in any contract, proposed contract or other matter, and is present at a meeting of the authority where the contract or other matter is under consideration, he must, as soon as practicable after the commencement of the meeting, disclose the fact of his interest, and not take part in the consideration or discussion of, or vote on any question with respect to, the contract or other matter.

In *Rands* v. *Olroyd* (1958) a councillor was a director of a concern which had decided not to enter into any contracts with the council while the director was a councillor. The councillor voted on council policy regarding tenders for building work and was held to have voted on a matter in which he had an interest.

2. Exemptions and Dispensations. Section 97 states the circumstances where s.94 will not apply. These include:

(*a*) where the councillor has an interest in a matter simply as a ratepayer or inhabitant of the area, or only as a consumer of water or passenger on a municipal transport undertaking;

(*b*) where the councillor has shares in a society or company to an amount not exceeding one thousand pounds or one-hundredth of the total issued share capital of the company (whichever is less);

(*c*) where the interest is so remote or insignificant that it cannot reasonably be regarded as likely to influence a member;

(*d*) where the Secretary of State (or the district council in the case of a parish or community council) has given a dispensation for the interested member to vote.

PROGRESS TEST 34

1. What is a pecuniary interest? (**1**)
2. When is an interested councillor entitled to vote? (**2**)

PART FIVE

PREPARATION FOR MEETINGS

CHAPTER XXXV

Practical Work of the Secretary

Although there are certain general rules to be followed when preparing for meetings and conferences, obviously the same set of rules cannot be applied in all cases, as the nature, purpose and place of the meeting may entail special treatment.

It is, therefore, proposed to deal with a number of separate cases, suggested by, or based upon, questions set by the principal professional secretarial bodies.

1. Timetable of arrangements for a meeting of an association or society, to which a well-known personality is to be invited as *guest speaker*.

The Retail Traders' Association

Meeting to be held on 30th June, 19.., to consider how the Retail Trade may best comply with recent consumer protection legislation.

Item No.	Date	Item	Remarks and/or action
1	19.. May 2	*Accommodation.* Confirm that a suitable hall is available for the meeting, and make a provisional booking.	County Hall, Park Street, E.C. booked provisionally for 30th June, 19..
2		Make provisional reservation at local hotel for guest speaker.	Provisional booking for 29 June.

Item No.	Date	Item	Remarks and/or action
3	19.. May 3	*Write guest speaker* (Mr. X) or his agent, inviting him to speak at the meeting and informing him of accommodation provisionally arranged.	May 5. Received acceptance from Mr. X's agent and agreement to hotel arrangements.
4	May 5	*Confirm hall and hotel bookings* for the dates provisionally agreed.	Acknowledge Mr. X's acceptance.
5	May 7	*Prepare agenda* for the meeting (*see* V) giving some particulars of the guest speaker and topic of his speech.	May 10. Final form of agenda approved by the Management Committee.
6	May 11	*Instruct printers.* Having drafted a form of notice, order supply of notices and agenda forms.	Supply of agenda and notice forms received 25 May.
7	May 27	*Convene meeting.* Post notice and copy of agenda to each member (and any others who are to make up the platform party), so as to comply with standing orders/rules as regards form, method of service, period of notice, etc., assumed to be 28 days' notice in this case.	Posted 27 May and certificate of posting obtained.
8	June 1	*Arrange for press coverage.* Issue invitation and send particulars of guest speaker to local newspaper(s), also copies of notices and agenda forms.	Arranged with *Daily Sun* and *Weekly News*.

XXXV. PRACTICAL WORK FOR THE SECRETARY

Item No.	Date	Item	Remarks and/or action
9	19.. June 1/8	*Arrangements at meeting hall.* Make all necessary arrangements for: (a) seating of platform party; (b) appointment of stewards; (c) notification to police and arrange parking facilities; (d) facilities for press representatives; (e) loudspeaker system.	Arranged and approved by Management Committee 9 June.
10	June 15	*Confirm travel arrangements with guest speaker.* Ascertain where and at what time he will arrive.	18 June. Confirmed. Mr. X to arrive City Airport 3 p.m., 29 June.
11	June 22	*Documents for meeting.* Prepare and have ready all documents, records, books, etc., likely to be required at meeting.	List prepared and checked.
12	June 29	*Reception of guest speaker*, by Chairman at airport.	Mr. X met with car and conducted to his hotel.
13	June 30	*Attend meeting hall*, and: (a) take documents, books, etc.; (b) check all arrangements.	Attended in morning. Checked.
14	June 30	*Transport of guest speaker* to meeting hall.	Mr. X fetched by car and met.

Follow-up arrangements

Frequently the convenors of a meeting rely not only upon the meeting but also upon the follow-up arrangements, in order to obtain the maximum benefit from it. It is not suggested that this would necessarily apply in the case of the association referred to in the foregoing example, but it would obviously be important where an association or society is wanting to use, say, a public meeting to spread its doctrine and increase its membership. For this purpose the undermentioned follow-up arrangements are suggested:

(a) *Press notices.* If the press had not been represented at the meeting, supply a copy of any important speech, or other material for publication.

(b) *Circulate copies of any important speech* (or a report of the meeting) to provincial branch secretaries (if any) who were not present at the meeting.

(c) *Any striking phrase or sentence* included in the principal speech may be "plugged" or adopted as the "gimmick" of the society or association, e.g. in its own quarterly bulletin, and in newspapers, periodicals, T.V. programmes, etc.

(d) *Provide a full account of the meeting*, including principal speeches, photographs, etc.

(e) *Stewards to make personal contacts* with people present at the meeting. e.g.:

(i) by encouraging them to join the association or society;

(ii) obtaining names and addresses of people wanting tickets for the next meeting, or literature, etc.

(f) *Distribute free literature* concerning the objects of the society or association. Such literature may be distributed by the stewards as people leave the meeting.

2. Arrangements for the conference of a manufacturing company
with overseas sales and service centres.

(a) *Prepare a draft* conference plan.
(b) *Submit draft plan to the board* of directors for approval.
(c) *Formal approval given* of the following plan:

Tuesday, 12th October, 19..		*Optional arrangements for wives and other invited guests:*
11 a.m.	Reception of conference members and invited guests by Chairman of the company.	
1 p.m.	Luncheon at Court Hotel.	
2.30 p.m.	Conference business.	Visit to Harolds for mannequin parade.
5 p.m.	Tea provided in annexe to conference hall.	

XXXV. PRACTICAL WORK FOR THE SECRETARY

Tuesday, 12th October, 19..
7 p.m.   Dinner at hotel, for those reserving accommodation at Court Hotel.

Wednesday, 13th October, 19..

10 a.m.	Conference business.	Conducted sightseeing tour of the City.
1 p.m.	Luncheon provided in annexe to conference hall.	
2.30 p.m.	Conference business.	Free for shopping, etc.
5 p.m.	Tea provided in annexe to conference hall.	
7 p.m.	Dinner at hotel, for those reserving accommodation at Court Hotel.	
8 p.m.	Theatre (musical show at Empire Theatre); or Dance at Court Hotel available to residents.	

Thursday, 14th October, 19..

510 a.m.	Conference business; last session.	Optional visit to Exhibition of Modern Art.
1 p.m.	Luncheon for conference members and guests provided at Court Hotel.	

(*d*) *Draft agenda* for the conference, and other documents.

(*e*) *Submit draft agenda and documents to the board* of directors for approval.

(*f*) *Formal approval given* of the following conference agenda:

Conference Agenda
and summaries of main points to be discussed

Tuesday, 12th October, 19..

2.30 p.m.   *Opening speech.* Mr. A. Blank, Chairman of the Company will open the Conference and welcome representatives from provincial and overseas centres.

2.45 p.m.   *Chairman's Report* on the Company's developments, and particularly on the success of the Sales Programme originated at the last Conference.

3 p.m.   *The main purpose of the present Conference.* After presenting his report, the Chairman will state the terms of reference of the Conference; namely:

"To look ahead to the day when we shall take a full and active part in the European Market, and to ensure that all sections of our organisation, sales, service and administration alike, will be ready to meet the extra demands that will then be made of them."

He will then call upon Mr. I. Hope, the Company's Sales Director, to state more fully the various ways in which the Conference members may assist, by pooling their ideas and making constructive suggestions, in achieving the principal purpose of the Conference.

4 p.m. *Further business of the Conference.* The Chairman will call upon Mr. E. Cann, the Company's Senior Technical Director, to explain the nature of the other business which, it is hoped, the Conference will be able to transact; in particular:

(i) *Restrictive practices* within the Company's manufacturing and transport divisions.

(ii) *Automation*—extension of its use within the organisation, the problems created, and their solutions.

4.20 p.m. Question time.
4.50 p.m. Close of day's proceedings.
5 p.m. Tea will be served in annexe to conference hall.

Wednesday, 13th October, 19..

10 a.m. *Chairman will open the day's business*, by repeating the terms of reference, namely:

"To look ahead to the day when we shall take a full and active part in the European Market ..."

Discussion.

11 a.m. Break for coffee, served in the annexe.
11.20 a.m. *Motions submitted* by Overseas representatives. Questions.
1 p.m. Luncheon, served in annexe to conference hall.
2.30 p.m. *Motions submitted* by provincial representatives. Questions.
3.30 p.m. *Chairman will thank members of the Conference* for the motions submitted and views expressed.
3.40 p.m. *Chairman will introduce the next business*, namely:

"Restrictive practices ..."

Discussion.

4.20 p.m. *Motions submitted* by provincial and overseas representatives.
Questions.
4.50 p.m. *Close* of day's proceedings.
5. p.m. Tea will be served in annexe to conference hall.

Thursday, 14th October, 19..

10 a.m. *Chairman will open the day's business*, namely:

"Automation—extension of its use ..."

Discussion.
11 a.m. Break for coffee, served in the annexe.
11.20 a.m. *Motions submitted* by provincial and overseas representatives.
Questions.
12.30 p.m. *Chairman will thank members of the Conference* for the motions submitted and views expressed.
12.40 p.m. *The Conference will close with a vote of thanks to be* proposed by the senior Overseas Sales Representative, Mr. A. B. Ramsing.
1 p.m. Luncheon, for Conference members and guests, at Court Hotel.

(*g*) *Arrange for printing of documents*, i.e. Conference agenda, invitation and application forms for tickets and accommodation, visits, etc.

(*h*) *Provisional reservations* for conference hall and hotel accommodation.

(*i*) *Invitations.* On receipt of documents from printers, issue invitations to provincial and overseas representatives, etc. (To be effective, acceptances must be received by a specified date.)

(*j*) *Firm reservations.* When acceptances of invitations are received and numbers to be accommodated at conference hall and hotel are known, make firm reservations.

(*k*) *Arrange visits* to places of interest, etc., and reserve seats where applicable.

(*l*) *Send conference tickets* to applicants, also (where applicable) receipts for payment in respect of hotel accommodation, etc.

NOTE: Other documents, such as the detailed agenda, conference handbook, theatre and admission tickets, etc., will be handed out (in a cardboard or plastic container) to members and guests at the reception.

(*m*) *Attend conference hall* to make all necessary arrangements *re* seating, facilities for press (if applicable), stewards, parking, microphones, etc.

NOTE: These ought to be attended to well in advance of the opening day of the conference.

(*n*) *Prepare documents*. List all documents required at the conference, arrange in order of use, and check.

(*o*) *Opening day of conference*.

(*i*) *In morning*. Take necessary documents to, and check arrangements at, the conference hall. Attend reception of conference members and guests.

(*ii*) *In afternoon*. Attend opening of conference.

3. Arrangements for the annual general meeting of a public company.

(*a*) *Draft the directors' report*. As soon as possible after audit of the company's final accounts, the secretary, having been instructed to do so, prepares a draft of the directors' report, the contents of which must follow the requirements of the Companies Act 1967 (ss.16 to 19, as amended by the Companies Acts 1980 and 1981). (See summaries of statutory and stock exchange requirements in Appendix II, Directors' Reports.)

(*b*) *Prepare a draft notice* of the annual general meeting, bearing in mind that not less than 21 days' notice is required (s.133).

NOTE: At this stage it is usually advisable to leave blank spaces for date of notice and date of the meeting, as the latter ought to be fixed by and given formal approval of, the board.

(*c*)*Arrange for printing of documents*. Unless it is intended to make use of the company's own form of reproduction, give instructions for the printing of notices, balance sheet, final accounts, and the directors' report

NOTE: The printers will be required only to set up the type at this stage, and to provide proofs for subsequent board approval.

(*d*) *Convene a board meeting* to deal with the following business and, where applicable, give formal approval by resolution:

(*i*) *Directors' report and audited accounts*. Submit a printers' proof of the directors' report and audited accounts for consideration and approval.

(*ii*) *Authorise the signing of directors' report and accounts* in accordance with requirements of the Articles (e.g. two directors

XXXV. PRACTICAL WORK OF THE SECRETARY 189

may sign the report and the secretary countersign it), and the audited balance sheet in accordance with the requirements of s.155, i.e. two directors, in the case of a *public* company.

(*iii*) *Approve transfers to various reserves*, where applicable.

(*iv*) *Recommend the payment of dividend(s)*, subject to approval of the company in general meeting.

(*v*) *Fix a date for the payment of dividend(s)*, if applicable.

(*vi*) *Register of members*. If it is decided to close the register of members, fix the date of closing and the period. Authorise the closing of the register and given instructions to advertise the closing in a newspaper circulating in the district in which the registered office is situate (s.115).

(*vii*) *Fix the date, time and place of the annual general meeting*, and give authority for the issue of notices, together with reports and accounts, to those so entitled.

(*viii*) *Proxies*. Consider whether proxy forms are to be sent along with the report and accounts; if so, authorise their issue.

(*ix*) *Press notices*. Consider whether to provide a report of the chairman's speech and of the proceedings of the meeting for publication in appropriate newspapers; if so decided, authorise the secretary to that effect.

NOTE: If press representatives are usually present at the company's annual general meetings, the above will not be applicable. Nevertheless, even though press representatives are expected to be present, it is usually advisable to provide them in advance with copies of the chairman's speech, to ensure accuracy.

(*e*) *Stock exchange requirements*. On the assumption that the company's shares are "listed", i.e. that the company has obtained permission to deal on the stock exchange:

(*i*) *Notify the stock exchange concerned*. On the day of the board meeting, at which the accounts were approved and dividend recommended, give the stock exchange all facts concerning the company's profits and dividends.

NOTE: A specimen form of Preliminary Announcement, drawn up by the London Stock Exchange with the co-operation of various professional bodies, sets out the minimum information that companies should give to their shareholders, the public at large, and the stock exchange concerned, in order to ensure uniformity of information

(*ii*) *Supply dividend particulars*, on printed form(s) provided by the stock exchange, to its Share and Loan Department. This is additional to the information provided in the preliminary announcement, and is required by the stock exchange for statistical purposes.

(*f*) *Press notices.* Supply the various newspapers (either directly or through the company's press agents) with the same information that was given to the stock exchange in the preliminary announcement—and at the same time.

(*g*) *Convene the annual general meeting:*

(*i*) Give final instructions for the printing of the directors' report and accounts, notices of the meeting—and for any other documents prepared by this time in draft form, e.g. chairman's speech, dividend warrants, proxy forms, etc.

(*ii*) On receipt of these documents from the printers:

(1) Send notices together with directors' reports and accounts to members entitled to attend the meeting.

(2) Send notice also to the company's auditors, as required by s.14(7) of the 1967 Act.

(3) Send copies of the directors' report and accounts *only* to members not entitled to attend the annual general meeting (e.g. holders of non-voting shares) and debenture holders.

(4) Send *four* copies of the directors' report and accounts to the Share and Loan Department of the stock exchange.

NOTE: These must be posted to the stock exchange at the same time as the notices and accompanying documents are posted to the members so entitled.

(5) If so decided (*see (f)* above), send, say, fifty copies of the report and accounts to the company's press agents for circulation to various newspapers.

(6) Obtain a certificate of posting in all of the above cases.

(*h*) *Accommodation.* If the meeting is to be held elsewhere than at the company's own premises, reserve a hall or room well in advance.

(*i*) *Preparation of dividend list.* On the assumption that the members will subsequently approve the board's recommendation at the annual general meeting, the work of preparing the dividend list may be commenced as soon as the closing date for dividends arrives.

(*j*) *Dividend warrants* may now be prepared from the dividend lists, again on the assumption that the members will approve the board's recommendation. The warrants will not, however, be despatched to members until after the annual general meeting.

(*k*) *Prepare an agenda.* The notice usually contains a brief agenda which is quite adequate for the main body of members attending, but a more detailed form of agenda may be prepared

XXXV. PRACTICAL WORK OF THE SECRETARY

which will contain the names of proposers and seconders of the various motions to be submitted at the meeting. These will be distributed to the directors and to all proposers and seconders as they arrive at the meeting.

NOTE: Alternatively, the motions to be submitted may be typed on separate slips and handed to the respective proposers before the meeting commences.

(*l*) *Prepare attendance sheets.* Unless an attendance book is kept for the purpose, prepare attendance sheets. To ensure that a true record is kept, both members (or their proxies) and press representatives should be requested to sign the sheet (or book) on admission.

NOTE: Where it is the practice to send admission tickets along with the notices, arrange for someone to collect them (after signature by the shareholders concerned), and give the same person the additional responsibility of ensuring that all persons attending sign the attendance sheet or book.

(*m*) *Prepare a list of proxies.* If proxy forms were issued with the notices, carefully examine them and check them with the share register (*see* XX, 9). Reject any which do not conform or which are received after the specified time for deposit, then prepare a list of valid proxies.

(*n*) *Arrangements at the meeting hall.* Make all necessary arrangements at the hall (or other appointed meeting place); for example:

(*i*) Appointment of stewards.
(*ii*) Ensure that seating is adequate.
(*iii*) Provide facilities for press representatives.
(*iv*) Check for heating, ventilation, lighting, etc.

(*o*) *Documents for the meeting.* Prepare and/or have available, all records, documents, registers, etc., that are likely to be required at the meeting; in particular:

(*i*) *Agenda*, i.e. spare copies of the brief form of agenda, also copies of the more detailed form of agenda for the chairman, directors, proposers and seconders, referred to in (*k*) above.

(*ii*) *Proxy cards and lists*, i.e. lists of valid proxies.

(*iii*) *Share register.* This may be required for the purpose of checking share holdings and voting power in the event of a vote by poll. (In the case of a large public company with several thousands of shareholders it would not, of course, be practicable to make the register available at the meeting.)

(*iv*) *Polling lists* may also be made available, if a poll is expected.

(*v*) *Copies of Companies Acts 1948–1981.* The secretary may need these for reference purposes.

(*vi*) *Copy of Memorandum of Association* of the company.

(*vii*) *Copy of Articles of Association* of the company.

(*viii*) *Directors' report and accounts.* A few spare copies of these should be available, also a signed copy of the accounts for inspection of the shareholders.

(*ix*) *Register of Directors and Secretaries.* This should be available for reference only, e.g. to ascertain dates of appointment, etc.

(*x*) *Register of Directors' Interests.* Anyone present at the meeting is entitled to inspect this register during the course of the meeting.

(*xi*) *Minute book.* The minute book of general meetings should be available, as *shareholders* are entitled to inspect it.

(*p*) *Attend the meeting hall.* On the day of the meeting, and well in advance of the time it is due to start:

(*i*) Send the above documents to the meeting hall.

(*ii*) Attend the hall, and check all arrangements referred to in (*n*) above.

PROGRESS TEST 35

1. What arrangements should the secretary make when a visiting speaker is to address a meeting? (**1**)

2. What follow-up arrangements must a secretary undertake after the meeting? (**1**)

3. Draft a timetable of events for a company conference showing the secretary's duties before and after the conference. (**2**)

4. What steps should a secretary take to prepare for a company's annual general meeting? (**3**)

5. List the events for which a secretary should make preparation which may occur during the annual general meeting. (**3**)

APPENDIX I

Glossary of Terms in Relation to Meetings

Acclamation. A form of voting, in which those present at a meeting indicate their approval of the motion in no uncertain manner by loud cheering or the clapping of hands, etc. It does not necessarily mean unanimity, but the small minority of dissenting voices (if any) are obviously overwhelmed.

Ad hoc. Literally "to this" or "for this"; that is, "for this purpose", e.g. an *ad hoc* committee is formed for a particular purpose.

Adjournment. The act of extending or continuing a *meeting* for the purpose of dealing with unfinished business, or of deferring the *debate* on a motion which is before a meeting.

Agenda. Literally means "things to be done", but commonly used to describe the agenda *paper*, which lists the items of business to be dealt with at a meeting.

Agenda paper. A list of items of business to be dealt with at a meeting, indicating the order in which the items will be dealt with—unless the order is altered by the will of the majority.

Amendment. A proposal to alter a motion which has been submitted to a meeting, e.g. by adding, inserting or deleting words of the original motion.

Ballot. A method of voting employed when secrecy is desired, e.g. in Parliamentary and other elections.

Bye-laws. Local laws set up by local authorities; also applied to the internal regulations of a corporate body or of an association.

"Clear days". Unless otherwise stated in the rules, the number of days specified as the length of time required to convene a meeting must be "clear days", i.e. they are to be *exclusive* of the day of service of the notice and of the day of the meeting: *Re Railway Sleepers Supply Co.* (1885).

Closure. One of the formal (procedural) motions, which is put in the form "That the question be now put", with the intention of curtailing discussion on the motion before the meeting and getting a decision upon it (*see also Guillotine* and *Kangaroo* forms of closure).

Committee. A person or body of persons to whom general or

specific duties have been delegated by a parent body, e.g. a committee in lunacy may consist of one person appointed by the court.

Debate. Discussion on a motion before a meeting, in which there is argument or reasoning between persons or groups of persons holding differing opinions, prior to putting the motion to the vote of the meeting.

Defamation. Any statement (written or by word of mouth), picture, effigy or gesture calculated to lower the individual to whom it refers in the estimation of the public or section of the public, or to bring him into ridicule or contempt.

Discussion. The general consideration of a subject before a meeting, in which, as far as possible, all persons may be allowed to air their views. Arising out of this discussion, two or more sets of persons holding differing opinions emerge, and this is the stage at which debate commences.

Division. The form of voting more commonly associated with the House of Commons, i.e. the members "divide", according to whether they are for or against the motion, by proceeding to the respective lobbies. The counting of the votes cast in this way is carried out by tellers.

Dropped motion. a term applied to a motion which, with the consent of the meeting, has been withdrawn, abandoned or allowed to lapse by the original mover. The term is also used to describe a motion which failed to find a seconder, i.e. where the rules require a seconder.

En bloc. When used in connection with meetings, this term usually refers to the voting of (say) a committee *en bloc*, i.e. electing or re-electing *all* members of a committee by the passing of *one* resolution. The rules sometimes prohibit this practice.

Ex officio. Literally, by virtue of office or position, as, for example, where a person attends a meeting not in his capacity of member but by virtue of his office; thus, the chairman of the board of a limited company may attend meetings of a committee appointed by the board, not because he is a member of the committee, but because of his chairmanship of the board.

Formal motion. A motion intended to alter the procedure of a meeting, e.g. to curtail discussion, to adjourn the meeting, etc., and not requiring any previous notice. If misused, it is referred to as a "dilatory" motion.

Form of proxy. A document in writing by which one person authorises another person to attend a meeting (or meetings) and vote on his behalf (*see also Proxy*).

Guillotine Closure. A form of closure used in the House of

Commons, in which a time limit is fixed for the debate on each section or stage of a bill. When the time limit expires, discussion ceases, whether concluded or not, and the chairman of the committee concerned has no power to refuse it.

In camera. Held in private, e.g. a meeting or Court from which the public are excluded.

Intra vires. Within the power of the person or body concerned.

Kangaroo closure. A method used in the House of Commons, whereby the chairman of a committee is empowered to "jump" from one amendment to another, omitting those which he judges to be of minor importance or repetitive. This obviates much unnecessary discussion, and saves a great deal of time.

Locus standi. Literally, a place of standing, i.e. the lawful or recognised right of a person to appear and to be heard.

Majority. Unless otherwise indicated, this may be taken to mean a "simple" majority, i.e. a number which is more than half of the whole number. Thus, a resolution is passed by a simple majority where five or more persons vote in its favour out of a total of nine actually voting.

Minutes. A written record of the business transacted at a meeting.

Month. According to the Interpretation Act 1978, a "month" means a *calendar* month, unless otherwise indicated. But a reference to "month" in a company's Articles of Association was held to mean *lunar* month, where the Articles made no provision to the contrary: *Bruner* v. *Moore* (1904).

Motion. A proposition or proposal put forward for discussion and decision at a meeting.

(*Mutatis mutandis.* With the necessary alterations.

Nem. con. An abbreviation of *nemine contradicente*, i.e. no one speaking against (a motion or proposal); without contradiction.

Nem. dis (*nemine dissentiente*). No one dissenting.

NOTE: *Nem. con.* and *nem dis.* do not necessarily imply that voting is unanimous.

Omnibus resolution. A resolution containing many parts or items. Unless the parts or items are closely connected, such a resolution is usually considered inadvisable, and may even be forbidden by the rules.

Open voting. Any form of voting "in public", e.g. on a vote by show of hands, where there is no attempt to preserve secrecy of the voting. It is, therefore, in complete contrast to voting by ballot.

Order of business. The intended order in which the items of business are to be taken at a meeting, as set out in the agenda paper. Nevertheless, it must be borne in mind that the order may be altered by resolution of the meeting.

Order of the Day. An Order of the Day is some business which the House of Commons has ordered to be considered on a particular day, such as the reading of a bill.

Order of speech. The order of speaking during debate as determined by the chairman. If, however, the order of speaking is disputed, the matter ought to be settled by vote of the meeting.

Ordinary business. What constitutes "ordinary business" is often defined in the rules, in which case any other business will be regarded as "special business".

Plenary power. Full power (for negotiation or decision); e.g. a person or committee may be granted plenary powers.

Point of order. At any meeting, a member may, at any time and without notice, interrupt debate by raising a "point of order", i.e. by drawing the chairman's attention to some irregularity in the proceedings, such as the use of offensive language, irrelevancy, breach of the rules, etc.

Poll. Although the word "poll" literally means "a head", i.e. the counting of heads, it is now generally used to describe the method of voting which gives members the right to record their votes proportionately to, say, shares of stock held.

NOTE: There is a common law right to demand a poll, unless excluded by the rules governing the meeting concerned: *R* v. *Wimbledon Local Board* (1882).

Postponement. The action of deferring or delaying a meeting to a later date. The postponement of a meeting which has been properly convened is not permissible at common law: *Smith* v. *Paringa Mines* (1906). The proper course is to hold the meeting and formally adjourn it, without transacting any business.

Previous question. One of the formal (or procedural) motions, which is usually put in the form "That the question be *not* now put".

Prima facie. Literally, at the first sight; highly probable on the face of it.

Privilege. A peculiar right, advantage, benefit or immunity. As used in relation to the law of defamation, it refers to either of two forms of defence, namely, absolute privilege and qualified privilege.

Procedural motion (see Formal motion).

Proxy. Literally, one acting for another, or a document giving authority to one person to act for another. Thus, it may refer to a person appointed to attend a meeting (or meetings) on behalf of the appointor and to vote on his behalf—or to the proxy form on which such authority is given.

Question. A subject for enquiry or discussion. Thus, a motion put to a meeting for its decision is usually referred to as the "question", e.g. the "previous question" refers to the original motion.

Quorum. The minimum number of persons entitled to be present at a meeting (or their proxies, if permitted) which the regulations require to be present in order that business of the meeting may be validly transacted.

Requisition. As used in relation to a requisitioned meeting, the action of calling for the convening of a meeting, e.g. a right is sometimes given in the rules entitling a certain specified minority of members to requisition the convening body to call a meeting. The word "requisition" is also used to describe the document in which the written demand is made.

Rescission. The rescission of a resolution is usually regarded as sufficiently important to merit special treatment; thus, the rules may provide that it cannot be rescinded until a certain time has elapsed and, even then, an exteded period of notice may be required for the meeting at which it is proposed to effect the rescission.

Resolution. Although the words "motion" and "resolution" are used indiscriminately, a motion is a proposal put to a meeting, whereas a resolution is the *acceptance* of that motion by the meeting.

Rider. An addition of a relative fact or theory to a motion. It is not an amendment, because it does not amend the motion but *adds* to it; and, whereas the addition of words in an amendment usually elucidate and amplify the motion, the addition of a rider *adds* a material fact—usually in the form of a recommendation. Unlike an amendment, a rider can be put either before or after the motion is finally put to the vote.

Riot. A tumultuous disturbance of the peace, possessing all of the following ingredients: (*a*) three or more persons; (*b*) a common purpose; (*c*) the execution or inception of that common purpose; (*d*) an intention to assist each other by force in executing the purpose; and (*e*) a display of force or violence calculated to alarm at least one person of reasonable firmness and courage.

"Rolled-up" plea. The defence of "fair comment" against an action for defamation is commonly in the form of a "rolled-up" plea, in the following words: "In so far as the words consist of allegations of fact, the same are true in substance and in fact; and, in so far as

they consist of expressions of opinion, they are fair comment made in good faith and without malice upon the said facts, which are matters of public interest."

Scrutineer. One who closely examines; for example, the chairman may appoint scrutineers to represent each side at an election, for the purpose of checking the validity of the votes. After the votes have been counted, and checked, the scrutineers complete a report to the chairman in which they state the result of the voting.

Second speech. Usually each member is allowed *one* speech upon each separate motion. As a rule, only the mover of the motion is allowed second speech; that is, he is given the right of reply.

> NOTE: The right to second speech is *not* usually given to the mover of an amendment.

Service by post. In some cases, the rules provide a formula for determining when a notice sent through the post is deemed to have been served. If, however, the rules make no such provision, the Interpretation Act 1978, will apply, i.e. unless the contrary is proved service is deemed to have been effected at the time at which a letter would be delivered in the ordinary course of post.

Sine die. Without an appointed day; indefinitely. Thus, a meeting adjourned *sine die* necessitates fresh notice for the adjourned meeting.

> NOTE: This provides an exception to the position at Common Law, namely, that fresh notice of an adjourned meeting need not be given, unless the rules demand it: *Wills* v. *Murray* (1850).

Special business. All business other than that which, according to the rules, constitutes "ordinary business'. Meetings convened for the purpose of transacting special business often require longer than the usual period of notice. The notice convening the meeting should be explicit, and must draw attention to the fact that special business is to be transacted.

Special proxy. A proxy appointed for one meeting only; the proxy form on which the authority is given requires *no* stamp. On the other hand, a "general" proxy covers more than one meeting, and the proxy form for this purpose must be stamped as a power of attorney, i.e. a 50p stamp.

Standing orders. The name given to the rules regulating the conduct and procedure of certain deliberative and legislative bodies, such as the permanent standing orders of local authorities.

Status quo. The existing state of affairs; thus, to "preserve the *status quo*" is to allow the original state of affairs to remain unchanged.

Sub committee. A committee appointed by the parent committee for a certain specific purpose, or to relieve the larger committee of some of its routine work. It usually consists of some of the members of the appointing committee, but specialist non-members may be co-opted to a sub-committee where necessary and where the rules permit.

Substantive motion. Literally, an independent motion. Thus, the term is applied to the motion which replaces the original one after amendments approved by the meeting have been incorporated in it. If the substantive motion is rejected, the original one is not revived.

Suspension of standing orders. Provision is usually made for the suspension of standing orders in cases of urgency or for special purposes. As a rule, a certain specified majority of the members is required to authorise the suspension, e.g. a two-thirds or three-fourths majority may be required.

Teller. One who "tells", e.g. one who counts votes. Two or more tellers may be appointed when a division takes place. In the House of Commons, for example, there are two tellers appointed for each party, and it is their duty to count the votes "for" and "against" as the members proceed to their respective lobbies.

Ultra vires. Beyond the legal power or authority of (say) a company; for example, a company may act "ultra vires" if it exceeds the authority it derives from the "objects" clause of its Memorandum of Association.

Unan. Unanimously, e.g. "carried unanimously" indicates that a motion or proposal has been agreed to by all present at the meeting.

Una voce. With one voice, i.e. unanimously. Another term used to indicate that all present agree to a motion or proposal put to the meeting.

Unlawful assembly. Although a meeting may be lawful in other respects, it may become an "unlawful assembly" if the conduct of its members is such as to give rise to fears of a breach of the peace.

Vice versa. The reverse; contrariwise; the terms or the case being reversed.

Waiver of notice. The process of waiving entitlement to notice of a meeting. Such waiver may be expressly given; for example, where *all* entitled to attend agree to excuse lack of notice. In many cases, however, the rules protect the convenors if they inadvertently omit to send notice to a member.

APPENDIX II

Examination Technique

PRELIMINARIES

1. Preparation. Ample preparation, followed by thorough revision to consolidate the knowledge already gained, is necessary for any examination. Without it, a list of examination hints is virtually useless. Nevertheless, even a well-prepared candidate can fail through faulty presentation of his work, waste of valuable time, and irrelevancy; it is for such a candidate that these hints have been compiled.

2. In the examination room. Even before he comes to grips with the actual questions on the examination paper, the candidate can improve upon, or mar, his chances; therefore, at this stage, the following points ought to be borne in mind:

(*a*) *Read carefully* the instructions on the outside cover of the answer book.

(*b*) *Supply the information required* on the outside cover, e.g. date, subject, candidate's letter and number.

(*c*) *Follow carefully the other instructions* as and when they become applicable, e.g. it is customary to require the candidate finally to arrange his answers in numerical order.

(*d*) *Written answers legibly* on both sides of the paper provided, but commence each answer on a fresh sheet. An instruction to this effect is usually given on the outside cover.

(*e*) *Number the answers.* Be careful to number the answers so as to indicate the questions to which they refer and, where applicable, continue the numbering on to any additional sheet or sheets.

(*f*) *Use the paper provided.* Usually the examining body provides headed paper, with spaces left for subject, and candidate's identification letter and number. This paper only must be used, and the spaces properly completed.

3. Planning the approach. Having followed and/or memorised the procedural instructions, the candidate may now turn to the examination paper itself. *This is the crucial stage of the examination*, and the following suggestions for a planned approach are not be be regarded as wasteful of time; just the reverse, in fact, as an answer which has been planned (and is, therefore, logically arranged) saves time in the writing of it and, moreover, avoids much repetion. Another important advantage is that the finished answer will be less haphazard, easier to mark; therefore, the examiner is less likely to miss the points you have attempted to make, and may even be sufficiently appreciative to award bonus marks for a well-planned answer.

(*a*) *Read carefully through the examination paper.* This enables the candidate to get a general impression of the nature and apparent difficulty (or relative simplicity) of the questions, from which he can plan his approach.

(*b*) *Read the instructions.* Return to the beginning of the paper to read (or re-read) the instructions, e.g. number of questions to be attempted overall and (where applicable) from each section of the paper; compulsory questions, if any; number of marks allotted to each question, where some questions carry higher marks than others, and any other special instructions.

(*c*) *Allot the available time* according to the number of questions to be answered, taking into account those cases where some questions earn higher marks than others. An allowance of, say, five or ten minutes ought to be made for the final reading through of the answers.

(*d*) *Choose the first question* to be attempted. Obviously, it is quite unnecessary to answer the questions in the same order as they appear in the paper, but the candidate must decide at this point whether to deal first with a compulsory question (where applicable), one of the questions earning higher marks, or one of the simpler (or shorter) questions earning lower marks. So long as the compulsory questions are not overlooked, the choice is not vitally important, although it is usually advisable to deal first with a question that the candidate feels is well within his ability to handle. A good start engenders confidence, and may well boost his morale.

(*e*) *Plan the answer* to the first question. Having read the question again in order to understand clearly what is required, it will probably be found that it consists of two, three or more distinct parts. Underline the key word of each part and then make a note of the various key words on a separate rough working sheet. Alongside, or underneath, each key word jot down your ideas at random, leaving space for any after-thoughts. Rearrange the various points you have made and commit them to your examination script in a logical sequence. In this way the candidate will ensure that each part of the question is dealt with; moreover, he is less likely to omit important points which the examiner is looking for in the answer.

Plan the answers to the remaining questions in the same way.

4. Rough notes on working papers. If the candidate uses a separate sheet (or sheets) for his rough notes, it should be securely attached to his examination script, but he must be careful to cancel the sheet or mark it clearly as "rough notes". Failure to do this might cause some confusion for the examiner—and prove disastrous for the candidate.

ANSWERING THE QUESTIONS

The foregoing hints might well be applied to practically any written examination, but it is now necessary to deal specifically with examinations in Meetings—Law and Practice. Questions on this subject are, obviously, capable of classification under these two broad headings.

1. Law of meetings. In answering questions of this type, the following points ought to be borne in mind:

(*a*) Always be careful to differentiate between the general and the particular; that is, between common law rules and the rules laid down by statute or the Articles of a limited company. It is a common fault of examination candidates to give a list of "rules" taken, perhaps, from Table A, and to give the impression that they are *general* rules.

(*b*) The examination candidate is required not only to know and understand the law of meetings, but also to be able to apply it. Consequently, most examination papers contain one or more questions which introduce a legal problem. Questions of this type are not necessarily capable of a decisive answer; if, however, the candidate gives a well-reasoned answer, he will certainly earn good marks.

(*c*) It is often advisable to cite cases to support statements or arguments, particularly in dealing with questions of this type. When citing cases, accuracy is, of course, essential; nevertheless, it is suggested that the candidate need not refrain from citing a case merely because he is not entirely certain of the full names of the parties to it, or of the date, e.g. *Eley* v. *Positive Government Security Life Assurance Co.* (1876) might reasonably be cited as "Eley's Case".

2. Preparation of documents, etc.

(*a*) *Notices:* If a question calls for the preparation of a notice of a *company's* general meeting, the special requirements of the Act in that connection must be taken into consideration. Unless these special requirements are known, the candidate would be well advised (if a choice is given) to prepare a notice for an unincorporated body.

(*b*) *Minutes:* When drafting minutes of a meeting, care must be taken not to fall into the common fault of report-writing. Arguments for and against a motion are *not* required, nor are the secretary's own comments on the decisions of the meeting. Ideally, minutes ought to be a well-balanced blending of both minutes of resolution and minutes of narration.

(*c*)*Resolutions:* Considerable care should be exercised in the drafting of specimen resolutions; in particular, it is important to ensure that the resolution becomes effective as and when it is intended to become effective. There is often some criticism of the "old-fashioned jargon" which is still frequently employed in the drafting of resolutions; nevertheless, the use of the phrase "... be and it is hereby ..." *does* ensure that the resolution concerned becomes immediately effective. On the other hand, candidates are advised *not* to use the phrase merely for the sake of using it; obviously, it must not be used in a resolution which is to have effect as from some future date.

APPENDIX III

Specimen Examination Questions

CHAPTER I

1. What determines whether a public meeting is lawful or unlawful? ICSA June 1983 (**2, 3, 5–7**)

2. What is a public meeting? How does a public meeting differe from a private meeting? Consider whether there is a right, direct or indirect, to hold a public meeting, making references, as appropriate, to statute and case law. ICSA June 1982 (Introduction, **1–3, 5, 6**)

3. A public meeting is defined as:
"Any meeting in a public place and any meeting which the public or a section thereof are permitted to attend, whether on payment or otherwise" (Public Order Act 1936)
Consider fully the significance, in the context, of "a public place" and "the public ... are permitted to attend", paying particular attention to the indirect right to hold public meetings. ICSA December 1980 (**2, 3, 6**)

4. Consider the right of a person to attend, and remain at
(*a*) a public meeting;
(*b*) a private meeting.
Illustrate your answer by reference to decided legal cases. ICSA June 1980 (Introduction, **2–11, 13, 14**)

5. Outline the rights of the press to attend meetings, making particular reference to the meetings of public bodies. Under what circumstances may the Press be excluded from meetings? Refer, as appropriate, to statute and case law. ICSA June 1981 (**13, 14**)

CHAPTER II

6. What is a meeting? What differences are there in the convening of public meetings and private meetings? ICSA December 1982 (Introduction, **1–8**)

7. For a meeting to take place there must be a plurality of persons (*Sharp* v. *Dawes* (1876)) and the meeting must have a chairman. Outline the circumstances where one person may constitute a meeting and consider briefly the functions and powers of the chairman of a meeting. ICSA December 1980 (Introduction, **1–8**)

8. "A meeting is the coming together of at least two persons for any lawful purpose" (*Sharp* v. *Dawes* (1876)). Explain fully the requisites of a valid meeting and outline any exceptions to the above statement. ICSA June 1980 (Introduction, **1–8**)

CHAPTER III

9. Consider the value of formal rules of debate to all types of organisations in which meetings are held, and explain briefly the matters which should be covered by such rules. ICSA June 1982 (**7**)

CHAPTER IV

10. Discuss fully the powers and duties of a chairman. ICSA June 1983 (**2, 3**)

CHAPTER V

11. You are to draft, in outline form only, the agenda for the annual meeting of an organisation of your selection. You are to explain in detail the reasons why any four of the items are on the agenda. ICSA June 1983 (**2, 3, 5**)

12. Consider fully the value of the agenda as a means of controlling a meeting. ICSA December 1971.

CHAPTER VI

13. By whom and to whom should notice of a meeting be given? Draft a typical notice of the Annual General Meeting for an organisation of your selection. ICSA June 1983 (**2, 3, 7**)

14. (*a*) Consider the importance of giving valid notice of a meeting, as appropriate to legal decisions;

(*b*) Outline the essential features of a valid notice. ICSA June 1982 (**2–4, 6, 7**)

15. Consider how the following might be convened:

(*a*) a political party meeting at which admission is by ticket only;

(*b*) the annual general meeting of a large professional association;

(*c*) the annual general meeting of a small amateur football club.

Draft the notice of the meeting, including outline agenda of EITHER the professional association OR the amateur football club. ICSA December 1980 (**2, 3, 8**)

CHAPTER VII

16. Explain the principle of the quorum in meetings and consider

the effect of the absence of a quorum at a meeting. ICSA December 1982 (**1–3**)

17. Consider the factors which determine the size of a quorum and the effect on business where a quorum is not present at a meeting. Under what circumstances can one person constitute a valid quorum? ICSA December 1979 (**1–3**)

18. Define "proxy" and "quorum" and consider fully whether a proxy holder can be reckoned in a quorum. ICSA December 1977 (**1–3**)

CHAPTER VIII

19. Explain the terms "original motion", "amendment", "substantive motion". Illustrate, by the use of two amendments, how a motion becomes substantive. ICSA June 1983 (**1, 3, 7, 10**)

20. What is an amendment to a motion? Outline the generally accepted rules governing amendments.

At the annual general meeting of an association, a proposal to pay an honorarium of £200 to the treasurer was amended twice to become a final figure of £400. Draft the amendments necessary to do this. ICSA June 1980 (**3, 7, 8, 10**)

CHAPTER IX

21. Explain the purpose of dilatory motions, outline their form and contrast a motion to adjourn a debate with a motion to adjourn a meeting. ICSA December 1981 (**1, 2, 4, 11, 12**)

22. Examine the value of formal (procedural) motions and consider in detail the significance of the "previous question". ICSA June 1981 (**1, 2, 3, 10**)

CHAPTER X

23. Outline the reasons which cause meetings to be adjourned. Explain, referring as appropriate to decided cases, how an adjournment is made. ICSA December 1979 (**1, 3, 4**)

24. Outline the difference between adjournment of a meeting and postponement of a meeting. Explain how, and when, a meeting may be adjourned, referring, as necessary, to legal decisions. ICSA December 1978 (**3, 4, 5**)

25. Consider the power of the chairman of a meeting (*i*) to reject an amendment to a motion, and (*ii*) to adjourn the meeting. ICSA June 1977 (**3, 4**)

CHAPTER XII

26. Explain the purpose of minutes. Illustrate by drafting two individual minutes, one of which relates to the re-election of the treasurer of either:

(*a*) a charitable organisation, or

(*b*) a professional organisation.

ICSA December 1982 (**2, 3, 4**)

27. An extract from the minute book of an amateur sports club read as follows:

"After discussion the chairman Mr. A.B. moved and the meeting agreed:

(*a*) the appointments for 1981/82 be Mr A.B. Chairman, Mr X.Y. Secretary, Mr P.Q. Treasurer, Messrs L.M. and F.G. Auditors at an honorarium of £300;

(*b*) membership registration and annual fees be increased to £5 and £10 respectively".

Consider the statement from the viewpoints of meetings procedure and of minute writing. Rewrite the passage in good minute form, making any assumptions you consider appropriate. ICSA June 1982 (**2, 3, 4**)

28. What information should be contained in the minutes of a meeting? Outline the essential features of good minute writing and explain how a report of a meeting differs from the minutes. ICSA June 1981 (**2, 3**)

CHAPTER XIII

29. The Arcadian Guild, a body with about 20,000 members, was granted a Royal Charter in 1973. One item of business of the 1982 Annual General Meeting was a recommendation by its Council that one of the Guild's properties should be sold to the Society for Games and Pursuits. A small but vociferous faction of members of the Guild was strongly opposed to the sale. Representatives of the Press and of the "local" radio were invited to the meeting by the General Secretary of the Guild acting on the instructions of the Council.

During debate on the item, Mr. X, a Spokesman for the faction stated "This proposed sale is evil. It is supported by the Council for their own interests who wish to sell to a Society which encourages killing and despoils the countryside. I call upon the Chairman to resign". The Chairman replied "The man is talking nonsense."

The Spokesman repeated the words on the "local" radio at 6 p.m.

that day. The meeting was reported in the "Daily Wrangler" the following morning when the Spokesman's statement and the Chairman's reply were reported verbatim. These statements were also reported verbatim in the next issues of the Guild's monthly journal and the Society's journal which is published every two months.

Consider whether, the Council, the Chairman and the Spokesman have been defamed and outline any possible defence to an action for defamation, in the circumstances. ICSA June 1983 (**10, 11, 13, 15**)

30. At a local authority meeting, a recommendation was received from its Education Committee that "in the best interests of the Authority's service and for reasons of professional competence, the contract of Mr. P.H. be terminated, with the payment of suitable compensation".

During debate, Councillor John Smith identified Mr. P.H. as Mr. Peter Hill, headmaster of one of the Authority's comprehensive schools. The decision of the Council was that the matter be referred back to Committee. In its report of the Council meeting, the local evening newspaper included a paragraph which stated "a recommendation to terminate the contract of Mr. Peter Hill, the headmaster of a local comprehensive school for reasons of professional competence was referred back".

Consider whether Mr. Hill has been defamed and outline the defences which could be made if an action were to be taken by Mr. Hill. ICSA December 1982 (**10, 11, 13, 15**)

CHAPTER XV

31. (*a*) Who is entitled to receive notice of a company's Annual General Meeting? What should be the contents of the notice?

(*b*) How is such notice served and what are the consequences of failure to give notice? ICSA June 1983 (**4–7**)

32. What is the significance of "clear days" in regard to notice of company meetings? What is special notice and for what purpose is it necessary? ICSA June 1980 (**7, 8, 11**)

33. With regard to company meetings explain fully "special notice" and "special business" and consider the purpose of a "special resolution". ICSA June 1979 (XVII, **7, 11, 12**)

CHAPTER XVI

34. What determines the quorum at company meetings; consider the significant features of the "disinterested quorum". ICSA June 1981 (**3–8**)

35. What factors determine the quorum at board meetings? Particular reference should be made to legal decisions. ICSA June 1978 (**3**(*c*), **5**(*b*), **7**)

36. When may one person be the quorum for a meeting? What is the effect of the absence of a quorum? ICSA June 1975 (VII, **1, 2, 3; 6**)

CHAPTER XVII

37. You are company secretary of a public limited company. At the request of the chairman of the company you are to write a memorandum to explain, with appropriate examples, the following terms:
(*i*) special business; (*ii*) special notice; (*iii*) special resolution. ICSA December 1982 (XV, **11, 12; 7**)

38. Distinguish briefly the kinds of resolution which may be passed at company meetings. Consider the significance of the chairman's declaration of the result of voting. ICSA June 1982 (**5–7, 10**)

39. Explain fully the difference between an ordinary resolution and a special resolution, indicating the circumstances in which each type of resolution is used. ICSA December 1981 (**5, 7**)

CHAPTER XVIII

40. Consider fully who has the right to vote at company meetings. ICSA December 1975 (**2, 3**)

41. Outline the extent of the voting rights which are usually attached to different classes of shares at company general meetings and indicate by whom such voting rights may be exercised. ICSA December 1973 (**1, 2, 3**)

CHAPTER XIX

42. What are the advantages and drawbacks to the board of directors of a public company of the right of shareholders to demand a poll at the Annual General Meeting? By whom must the demand be made and when must the poll be taken? ICSA December 1980 (XVII, **8**; XVIII, **1–2; 1–4**)

43. You are secretary of a public company which has adopted Table A. It is likely that at the forthcoming annual general meeting a poll will be held on the re-election of one of the directors.

Your chairman has requested you to write informing him who has the right to demand a poll and to outline the procedure which he should follow at the meeting if a poll should be demanded. ICSA December 1978 (XVIII, 2; 1–4)

44. Mr. B. holds 6 per cent. and his wife Mrs. B. 2 per cent. of the issued ordinary share capital in X.Y.Z. Ltd., a public company which has adopted Table A. Mr. B.'s son, Mr. B.1 holds 100 ordinary shares in the company. At the 1976 Annual General Meeting of the company, at which the correct procedures were followed, Mr. B. was removed from office. One month after Mr. B.'s removal the Directors of X.Y.Z. Ltd. co-opted Mr. R. to the Board. Mr. R.'s formal appointment as a Director was made at the 1977 Annual General Meeting.

The business of the 1978 Annual General Meeting included a resolution proposed by Mr. B., seconded by Mrs. B., for which the correct notice was given, to remove Mr. R. from office. One week before the date of the meeting Mr. B. deposited with the Company, proxies in favour of his sons Mr. B.1 and Mr. B.2 and their wives.

Mr. B. was not present at the meeting, but Mrs. B. attended, as did Mr. and Mrs. B.1 and Mr. and Mrs. B.2. The resolution to remove Mr. R. was lost on a show of hands. Immediately Mrs. B., Mr. and Mrs. B.1 and Mr. and Mrs. B.2 demanded a poll which was taken forthwith. On the poll the resolution was passed.

Consider fully whether the decision to remove Mr. R. from office is valid. You should give appropriate legal references. ICSA June 1978 (XVIII, 2; 1–4; XX, 5)

CHAPTER XX

45. What is the value of, and also the disadvantage to, a shareholder of the right to appoint another person to act at a company meeting on the shareholder's behalf? ICSA June 1983 (3–9)

46. What is a proxy? Consider the differences between corporation representatives and proxy holders in regard to appointment and to rights at company meetings. ICSA June 1981 (XVI, 3, 4; XVIII, 2; 12)

CHAPTER XXI

47. Why is there an obligation to keep minutes of company general meetings? Where should such minutes be kept and who has the right to inspect them? ICSA December 1982 (1–3)

48. You are required to draft the full minutes of the annual general meeting of a company at which a director was removed from office and the retiring auditors were not reappointed. ICSA June 1976 (XII, 2–4; 2, 3)

CHAPTER XXII

49. What are the requirements for a company to hold an annual general meeting? Outline the items of ordinary business transacted at such a meeting. ICSA December 1982 (**2–5**)

50. Consider fully the purpose and powers of company general meetings including the annual general meeting. ICSA December 1980 (XIV, **7–9**; **1–5**)

51. You are secretary of a public company which is to hold its annual general meeting in two months' time. Three months ago, following a boardroom disagreement about development policy, the present chairman, an existing board member, replaced the former chairman who resigned his directorship. You are required to outline the *special* arrangements you will make for the annual general meeting which you expect will be acrimonious. ICSA December 1979 (XX, **6, 7, 10**; XXXV, **3**)

CHAPTER XXIII

52. By whom, how and for what reasons may extraordinary general meetings of companies be convened? ICSA June 1981 (**1, 3**)

53. Outline the rights of shareholders: to requisition a company meeting; to introduce resolutions for consideration at a company's Annual General Meeting; to circulate statements. ICSA June 1978 (XVII, **11**; **1, 3**)

CHAPTER XXVI

54. Consider the value of the committee system as regards meetings, and outline the main classes of committee which may be for me. ICSA June 1975 (**4,6**)

55. As secretary of your organisation, you have been asked to assist in setting up an office Joint Advisory Committee. Explain how you would proceed, adding your comments on the purpose, uses and limitations of such a committee. ICSA December 1972 (**4, 5, 7**)

CHAPTER XXVII

56. Outline the nature and sequence of meetings of members which are held in a members' voluntary winding up of a company. Refer to the convention, business and chairmanship of the meetings. ICSA December 1982 (**1–6**)

57. What are the regulations with regard to proxies for meetings of creditors in a creditors' voluntary winding up? ICSA December 1972 **(8)**

58. What meetings must be called and who is responsible for calling them in a creditors' voluntary winding up? CIS December 1969 **(6, 8)**

Index

absence of quorum, 17
absolute privilege, 68
accidental omission to send notices, 16, 35
acclamation, 20, 193
accounts, liquidator's presentation, 161
addressing the chair, 26
ad hoc, 193
   committee, 148, 178, 193
adjourned business, 51, 52
adjourned meeting
   notice of, 56
   quorum of, 95
   validity of proxies at, 57, 122
adjournment, 21, 51, 52, 56, 193
   of debate, 21, 51
   of meeting, 21, 26, 52, 56
   cases relating to, 57
   reasons for, 26, 56
   to take poll, 26
   winding up rules regarding, 154
admission charges, 2
admission of press to meetings, 12, 13
admission to meetings, 12, 13
advertisement of liquidator's appointment, 155
agenda, 28, 95, 193
   definition, 28, 193
   form, 28, 85
agenda paper(s), 28, 193
   chairman's copy, 28, 85
   contents, 28, 29
   definition, 28, 193
   detailed, 28, 31, 32, 85
   form, 28, 85
   preparation, 29, 30
   retention, 33
   "skeleton", 28, 30, 85
alteration of
   minutes, 64
   rules of meeting, 19
ambiguous notice, 16, 27
amendments, 42, 55, 102, 193
   chairman's refusal of, 17
   definition, 42, 193
   form, 21, 43
   inadmissible, 49
   negative, 43
   of substantive motion, 45
   order of dealing with, 7, 21, 45
   parliamentary method, 46
   "popular" method, 45
   rules governing, 43
   to amendments, 21, 44
   to formal motion, 49
   to special/extraordinary resolution, 44
   voting on, 44, 55
   withdrawal of, 44
annual accounts, presentation of, 127
annual general meetings, 126
   arrangements, 188
   attendance sheets, 191
   business of, 127
   circulation of resolutions, 108
   convening, 90, 126, 190
   effect of default in holding, 127
   documents available, 190
   list of proxies for, 122
   notice of, 90
   preparation, 128, 188
   preparation of agenda, 190
   press notices, 189
   proxies at, 189
   statutory provisions, 127
   when held, 127
annual report and accounts
   preparation, 188, 189
   presentation, 127
apology and payment into court, 70
appointment of officials, 19
arrangement with company's creditors, 159
arrest without warrant, 6
Articles of Association, alteration of, 105

INDEX

assault on removal from meeting, 12
attendance at board meetings, 141
auditors
   appointment, 139
   entitlement to notice, 86
   report, 31
   resignation, 91, 131
   removal of, 93
"aye" or "nay" voting, 20

balance sheet, signing, 188
ballot, 20, 193
bankers, appointment of, 139
billposting, 34
board meetings, 86, 138–143
   attendance, 141, 143
   business of, 140
   business of first, 138
   conduct, 113, 140
   convening, 141, 188
   first, 138
   minutes, 124
   names of proposers and seconders, 60
   power to appoint committees, 141
   purpose, 138
   quorum, 95, 96, 142
   resolutions in writing, 141
   voting at, 113, 141
books, disposal of, 104
breach of the peace, 7
broadcasting, 34, 66
brokers, appointment of, 139
business
   order of, 19
   ordinary, 19
   special, 93
bye-laws, 193

casting vote, 19, 25, 113, 174, 177
certificate of incorporation, 138
chairman, 23
   addressing the, 26
   announcing result of poll, 116
   appointment, 23
   courtesy towards, 26
   declaration of voting results, 108
   deputy, 23
   duties, 24, 25, 48, 49
   female, 26
   impartiality, 23
   misconduct of meetings, 17
   of committee, 145
   of meetings in winding up, 152
   powers, 19, 25, 48, 56
   qualifications, 23, 24
   remedies available to, 26
   removal, 26, 27
change of company's name, 83
"chuckers out", 5
class meetings, 96, 132
   quorum of, 132
class resolutions, 132
class rights, variation of, 132, 133
"clear days" notice, 90, 193
closure motion, 50, 193
committee of inspection
   appointment of, 155, 159
   function of, 155, 159
   in winding up, 155, 159
   meetings of, 155, 159
committee meetings, 80, 145, 146, 147
   admission of press, 12
   proposers and seconders, 60
   quorum of, 96, 145, 146
   specimen minutes, 61
   standing orders, 178
committee system, 146
committees, 21, 22, 145, 193
   appointment of, 21, 22, 80, 145, 178, 193
   classification, 147
   constitution, 22
   functions, 147, 148
   minutes, 179
   powers, 21, 22, 146
   recommendations referred back to, 52, 53
   standing, 147
   types, 147, 148, 178
commons, meetings held on, 2
common seal, adoption of, 45
companies, 75
   contractual capacity, 78, 79
   legal status, 77, 78
   public and private, 76, 77
   registration, 75, 76
company law, 75
company name, alteration of, 105
conference
   agenda, 184
   arrangements for, 184
   chairman's duties, 184
contracts, director's interest in, 97
convening of meetings, of board of directors, 90, 141, 188

INDEX

Corrupt and Illegal Practices Prevention Act 1883, 5
"count out", 39, 57
court's power
  to convene meeting, 129
  quorum of meeting convened by, 95
  re requisitioned meeting, 109
  re variation of class rights, 132, 133
  sanction to compromise with creditors, 160
creditors and contributories
  compromise with, 160
  meetings, 80, 151

date of meeting, 35, 86
debate, 20, 51, 194
  conduct of, 20, 51
  definition, 20, 194
  rules governing, 20, 51
declaration of
  poll, 115, 116
  solvency, 159
defamation, 65 *et seq*
  by innuendo, 72, 75
  definition, 65, 194
  protection for newspapers, 67, 70
  unintentional, 69
Defamation Act 1952, 65, 66, 67
defamatory statements, 65
  defences against, 67
Department of Trade
  appointment of inspectors, 105
  power to convene, 91, 127
  quorum of meeting convened by, 142
deputy chairman, 19
directors
  appointment of first, 138
  assignment of office, 105
  attendance, 143
  authority to convene, 82, 90
  definition, 138
  disclosure of "interests", 97
  draft report of, 188
  "over-age", 93
  report, contents of, 165
  report and accounts, resolution to adopt, 188
  resolution for election, 32
  resolution to give unlimited liability, 105
  responsibility at board meetings, 138
  special notice to remove, 93
dividend
  recommendation of, 190
  resolution adopting, 31
dividend list, preparation of, 191
dividend warrant, 192
division, 20, 194

ejection from a meeting, 12
election of
  auditors, 139
  chairman, 138
  directors, 32, 138
  secretary, 138
en bloc, 194
entitlement to notice, 35, 85
equality of
  opportunity to speak, 20, 24
  votes, 24
evidence, minutes as, 64
executive committees, 147
ex officio, 194

fair comment, 67

"gag", 50
guillotine closure, 50, 194

highway, meetings on the, 1, 2
Home Office report *re* meetings on private premises, 9

innuendo, 72, 75
interest out of capital, resolution to pay, 105
Interpretation Act 1978, 36, 97
intolerant speakers, 5
irregularities of chairman's appointment, 17
irrelevance, 25

joint committee, 142
joint holders' entitlement to notice, 86
justification, plea of, 67

kangaroo closure, 50, 195

lady chairman, 26
libel
  and slander compared, 66
  legal action for, 66
  plea of, 66
Libel Act 1843, 70
licence conferred by admission charge, 12

INDEX

liquidation, *see* winding up
liquidator
  appointment of provisional, 154
  in creditors' voluntary winding up, 159
  in members' voluntary winding up, 159
  in sanctioning compromise with creditors, 159
  in transfer or sale of assets, 105
  secretary as, 149
  in winding up by court, 149
local authorities' meetings, 12, 13, 173–80
  chairman, 174
  conduct, 173
  minutes, 175
  quorum, 174
  type of meetings, 173
Local Authorities (Admission of Press to Meetings) Act 1908, 12
local government structure, 171, 172
Lord Campbell's Act, 70

majorities, 103
  winding up rules *re*, 153
meeting hall, arrangements prior to meeting, 182, 191
meetings
  annual general, 80
  board, 80, 138–43
  class, 80, 132–36
  committee, 80, 145–47
  company; kinds of, 75–7, 85
  constitution, 17
  convening, 17, 34, 36, 90, 126, 141, 162, 188, 190
  definition, 1, 15
  disorder at, 5, 20, 25
  documents required, 190
  extraordinary general, 80, 129–31
  follow-up arrangements, 183
  in private places, 9
  in public places, 8
  interruption of, 3, 4
  in voluntary winding up, 157–63
  in winding up by the court, 149–56
  minutes, 59, 124
  of committee of inspection, 155
  of creditors in case of insolvency, 86
  of liquidator, 156, 161, 162, 163
  preparation for, 34, 181, 188
  private, 1
  procedure at, 54
  public, 1
  regulations governing, 17, 19–22
  removal from, 2, 5, 24
  unlawful, 2
  valid, 15, 16
  voting at, 19, 55, 112
members' rights to
  circulate statements, 108
  demand a poll, 112
  introduce resolutions, 108
  requisition a meeting, 108, 130
Memorandum of Association,
  resolution to alter, 105
minorities
  power to requisition meetings, 109, 130
  protection of, 132
minute book
  forms, 62, 124
  safeguards for, 22, 24, 63
  statutory requirements, 124
minutes, 22, 59, 195
  adoption, 63
  alteration, 64
  as evidence, 64, 125, 175, 179
  compared with reports, 60
  contents, 59
  definition, 59
  essentials, 60
  inspection and copies of, 126
  of narration, 59
  of resolution/decision, 59
  reading the, 63
  resolution in writing, 141
  specimens of, 61
  statutory requirements, 126, 175
  "taken as read", 63
  winding up rules *re*, 154
minute writing, essentials of, 60
month, interpretation of, 195
motion, 41, 54, 102
  definition, 41, 102, 195
  "dilatory", 46, 48
  disposal, 21, 42
  "dropped", 21, 42
  for adjournment, 52
  formal, 46, 48–54
  form, 21, 41
  "next business", 49
  presentation, 41
  seconding, 20, 41
  "shelved", 21, 42

submitted in writing, 21, 41
substansive, 42, 46, 55
withdrawal of, 20

newspapers
  advertising in, 151
  definition, 72
  qualified privilege, 70
notice, 34, 86
  of liquidator's appointment, 154, 159
  special, 93
notice of meetings, 34, 56
  ambiguity of, 16, 37
  contents, 34, 35, 87
  definition, 34
  entitlement to, 35, 86
  form, 19, 34
  inadequate/short, 16, 37, 105
  in winding up by court, 151
  omission of contents, 16, 37
  on notice board, 34
  period of, 19, 35, 36, 92
  reading, 31
  service of, 34, 36, 89
  special, 93
  special business in, 35, 93
  specimen of, 36, 37
  statement *re* proxies in, 88
  "taken as read", 31
  unauthorised issue of, 16, 37
  waiver of, 15, 35, 86, 199
  winding up rules *re*, 151
notices, 34

officers, appointment of, 19
official receiver
  as provisional liquidator, 150
  preliminary report of, 150
omission to send notice, 15, 35
omnibus resolution, 195
oral consent/negation, 20
order, preservation of, 4, 5
order of
  business, 19, 24, 195
  speaking, 20, 195
  the day, 195
ordinary business, 19, 195
ordinary resolution, 103
  for voluntary winding up, 157
  majority required for, 103
  when used, 103
organised opposition, 4

parks, meetings held in, 1
parliamentary method of
  dealing with amendments, 46
  voting, 20
period of notice, 92
petition for winding up, 149, 150
place of meeting, legality of, 1, 2
platform party, arrangements for, 183
plenary power, 196
point of order, 196
  chairman's decision *re*, 19, 25
police powers at meetings, 9–11
political meetings, offences committed at, 10
political organisations, 6
  uniforms, 6
poll, 20, 114, 196
  common law right to demand, 20, 26, 114
  procedure on taking, 114, 115
  proxy rights, 114
  statutory right to demand, 114
  Table A provisions *re*, 114
polling list, 115
postponement, 57, 196
preliminary announcement, 190
president, status of, 24
press, right of admission to meetings, 12, 13
"previous question", 41, 51, 196
private premises, 10
  defined, 10
privilege, 196
  qualified; loss of, 72
  types of, 68
privileged communication, 68
privileged occasion, 68
procedural motion, 48, 196
  definition of, 48, 196
  examples of, 49
  purposes of, 48
procedure at meetings, 54
processions, public, 6
  definition of, 9
  under Public Order Act 1936, 7
promoter's rights at meetings, 11
proposal, 102
proposers, names of, 59
protection of minorities, 132
provisional liquidator, 150
proxies, 22, 118–23
  at common law, 118
  at private company meetings, 118

definition, 118
deposit, 21, 119
form of, 21, 119, 120
forms, issue of, 119
list of, 122, 191
power to appoint, 21, 88
provision of Act *re*, 118
provision of Table A *re*, 120
rejection, 121
revocation, 121
rights of, 118
stamp duty on, 121
stock exchange regulations *re*, 120
two-way, 21, 120
under seal, 120
validity at adjourned meeting, 122
winding up rules *re*, 153
Public Bodies (Admission to Meetings) Act 1960, 13
public highway, meetings on, 1, 2
public meetings
  definition of, 1
  obstruction in, 2
  qualified privilege *re* proceedings at, 72
  violence at, 2
Public Meetings Act 1908, 56
Public Order Act 1936, 6–9
public place
  definition of, 8
  meetings held in, 8
public processions, definition of, 9
publication, unnecessary, 68

qualified privilege, 68, 70–2
  Defamation Act 1952, *re*, 68, 70
quasi-military organisations, 6
quorum, 35, 95, 197
  absence of, 39, 40
  Company Act's provisions *re*, 95
  for committee meetings, 96, 145
  constitution of, 19, 95
  definition of, 39, 95
  disinterested, 97, 142
  failure to maintain, 17, 39, 56, 100
  failure to muster, 17, 39, 56
  for meeting convened by Department of Trade and Industry, 97
  incompetent, 40
  of board meetings, 95, 96, 141, 142
  of meeting convened by Court, 97
  of meetings on winding up, 149
  of one person, 1, 96

stock exchange regulations, 98
Table A provisions *re*, 95, 97
winding up rules *re*, 152
recommendation of committee, 52
reduction of capital, resolution for, 105
reference back to committee, 52
refusal to leave meeting, 11
register of
  directors and secretaries, 192
  directors' interests, 192
  members, 191
registrar of companies, documents to be filed with, 106
registration of documents, resolutions *re*, 106
regulations governing meetings in, 19
  creditors' winding up, 162
  members winding up, 162
  winding up by Court, 149–56
reply, right of, 20, 44
reports and minutes compared, 60
reports
  at meetings, 188, 189
  qualified privilege given to, 70
representative voters' entitlement to notice, 86
requisition, 197
requisitioned meetings
  directors' duties and liabilities *re*, 129
  members' rights *re*, 109, 129–130
recession, definition of, 197
reserve liability, resolution to create, 105
resolution, 21, 102, 197
  agreed to by all members, 108
  binding all members of a class, 132
  chairman's declaration *re*, 108
  circulation, 109
  definition of, 102, 197
  extraordinary, 44, 103–5, 129, 132, 157, 159
  filing of, 105
  form of, 21
  for winding up, 153
  in writing, 21
  kinds of, 102
  notice of, 102
  of board, in writing, 141
  ordinary, 103
  registration of, 105
  recession of, 22, 197
  special, 105–8
  specimens of, 31, 32, 45, 46, 116

INDEX

winding up rules *re*, 153
rider, 43, 197
right to hold meetings, 2
riot, 4, 197
rolled-up plea, 198
rout, 4

scrutineer(s)
  appointment, 115
  definition, 198
  report of, 115
second speech, 20, 44, 198
seconders, 41, 59
seconding, 20, 41, 44
secretary
  appointment of company, 138
  in preparing for meetings, 181–92
  instructions to, 139
seditious assembly, 4
Seditious Meetings Act 1817, 4
"sense" of a meeting, ascertainment of, 17, 24
service by post, 89, 173, 174, 198
shareholders' rights, 109, 110, 112, 129
short notice excused, 86, 93
slander, 65, 66
Slander of Women Act 1891, 66
"slanging match", 5
solicitors, appointment of, 139
special business, 19, 93, 198
  manager, 150
  notice, 92, 93
special resolutions, 105
  chairman's declaration *re*, 108
  copy required in Articles, 105
  definition of, 105
  for voluntary winding up, 157
  period of notice for, 105
  registration of copies, 106
  specimens of, 157
  stock exchange requirements, 105
  when required, 105, 106
specimen resolutions, 31, 32, 45, 46, 116
speech, order of, 20
  second, 20, 44, 198
  time limit for, 20
standing orders, 175, 178, 198
statement of affairs, 151
statements privileged under Defamation Act 1952, 70
statutory declaration of solvency, 159
stewards at public meetings, 4, 184

stock exchange requirements *re*
  accounts, 189
  copies of resolutions, 104, 106
  directors' reports, 169
  disinterested quorum, 97
  dividend particulars, 189
  proxies, 120
sub-committee, 148, 199
  "whispering", 5
substantive motion, 42, 46, 55, 199
suspension of rules, 22
  of standing orders, 179, 199

Table A provisions *re*
  board meetings, 138–43
  proxies, 112
  special business, 93, 94
  varying class rights, 132
  voting rights, 113
  waiver of notice, 86, 87
trespassers, 000
two meetings, one notice, 37

unauthorised issue of notice, 00
uniforms, prohibition on wearing, 6
unlawful assembly, 2–4, 199

variation of members' rights, 132
verbal notice, 34
voting, 20, 112
  at board meetings, 112, 113
  Company Act's provisions *re*, 112
  methods of, 20, 112
  open, 195
  Table A provisions *re*, 112
  unanimous, 20, 199

warrant, arrest without, 6
weapons, offensive, 7
winding up by the Court, 149
  adjournment of meetings in, 154
  chairman of meetings in, 152
  commencement of, 150
  committee of inspection in, 155
  convening of meetings, 151, 152
  first meetings of creditors and contributories, 151
  hearing of petition for, 150
  liquidator's appointment, 154
  meetings in, 151
  notice of meetings in, 151
  official receiver's report, 151

place of meetings in, 152
procedure in, 149
proxies for meetings in, 153
quorum for meetings in, 152
resolutions at meetings in, 153
statement of affairs in, 151
winding up, voluntary, 157
  circumstances for, 157
  commencement of, 158
  conclusion of, 160
  convening of meetings, 152, 159
  creditors' meetings in, 159, 162
  declaration of solvency in, 159
  dissolution of company, 158
  filing copy of resolution, 158
  forms of, 149
  general meetings of company, 159
  legislation, 83
  liquidator, appointment of, 154
  liquidator's duties in, 155
  notice of resolution in, 158
  procedure in creditors', 149
  procedure in members', 159
  resolutions required for, 157
  specimen resolutions for, 157

Details of some other M&E
related books can be found
on the following pages.

For a full list of titles and prices write for the
complimentary Macdonald & Evans Business Studies
catalogue available from Department BP1,
Macdonald & Evans Ltd., Estover,
Plymouth PL6 7PZ

Capital Gains Tax
VERA DI PALMA

The amount of capital gains tax legislation is substantial and makes great demands on the student already heavily committed in other subjects. This HANDBOOK is intended for such students; every area of the subject in which they are likely to be examined is included and an appendix contains sample questions from the past papers of the relevant professional bodies. " Vera di Palma, one of our most distinguished authorities on the subject, is a reliable guide picking her way through the complicated provisions with a confidence which is passed on to the reader." *Times Educational Supplement* Recommended by the Association of International Accountants, the Institute of Taxation, the Institute of Bankers and the Institute of Chartered Secretaries and Administrators.

Company Law
M.C. OLIVER

"To pack into a pocket-sized book . . . the wealth of detail required, at least for examination purposes, of aspiring company secretaries, accountants and students of business management is no mean achievement in itself; add to this the bonus of progress tests at the end of each chapter, a selection of test papers and the author's comforting advice on learning and examination technique, and the reasons for the book's continuing popularity are clear." *The Solicitors' Journal* Recommended by numerous professional bodies, including the Institute of Bankers, the Institute of Commercial Management, the Institute of Cost and Management Accountants, the Association of Cost and Executive Accountants, and the Association of Accounting Technicians.

Company Secretarial Practice
L. HALL, *revised by* G.M. THOM

This HANDBOOK has been specifically written to meet the requirements of students preparing for the final examinations of the Institute of Chartered Secretaries and Administrators. It also covers the corresponding syllabus of Polytechnic Diplomas by which students may earn exemption from certain of the Institute's examinations. In addition, students preparing for the Higher Stage Company Secretarial

Practice examination of the London Chamber of Commerce and Industry will find it useful supplementary reading. This revision takes full account of the latest company legislation and much of the material formerly contained in the appendixes is now included in the main body of the text. Recommended by the Institute of Business and Technical Management.

Illustrated

A Dictionary of Law
L.B. CURZON

An understanding of complex legal terminology is an essential requirement for all those wishing to pursue a career in the law or indeed for those studying some aspect of the legal system in the process of qualifying for other professions. This comprehensive dictionary provides an up-to-date guide for students at home and abroad to the specialised vocabulary of the principles, practices and procedures of English law. It is also hoped that its clear definitions will prove of interest and use to the general reader. The nature of each entry varies from the straightforward to reference to reports and other legal literature. The reader's attention is frequently drawn to statutes and cases as a stimulant to further exploration of the topic. For this new edition the text has been thoroughly revised and updated, and in view of the increasing use of delayed commencement provisions the law is stated wherever possible as if all affected statutes were fully in force. One of the M&E Professional Dictionaries series. "Hopefully, this work will not only find its way to students, but also to practitioners' libraries as an excellent book of quick reference." *Justice of the Peace*

The Law of Meetings
SIR SEBAG SHAW &
JUDGE E. DENNIS SMITH

The object of this book is to provide a comprehensive survey of the rules, legal and conventional, which regulate the constitution and conduct of meetings. The information is presented in a logical fashion showing the development from common law and general custom to the often intricate regulations peculiar to particular bodies. The reason for a particular rule is indicated, as well as its source, thus making the book an invaluable reference source for both the student and the layman. "This standard work should be of interest and value to many others apart from students and committee secretaries and chairmen." *The Law Teacher* Recommended by the Institute of Chartered Secretaries and Administrators and the Association of International Accountants.

Casebound

Practical Business Law
A. ARORA

Part of the M&E Higher Business Education series this book presents the fundamental elements of commercial law in a systematic and progressive manner for advanced business students who are approaching the subject for the first time. It has been written primarily for students engaged in the different professional and vocational courses in which business law is a component, such as accountancy, banking and insurance, civil and production engineering and business management. In addition it will provide a useful introduction to commercial law for students reading for a degree in law or preparing for one of the professional law examinations. Since the general rules of contract law underlie all commercial transactions, the book begins with a general account of the law of contract and then proceeds to deal with the different types of transaction, treating each in as much detail as appropriate for the student who has yet to specialise. Each chapter is provided with a synopsis of the contents and concludes with a set of revision questions designed to test the student's grasp of the material under study.